Interlude, n break, breathing-space, breathing-time, delay, episode, halt, hiatus, intermission, interval, pause, respite, rest, spell, stop, stoppage, wait.
--*Chambers Pocket Thesaurus*, 1992

Cambodian Interlude

Inside the United Nations' 1993 Election

Tom Riddle
former UNTAC
Computer Liaison Officer

Orchid Press
Bangkok 2000

Tom Riddle:
Cambodian Interlude
Inside the United Nations' 1993 Election

First published: 1997
Reprinted: 2000

ORCHID PRESS
P.O. Box 19
Yuttitham Post Office
Bangkok 10907, Thailand

Cover photo by David Portnoy/Black Star.
Cover design by Sujinda Khantayalongkoch.
Book design by Tom Riddle.

Lyrics from Don McLean's American Pie reproduced by kind
permission of MCA Music Australia Pty Ltd.

Printed on acid-free, long life library paper which meets the specifications of
ISO 9706/1994

ISBN: 974-8299-36-8

Dedicated to the families of

Ty Sary
Hang Vicheth
Lay Sok Phiep
Atsuhito Nakata

members of the UNTAC Electoral Component
killed in the line of duty

and

to the expatriate men and women
of the non-governmental organizations
of Cambodia.

Contents

Acknowledgments

UNTAC's Electoral Component had a bi-weekly newsletter, *Free Choice*. The staff of *Free Choice*, Leah Melnick, Sara Colm, Deborah Hopper, Gitaka Noyes, Niphat Taptagaporn, and Johnathan Stromseth kept everyone informed, even if it meant scaring them, about what was going on in Cambodia. I used their newsletter, along with the anonymous handouts and fact sheets that the UN gave to the staff, to double check the events described here. Three Cambodians wrote me from Cambodia to clarify and verify certain points; I promised them anonymity, but I want to acknowledge their help. Mrs. Thidarat Nakkyo, a Khmer-speaking Thai who worked with UNTAC, helped with Khmer pronunciation.

This book was written in the town of Panat Nikhom, Thailand, immediately after I left Cambodia. On the second floor of my three-dollar-a-night hotel lived the only other foreign resident, Terry Underhill. By chance, he was a former technical writer from England. As the first person to read the book, he made many helpful suggestions. Copy editing was done by James Eckardt and Bret Thorn of *Manager Magazine* and by Dr. Bill Berg, whom I first met during his Fulbright Lectureship in the university where I was a lecturer in anthropology. David Portnoy, who spent two years photographing Cambodia, opened up his picture library to me and took charge of the photo layout. And Hong Kong-based photographer John Westhrop gave permission to reprint his photograph of traffic in Phnom Penh. The picture earlier appeared in the *Phnom Penh Post*.

I alone am to blame for any inaccuracies in the historical or personal events described herein. However, except for a few name changes, this is the way it was.

Introduction

I arrived in 'Cambodia on Saturday, March 22, 1992 and left sixteen months later on Sunday, July 25, 1993. I came only a week after the United Nations Transitional Authority officially began work, and stayed until the first soldiers departed two months after the UN-supervised election. I arrived when wearing a UN cap still put you at the head of the queue, and before the locals began manufacturing them in their sweat shops and selling them in the market. I arrived when the Cambodian people still believed that the UN was going to end their nightmare by bringing peace to their country.

Things were then a horrible mess. Nevertheless, everyone believed it was a less horrible mess than that made by Pol Pot and his Khmer Rouge during their experiment in communal living from April 1975 to early 1979. The Pol Pot years had left a million people dead in what had been a picturesque country of eight million nestled between Thailand, Vietnam, Laos, and the Gulf of Thailand.

In the early '80s I worked as a teacher in the refugee camps of Southeast Asia. In my classes I met a few of the hundred thousand *Khmer*, as Cambodians like to call themselves, who were on their way to the USA. I liked them and thought that someday I would like to visit their country, then occupied by the Vietnamese army and isolated from the international community. In 1989, I picked up a master's degree in anthropology from the University of Hawaii, but dropped out when faced with getting a Ph.D. Two years later, I was hanging around Hawaii, waiting for my future to crystallize, and still hoped to one day visit Cambodia.

Then, in October, 1991, the television news reported that after years of negotiations and the withdrawal of the Vietnamese troops, a *Comprehensive Political Settlement of the Cambodia Conflict* had been signed in Paris. Under the terms of the settlement, better known as "The Paris Peace Agreement," the UN was going to virtually govern Cambodia until elections could be held and a new government put in place. It was to be the biggest operation in the history of the United Nations.

A couple months later I telephoned the United Nations Volunteers to ask for an application. I knew that the UNVs were the Peace Corps of the UN and if anyone would go into the "heart of darkness" it would be them. I told the UNV desk officer that I was only interested in Cambodia. She told me to forget it—the last thing Cambodia needed was an anthropologist. I applied anyway, but somehow never managed to complete the letters of reference or other details.

One night a few weeks later a woman from Geneva telephoned me in Honolulu.

"Can I speak to a Mr. Thomas?"

"This is Mr. Thomas."

Blah...blah...blah..."when do you want to go to Cambodia?"

"Tomorrow."

"We need someone who can go right away."

"I said 'tomorrow'."

"The language classes have already begun with the first group of Volunteers, so we want to get you in as soon as possible."

"How about 'tonight'?"

She explained that with the election coming up, the UN needed people to go out into the Cambodian countryside, organize the voting districts, and register people to vote.

"Have you finished the application?" she asked.

"No, not yet."

"Never mind. You'll need to do the medical, though."

"Okay. So I lift off in two weeks?"

"More like a week, ten days max."

"Gotcha."

I immediately phoned a Cambodian-American friend with the news. He told me that his wife would never let him go back to Cambodia— she thought it was too dangerous. "But if the UN is there, it might be safe," he decided. "So go."

Geneva faxed me the medical form and job description.

They called me back that night. "Wait a minute," I said, "it says here that you want a demographer and a statistician."

"You have a degree in social sciences. We thought that was close enough."

My Ph.D. proposal had been on alcohol abuse in the South Pacific.

They called again two nights later.

Geneva: "The computer man quit."

America: "So?"

Geneva: "We see that you have lots of computer experience. How would you like to be the new computer man?"

America: "Why not?"

Geneva: "We'll fax the job description."

The fax said, *"Analyst Programmer. University degree in computer science, programming or systems analysis, preferably with emphasis on treatment of sociological data...five years or more of professional experience."*

Once I had taught word-processing to the housekeepers of the Sheraton Waikiki. But if the UN thought I was qualified, I was qualified. That shows what a university degree will do for you.

A week later I left for Cambodia.

Cambodia

Cambodia is about
the size of Missouri

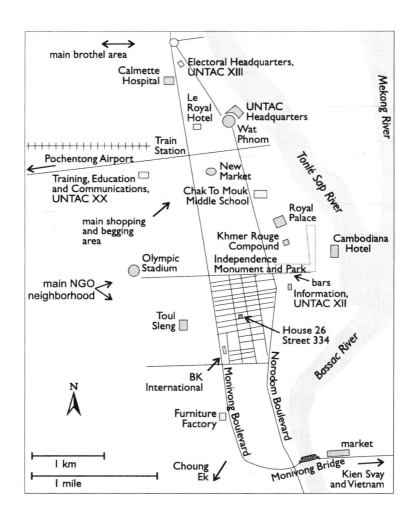

main brothel area

Calmette Hospital

Electoral Headquarters, UNTAC XIII

Le Royal Hotel

UNTAC Headquarters

Wat Phnom

Train Station

Pochentong Airport

Training, Education and Communications, UNTAC XX

New Market

Chak To Mouk Middle School

main shopping and begging area

Royal Palace

Khmer Rouge Compound

Cambodiana Hotel

Olympic Stadium

Independence Monument and Park

main NGO neighborhood

bars

Information, UNTAC XII

Toul Sleng

House 26 Street 334

Monivong Boulevard

Norodom Boulevard

Bassac River

BK International

Furniture Factory

N

market

I km

I mile

Choung Ek

Monivong Bridge

Kien Svay and Vietnam

Mekong River

Tonlé Sap River

UNTAC's Phnom Penh

maps and illustrations by the author

1 It's All Fun and Games
March - May 1992

In Bangkok at 5:30 A.M., men dressed uncomfortably in business suits are waiting to board the Bangkok Airways flight to Phnom Penh. These men, who have beside them round middle-aged wives wearing silk dresses, are not United Nations officials. They are Cambodians who have lived overseas for some years, and they are now going home, some for a visit, some for good. The business suits seem to be the mandatory costume of returning Cambodian men.

One hour later, the heat blasts me as I step off the plane at Phnom Penh's tiny airport. Instantly, I am hot and sticky. After passing through customs, I do not see any more suits. Now is the middle of Cambodia's dry season and a business suit, even for a United Nations official, would be insufferably hot.

The paved two-lane road from Pochentong Airport into Phnom Penh is filled with cars, motorcycles, trucks, bicycle rickshaws, pony carts, oxcarts, bicycles, and pedestrians. In Cambodia, drivers must drive on the right-hand side of the road, as they do in the United States. But if you want to drive on the left, that's fine too. In fact, people can drive any way they want: basically, there are no rules. For example, there are stop lights at a few major cross streets, but drivers stop only if they want to. If there is traffic entering the intersection and someone wants to go, he just goes—the other drivers stop for him or he stops suddenly for the other drivers. Eventually, the chicken crosses the road.

Riding into town and later walking the streets, I am amazed by what even the most casual pedestrian sees:

—a man carrying three car tires around his middle as he drives his motorcycle. His fingertips barely reach the handle bars.

—a motorcycle that is so over-packed with dozens of live chickens hanging by their bound feet that the bike and driver look like one giant flying chicken.

—a tiny motorbike with six people on it. They are a family—father, mother, two kids, and a baby on the hip of each parent.

—a one-passenger bicycle rickshaw carrying an entire elementary school class. Other rickshaws carry a sheet of plate glass the size of a door, a load of bricks, a bed. You name it—they carry it.

The roads are so jammed that no one can go much faster than a bicycle rickshaw, which means that when people hit each other, they usually walk away from it. I'm told that outside the city, however, with no limit to the number of passengers a bus or pickup truck can carry, or how fast it can travel, huge bloody traffic accidents occur when the overloaded and top-heavy vehicles hit something or overturn.

In this city of about a million people, many of the cars and trucks are white United Nations vehicles, or they belong to an NGO, a non-governmental organization: CARE, Save the Children, Lutheran World Service, Church World Service, American Red Cross, Swiss Red Cross, Swedish Red Cross, American Friends Service Committee, Quaker Service Australia, World Vision, World Concern, World Family Hawaii, Handicap International, UNICEF.... Even the Transcendental Meditation guru, the Maharishi, has an NGO in Phnom Penh.

Occasionally, I see huge white trucks that look like ships on wheels. These are the UN military personnel carriers, designed for traveling over land mines: the mine explodes, the shrapnel deflects off the thick metal "keel" of the truck, and no one gets killed, at least in theory. Cambodia is notorious for its land mines and unknown millions of them are buried in unknown places waiting to go off. Every month about two hundred people—many of them children—take one wrong step and lose a limb or two. One in 237 Cambodians is missing a limb.

Along the downtown streets—jammed into nondescript three-story concrete buildings—are shops, hotels, beauty parlors, travel agencies, banks, government buildings, restaurants, and movie theaters. In the poshest sections of downtown are the beggars: widows with children and soldiers with crutches. The soldiers clearly were not riding in UN military personnel carriers when they crossed mine fields. With 40 percent of Cambodian households headed by women, widows with children seem to be the norm. Their husbands starved to death, stepped on land mines, died in battle, or were murdered. Cambodia is the land of missing limbs and lonely hearts. Anyway, the beggars are tolerated, and even the shopkeepers sometimes give them handouts.

Clerks in the shops downtown earn twice the average per capita income of US $180 a year—they earn twenty thousand Cambodian *riels* or about thirty American dollars a month, enough to buy dinner for two in one of the better restaurants in Phnom Penh. Cambodia, I gradually discover in different ways and over and over again, is one of the poorest countries in the world.

Past the shops of this surprisingly flat city, nicely laid out by the French in even blocks of numbered streets with an occasional roundabout, are the residential districts. In the residential districts are many large and elegant concrete and brick houses. Or, if they are not elegant now, they are probably being renovated. This is construction worker paradise. No street is too small or too settled not to have a Vietnamese-led construction crew at work. What's the rush? With so many foreigners coming to town, landlords know they can rent a large house for three or four or even five thousand U.S. dollars a month. American dollars are the preferred currency, considered more stable than the fluctuating Cambodian riel. All this means that most Cambodians can't afford decent housing, that foreign governments and non-governmental organizations spend a large part of their budgets on housing and office space, and that a landlord can make in one month what a store clerk makes in eight years. These newly renovated buildings have electricity and air conditioning that may or may not function. When it is not functioning, the residents complain of roasting like baked chickens in their modern, airless concrete ovens.

Of course, not everyone lives in a residential neighborhood on the edge of renovation. Most people live in less upscale housing: a noisy, crowded tenement building; a dusty, deteriorating house; a thatched hut; a bicycle rickshaw; or a piece of cardboard laid flat on the sidewalk. People who camp out along the main streets are what the international community calls IDPs—"internally displaced persons." That means there was recent fighting near their homes, and rather than be target practice for this year's enemy, they have fled into the city. The UN estimates that there are 180,000 IDPs scattered throughout Cambodia.

There is an abundance of food in the markets and in the restaurants. Restaurants of one sort or another are all over town. The restaurants are clean—if they weren't, no one would eat in them. They have, however, their own standards of cleanliness. Most restaurants are open to the dusty roads, flies are everywhere, the kitchens are black, the utensils are greasy, the cooks smoke as they prepare the food, the tap water is not potable, and people don't care much about washing their hands. The standards of cleanliness are such that in the roadside restaurants, where I sometimes dine with the rickshaw drivers, everyone can drink from the same cup. When sharing a cup with my fellow diners, I find it useful to consider that the germ theory, like the Big Bang or creation theory, is just a theory and, as such, is open to debate. Nevertheless, some of the NGO people say that there is a relationship between the sanitary standards in Cambodia and the fact that 20 percent of the children never reach the age of five.

Unlike the Thais, the easygoing Cambodians do not use much chili, ginger, or garlic in their cooking. Here, the big spice is grease, and the fish, vegetable, egg, and meat dishes sold in the roadside restaurants are covered in it. Surprisingly, though, almost all restaurants sell Becks, Tiger, and Heineken beers, with a few stocking Miller Draft, all for the same price as the imported Coca-Cola.

The Cambodian people are clean as well. Many people bathe outdoors from a tap or basin because, one way or another, everyone here likes to look neat and clean. Bathing in the street, by the way, is not considered immodest as the bathers cover themselves with a *kramaa*, or wrap-around skirt. Modesty does not end at the bath, either—almost no one wears shorts, and women do not expose anything above their calves. I'm told that many Cambodian women are so modest that they do not undress completely, ever.

The French may have laid out this city, but it was founded by a Cambodian lady, Mrs. Penh. One day in the legendary past, Mrs. Penh found a bronze Buddha statue on a little hill or *phnom* in what is now Phnom Penh. With this auspicious omen in mind, people settled there, calling the area Mrs. Penh's Phnom (pronounced *Misses Pen's Pa-nome*), or Phnom Penh for short. Today, her ashes are buried on the little hill. Across from that hill, now called Wat Phnom, is UNTAC headquarters.

In 1434 the Khmer kings thought that this particular place—where the Tonlé Sap, Bassac, and Mekong rivers meet—would be a charming place to settle and to get away from marauding Thai armies. So the Khmer Kings left behind their old capital, Angkor Thom, which was just down the road from their twelfth-century masterpiece, Angkor Wat, and came here. In 1884 the French stepped into Phnom Penh and built the Cambodian Royal Palace, based on the Thai Royal Palace, plus government buildings and many of the older villas in town. The French bowed out in 1954, as they granted independence to the Kingdom of Cambodia under King Sihanouk, known in 1992 as Prince Sihanouk.

In 1970, the Americans came into the newly declared "Khmer Republic" after Sihanouk was ousted in what he believed was an American-inspired coup d'état. While the Americans were here, they killed at least a few hundred thousand Cambodians by dropping 150,000 tons of bombs on them*—much more than they dropped on Japan during World War II. From high altitudes huge B-52 bombers carpet-bombed the helpless Cambodians who had the misfortune of living along what the Americans believed was the major North Vietnamese supply route to South Vietnam, the Ho Chi Minh trail. Henry Kissinger and Richard Nixon never gave those people a second thought. Why should they? Living in isolated jungle communities, the rural Cambodians had no political significance. Little did Kissinger and Nixon realize, however, the effect that the TNT and napalm falling from the sky like monsoon rain would have on the survivors. Some would join forces with a man who had once, thanks to a Cambodian government scholarship, studied radio electronics in Paris. That man was Saloth Sar, better known by his *nom de guerre*, Pol Pot.

Pol Pot's forces, which conducted a terrifying artillery barrage of Phnom Penh, convinced the Americans to leave. A few days later, on April 17, 1975, the Khmer Rouge entered Phnom Penh, and the country became Democratic Kampuchea. One of the first things the new government did was ask all residents of Phnom Penh to leave their city in order to save themselves from the legendary American carpet bombing. This people did, thinking that they were to return in a few days. But there was no bombing and the people were not going back. Instead, everyone was ordered to take up a new profession—agriculture. Phnom Penh suddenly took on the air of a quiet country town. The only people around were the Chinese Embassy staff, Prince Sihanouk under house arrest, and Pol Pot and company—about 30,000 people, down from 2.5 million in 1975. Mr. Pot set himself up in the large rest house that would later become UN headquarters.

Some of Pol Pot's henchmen set up shop in a high school and turned it into the notorious torture chamber, Security Office 21. So, except for the screams coming out of "S21," Phnom Penh was a virtual ghost-city from April 17, 1975 until January 7, 1979, the day the Vietnamese "liberated" the city, even though there was essentially no one to liberate. The day before, Prince Sihanouk had flown to Beijing and, earlier that morning, Pol Pot had flown off in a helicopter bound for Thailand.

Cambodia then became The People's Republic of Kampuchea. Five months later, in May 1979, a man who would one day become my friend and UNTAC colleague, Sergei Ajadjanov, entered Phnom Penh as a Khmer-speaking Russian diplomat.

He found the streets virtually deserted—people were afraid to come into the city. In those days, according to Sergei, you could walk into a house and see coffee cups on the table where the occupants had left them four years before. Slowly, though, Cambodian people returned to Phnom Penh, but only in the daytime. They would come early in the morning, loot all day, and in the evening cart their booty back to the outskirts of the city. Sergei asked the Vietnamese why they did not stop the looting. They told him that the people were desperately in need and that they, the Vietnamese, were unable to give them anything except what was left in the city. The Vietnamese claimed that if they blockaded the city, people would call them "occupiers" when, in fact, they were "liberators." Thus, the looting continued until all the shutters and doors and coffee cups that anyone ever wanted were carted off or destroyed. Gradually, though, people started coming back into the city to live. Most were squatters. What happened to the original owners? Did they find their houses? Were they dead? Scattered? Who knows? A Cambodian man I met in Hawaii said that around this time he found his old house in Phnom Penh. It had been thoroughly ransacked. The looters, however, had left a picture of his mother that he picked up and carried with him to Hawaii. Meanwhile, according to Sergei, the Vietnamese, without much shooting, restored order to the city. Life returned to Phnom Penh until it became the unpleasant noisy mess that we have today in a country that has been known since 1989, the year the Vietnamese troops withdrew, as the State of Cambodia.

And now, in March 1992, there is UNTAC (*un-tack*), the United Nations Transitional Authority in Cambodia.

Cambodia is going to have an election. To have an election there must be voters. But where are the voters and how many are there? If no one knows, how can the potential voters be registered or given polling stations? That is why UNTAC created an Advanced Electoral Planning Unit, AEPU, to take a thorough census of possible voters, and that is why I am here.

The AEPU is part of the Electoral Component, which is headed by a former law professor, Reginald Austin, a white Zimbabwean. The other UNTAC components are Military, Human Rights, Civil Administration, Civilian Police, Repatriation, and Rehabilitation. The Military and Electoral are the biggest components.

The Military, consisting of battalions from eleven different countries (the Netherlands, Bangladesh, Pakistan, Uruguay, India, Indonesia, France, Malaysia, Bulgaria, Tunisia, and Ghana), are going to act as peacekeepers. To keep the peace, the UN soldiers will protect the soldiers of the four factions who have signed the Paris Peace Agreement once they surrender their arms and enter holding centers, an event that is scheduled to begin on June 15. Three of the factions—Prince Sihanouk's, Son Sann's (who was once Sihanouk's prime minister), and

---

* See *Sideshow* by William Shawcross for a complete account of the bombing.

Pol Pot's—together waged war for years against the fourth faction, the Vietnamese-installed government. Once in the holding centers, the soldiers will be taught skills needed in a country at peace. After 70 percent of the soldiers from all four factions are in camps, and "a neutral political environment" is in place, the United Nations will supervise a "free and fair" election that will lay the foundations for a democratic government. "Democratic government" is the system by which people in the last quarter of the twentieth century should, everyone says, want to be governed.

The plan sounds great.

As part of the Agreement and to help achieve "a neutral political environment," the country is now governed by a Supreme National Council made up of representatives of the four factions and headed by the one man whom everyone respects, 70-year-old Prince Norodom Sihanouk. But he is not the head of UNTAC. The head of UNTAC is Mr. Yasushi Akashi, a Japanese diplomat who speaks English with only a slight accent. I know this because by chance I met him one day as he was driving around the city looking for a place to live. I just happened to be walking down a quiet street when his car stopped beside me and he stepped out. Just to be polite, I introduced myself and told him, as his bodyguards looked on, that I was a United Nations Volunteer. He complimented me on this fact and asked if I was taking malaria medicine. I told him that I was not. He advised me to stay healthy; I promised to try. As we parted, he wished me luck. Mr. Akashi must be in his sixties and—with his watery eyes, glasses, and thin hair combed neatly to the side—adds new meaning to the word "unassuming." At one point the UN was considering asking Margaret Thatcher to run this mission, but opted for an Asian since Cambodia is in Asia and, by chance, the biggest donor to UNTAC is Japan. No one ever accused Mrs. Thatcher of being unassuming.

This is March. In the wet season, May to November, many of the roads will be impassable, so the best time for the election will be mid-dry season—February 1993.

SETTLING IN AND SHIPPING OUT

As soon as I arrived in my hotel, I was informed that, since there were not yet any computers in the Advanced Electoral Planning Unit, I would have about a month to devote to studying the Khmer language and culture. How relaxing. I settled into the homey Le Royal Hotel, which was where the *New York Times* reporter Sydney Schanburg stayed in 1975, as anyone who has seen the movie *The Killing Fields* knows. The swimming pool was still in the back, and the hotel was, in a quaint and rustic way, pleasant. I had an air conditioner in my room, which worked half the time, and one of the hotel housekeepers washed my shirts and pants for fifty American cents each, thus almost doubling her salary from the hotel if I changed clothes five times a week. I had to wash my own underwear. The French built Le Royal in the 1930s to be Cambodia's premier hotel. There were high ceilings, wide wooden polished banisters that curved down the stairs, and in my spacious bathroom was something that a country bumpkin like myself had never seen before—a bidet.

On my second full day in Cambodia, I joined the United Nations Volunteers' language and culture classes. The UNV administrators had spared no expense to set up the finest language classes that money could buy. To that end, they had hired the eminent linguist Mr. Til Ting from Australia. Mr. Ting, a Cambodian by birth, had studied advanced language teaching techniques at an Australian university, but decided to use the same teaching technique that Cambodian schools employed: write furiously on the blackboard, have the students copy it, again write furiously on the blackboard, have the students copy it, and do this all day. In this way Mr. Ting was able to skip drills, role plays, dialogues, and any kind of class participation. According to the 18 other students in class, the "I write/you copy" technique was practiced all morning, every morning.

The culture class was in the afternoon. Today's topic was women. As a few of the men in the class, like myself, were not married, Mr. Ting lost no time in informing us of the way to tell a good Cambodian woman from a bad one: a bad one will always give herself away by dragging the heels of her sandals as she walks. He demonstrated this and told us to listen for the telltale sound—scuff, scrape, scuff, scrape. While on the topic of women, Mr. Ting told us that prostitution was not indigenous to Cambodia, as it is to the rest of Asia. Indeed, according to Mr. Ting, the hedonistic French introduced the world's oldest profession to Cambodia in the last century to keep their soldiers from getting too homesick. But once the French started the ball rolling, the Cambodians could not stop it, and that is why today, according to the men outside Le Royal Hotel, the rickshaw drivers can get laid for two dollars behind the train station.

By evening I was exhausted. Back in the hotel I found a message waiting for me: "Mr. Tom is to report immediately for full time duties in the Advanced Electoral Planning Unit." Thus ended my first and last day in the language·and culture classes.

The next day I reported for work and met my boss, Hugo. Hugo was from Bulgaria and spoke English with what sounded to me like a Count Dracula accent. He explained that he had left Bulgaria for the United Nations in New York and now his wife and kids were in Connecticut. The UN had sent him to Cambodia two weeks ago. I talked to him for twenty minutes. He chain smoked and seemed a little haggard for someone about my age, but pleasant enough. After our meeting, he went to the "field" for three days. Four days later I had another thirty minute meeting with him before he went off for a week. But never mind, the computers had suddenly arrived, and it was my job to set them up. Okay, no problem. Then it was my job to train the other five people on the staff. Okay, no problem.

Everything proceeded smoothly...

I gradually discovered why I had been yanked out of the language and culture classes. The plan was that the people in the classes would, in a few weeks, leave Phnom Penh for the provinces where they would take a detailed census of potential voters, but before they went there other people would blaze a path for them. "Other people," I learned, included me.

Thus, in April 1992, my mission was to be part of a team that would travel to different provinces and gather from Cambodian government officials whatever statistics were already available about the four million potential voters in the provinces.

So good-bye Phnom Penh and...

HELLO KAMPONG CHHNANG

My first field trip was with my Russian comrade, Sergei, and a UNV cartographer. All six cartographers in the Electoral Component, it turned out, were UNVs who, like me, had been excused from the language and culture classes.

Sergei was the first Russian diplomat I had ever met, and I immediately liked him. With his round body and intelligent face, he looked remarkably like Napoleon Bonaparte. Still the diplomat, Sergei enthusiastically shook hands with everyone in the office the first thing every morning. He complemented his diplomatic demeanor by smoking his cigarettes through a cigarette holder.

We were going to Kampong Chhnang (*Kam-boong Cha-nang*), the provincial capital of the province of the same name. Kampong Chhnang is only 87 kilometers from Phnom Penh, and a major national road, Highway 5, links it with the capital, so it should have been easy to get there. On the outskirts of Phnom Penh, however, we found that our wide boulevard suddenly deteriorated into a two-, then a one-and-a-half-, then a one-lane country road filled with cars and motorcycles and ox-carts heaped with straw to protect crockery on its way to market in Phnom Penh. The oxcart drivers sat under their thatched sun roofs in-haling the dust stirred up by the motorized vehicles. Our Nissan Patrol was air-conditioned. Sergei drove while the cartographer and I pestered him with endless questions about Cambodia, all of which he patiently answered.

After less than an hour the traffic thinned out. Most of the houses turned from wood and brick to thatch and bamboo. Along the road, though, vendors were still selling soft drinks and coconuts. This was the dry season and it was scorchingly hot. For long stretches the road was not even minimally paved, and every bridge crossing became an adven-ture. The UN had somehow calculated that there were 4,100 bridges in Cambodia in need of repair, and many of these, with large holes in them where boards or sections of pavement were missing, seemed to be on the road to Kampong Chhnang. The bridges provided a source of em-ployment for local young men, especially those young men who were missing limbs, by giving them the opportunity to direct vehicles, using hand signals, around the holes. The drivers, anxious that their vehicles not become wedged into a hole or slip off the bridge into the ravine below, followed the hand signals with rapt attention. If a vehicle reached the other side, the driver heaved a sigh of relief and slipped the men some money.

Road maintenance was a source of employment as well, although it was mainly for little boys. Road maintenance consisted of positioning a ten-year-old every few hundred meters behind a little tripod of sticks so drivers knew that ahead were CHILDREN WORKING. In his work area each boy would throw some dirt or loose rocks into a few pot holes. This road maintenance crew was serviced by a man who rode a bicycle with two buckets of drinking water slung on the back. He would stop now and then to give the children a drink and thus keep them from dying of dehydration.

In the refugee camps, my students had dreamily told me how, as chil-dren, they had tended the farm animals in places like this. They had made it seem so wonderfully bucolic. But now, in the middle of the dry season, everything but the upper leaves of the shade trees growing sparsely along the road and the palm trees bordering the dry rice fields was brown, hot, and dusty. As I looked at the children tending the water buffalos and cattle, I wondered if this was really worth fighting over.

A checkerboard of rice fields and ponds, as seen from the Phnom Chisor temple, illustrates the extensive irrigation system that the ancient Cambodians developed to support their civilization.

The Vietnamese-installed government put on display some of the thousands of skulls it dug out of the Choeung Ek "killing field" just outside of Phnom Penh.

The road was bad, but by 10:30 we reached Kampong Chhnang. Naturally, the provincial authorities did not know we were coming, but they seemed glad to see us. We all shook hands and promptly sat down around a large conference table where Sergei, using his diplomatic and linguistic skills, performed the introduction: "We are from UNTAC, the United Nations Transitional Authority in Cambodia. We are here to help the Cambodian people have free and fair elections in early 1993. We are now in the preliminary planning stages and would be happy to have any information you can give us on provincial, district, commune, and village names and populations. Furthermore, our cartographer would like to see any maps you might have so that he can find district and commune boundaries to help establish voting precincts." Cambodians apparently like formal introductions, and the government officials nodded in approval.

The office was hot, with no electricity, and the office tea lady, the only woman there, placed glasses of ice-water, from the local ice factory, in front of us. The cartographer and I sipped the water while Sergei and the Khmer officials smoked.

The government officials said that even on such short notice they could help us. They just needed the rest of the day to prepare.

"Yes, very well, thank you. And accommodation?"

"We will take you to the hotel."

The hotel was state-run, so the people who ran it were paid almost nothing and felt they should work accordingly. Consequently, the hallways were nearly as dusty as the road, the floor had not been swept for months, and toilet and shower cleaning had been put on indefinite hold. Nevertheless, the mosquito-netted beds had clean sheets, and on a personal level the staff was very helpful and friendly. All the rooms opened up onto tiny balconies and shared a basic motif in that the floors, walls, and ceilings were the same color—dusty concrete gray.

The hotel was just a few meters from the market, and our rooms overlooked the Tonlé Sap River. Both sides of the broad, barely flowing river were lined with low lying Vietnamese fishing/house boats. The Vietnamese, most of whom had sailed in from Vietnam, claim to like that kind of life as much as the ethnic Cambodians prefer to live on land.

In the afternoon, after bargaining with a local fisherman, we arranged to take a cruise upstream. From our motorized canoe we did not see a single metal roof on the house boats along the river—everywhere was thatch. Except for an occasional TV antenna, it could have been a scene from Francis Ford Coppola's film *Apocalypse Now*.

Our boatman brought us back just before sunset. With the heat of the day now eased up a bit, we decided to go for a walk downstream along the river bank. Again there were only Vietnamese living along the river, but here their houses were perched high on stilts in preparation for the coming wet season and high water. The barefoot and shirtless children acted as if they had never seen a foreigner before, and perhaps they hadn't. They crowded around us and created a commotion of laughter and screaming. Grandmothers yelled at them to behave, but they were out of control.

At one point we crossed a deep gully on a rickety bridge that was just half a dozen unevenly spaced two-by-fours wide with no hand railings for fifteen meters or so. In the middle, the bridge swayed back and forth, and we wondered if the next step was going to be our last, though the locals passed us in both directions without hesitating.

After crossing the bridge we heard a shot, a high caliber rifle of some sort. The people weren't diving down, so okay. But what was it? Then another shot, and three more. The people were quiet, looking for where the shots had come from. Slowly they walked towards the shooting, and slowly we followed. What was it? A domestic dispute? A robbery? No, someone was cooking dinner, and in the ashes, for reasons no one could explain, were five bullets. Two militia men heard the shots and came to investigate. They were civilians—Cambodians—with military caps, heavy shirts, and automatic rifles. They saw that nothing was wrong. I asked them if they would mind posing for a picture. Not at all. One of them, seemingly out of habit, kept his finger atop the barrel of his gun.

Back at the market, we stopped in a small floating riverside restaurant to have a beer. The Vietnamese waitresses were very friendly. They wanted to know our names and asked us to come back that night for a visit. Two waitresses danced the Cha-cha-cha together. One came over and looked at me with an expression of complete emptiness that said, "For ten dollars, honey, I'm yours." She was a honey herself, but my life was empty enough already.

We went back to the hotel. Sergei had his fourth and fifth showers of the day and introduced us to the only other guests—three women who worked at the local bank. Theoretically they received the standard government salary of twenty thousand riels (about thirty dollars) every month, but they said they frequently went for three months without getting paid. They had been living in the dirty hotel for a year, although a glance about their room gave the impression that they had just breezed in the night before and had not yet found time to unpack. One of them had the bulging bloodshot eyes and the sallow skin that comes from years of malnutrition. She also laughed like a hyena; it was driving me crazy.

But maintaining sanity soon became secondary to coping with diarrhea. I woke up in the middle of the night with stomach pains in a hot, dark, and airless concrete box. The toilet was outside the room, down the hall, and down a flight of slippery concrete stairs. I hung my flashlight from a piece of string around my neck, squatted over the hole in the floor and wondered what I was doing in Cambodia.

In the morning my head was still spinning and the diarrhea would not stop. Sergei told me to eat plain rice soup, reminded me that I had plenty to do in Cambodia, and urged me to forget about the diarrhea. That much was clear.

We drove back to provincial headquarters. There a confident Khmer official, the special deputy in charge of relations with UNTAC, told us that not only were we the first delegation from UNTAC ever to visit his province, we were also his first official duties.

The deputy, after several of Sergei's cigarettes, showed us his work. As there were no photocopy machines, everything was either a handwritten document or a carbon copy that had been typed in Khmer with great neatness on unbelievably thin paper. He read the statistics in Khmer, Sergei wrote them on paper, and I immediately typed them into our notebook computer. I knew the Khmer numbers by now and could keep up with him if he read the numbers as "1-2-5-9," but if he said, "One thousand two hundred and fifty-nine," I was lost. Fortunately Sergei never missed a beat, and I could read his handwriting. In the course of the morning at the provincial headquarters, and later in a dusty district office, we came to realize that the government officials had made it their business to keep track of people. They knew how many people were under their control, where those people went when they moved, and who was a stranger in the area.

In the morning our cordial host, the deputy, had announced that he would be throwing a banquet in our honor that evening. But by late afternoon that promise had been forgotten and replaced by an invitation to drink a special palm wine, or toddy. He explained that the sap of the most special palm trees yielded the most delicious juice after 9 P.M., and that he would bring it to us at ten o'clock sharp. I was sure that I would be asleep by nine. But at eight o'clock, just as I was preparing for bed, he showed up at the hotel and said that we should follow him to his house where the palm wine was waiting.

We drove a good distance into the bush over a road that could have been a test track for lunar landing vehicles. Upon arrival, we were ushered upstairs to the wooden porch of his one-room house illuminated by a fluorescent light attached to a car battery. The most special palm wine was waiting along with a case of Miller Draft Beer in case of emergency.

After a few glasses of toddy and a couple of cans of beer to wash it down, our host declared, speaking English for the first time, that I was his long lost brother. He explained how he had worked with the Americans before 1975 and how he still had fond memories of them and affection for all of their relatives. He further declared that if I were assigned to work in his province it would be one of the greatest days of his life. Now that he knew me "very well," he could add that he was sure that the two of us working together could ensure a successful election in Kampong Chhnang. Finally, now that we were half-drunk and brothers, he felt he could tell me that he was the English teacher of Miss Chana, the lady with bloodshot eyes who lived in our hotel and who had joined us for the outing. With everyone in high spirits, Chana, in violation of the highest standards of Cambodian morality, was now finishing a can of beer herself. Confident and after much prodding by her teacher, she, too, began to speak English with me. "Very yell sank you," she said.

Meanwhile the neighbors had crept out of the shadows to have a look at the first foreigners ever to visit their neighborhood. The Cambodian children, unlike the Vietnamese children, stayed quiet.

We left the province the next day with warm good-byes from everyone, and my brother, the deputy, hitched a ride with us to Phnom Penh.

Journey to Battambang and Banteay Meanchey

Five days later Sergei and I were sent on our second mission: to Battambang (*Bat-tam-bong*) and Banteay Meanchey (*Ban-tee Mee-an-choy*) provinces. This was a special mission: two teams would fly up on a United Nations cargo plane and case out both provinces.

Our plane was the cattle car of the air, a C160, the door of which hinged down from the back like the jaw of a crocodile so that it could be loaded with cattle or, in this case, file cabinets, boxes of medicine, luggage, and other essentials. Passengers sat in long canvas awnings that ran down both sides of the fuselage. The windows were like the oddly scattered portholes of a ship.

Our names were not on the passenger manifest, thanks to a bureaucratic mix-up, but as we had UNTAC ID's, we could squeeze on. We sat down and immediately felt as if we had been locked in a car with the windows rolled up on a hot sunny day. We baked for a few minutes before starting to move. As we did, with no air conditioning and no cabin insulation, the roar of the engines filled the plane until conversation became impossible. After a long taxi, we were airborne. When the plane reached cruising altitude, it cooled down.

After forty-five minutes we landed in Battambang where our driver, the former chauffeur to the Polish ambassador, was waiting for us. He had driven up from Phnom Penh the day before. Battambang is the second largest city in Cambodia—you can ride a bicycle across it in half an hour. It also has some old-world charm, with wide shaded streets that the French laid out so that the main streets run parallel to the river. In the middle of town was a huge white 19th-century French governor's mansion with flowers surrounding it and two 19th-century cannons at the gate. We were ushered inside and promptly shuffled away from the bustle of the mansion to a quiet conference room. We sat down around a huge polished hardwood table where we waited and wondered what was going on.

Battambang province borders Thailand, and it was from here that many refugees fled to Thailand in 1979 and the early eighties. Now, however, thanks to the Paris Peace Agreement and the United Nations, 370,000 of these refugees, called returnees, were coming home from Thailand. With people under UN protection coming in, Battambang was enjoying a change of fortune. UNTAC was pumping money into it for roads, housing, police protection for the returnees, well digging, and other infrastructural improvements. Hence the bustle and polish of the local authorities.

We were beginning to wonder if we had been forgotten when Mr. Governor himself strolled in. We stood up and everyone shook hands. I immediately sensed that the governor, unlike my friend in Kampong Chhnang, would never think that I was his long lost brother. He looked like a fat Cheshire cat. He sat down in his favorite chair, yawned, smoked a cigarette, and studied the ceiling as Sergei explained our mission. Clearly, he was not very interested in us. Nevertheless, in an offhand way, he wished us well and assigned one of his lieutenants to help us. As we were leaving, we met two other United Nations delegations who were waiting to see the governor—a group of Indonesian police and the legal advisor of the United Nations High Commissioner for Refugees. To the governor, we had been just another pain in the butt.

The governor's lieutenant housed us, for a nominal fee, in the government guesthouse. It was the Hilton after Kampong Chhnang—large clean rooms, tiled floors, air conditioning, and three to five beds in each room. We set our bags down and promptly went to lunch.

Battambang had one restaurant fancy enough to provide menus. The Blue River restaurant overlooked the Battambang River which was muddy brown and whose bank, as was the Cambodian custom, served as the restaurant's garbage dump. Everything fit into place. The restaurant—crowded with unarmed UN soldiers and police, NGO workers, and a few Cambodians—featured a television that blared rock videos from nearby Thailand.

In the afternoon we had another meeting with government officials and, as usual, Sergei wrote down population statistics while I entered the data into the computer.

That night we went back to the restaurant. This time a dance band with a female lead singer played syrupy Khmer love songs as two waitresses slow danced together. I did not see any Vietnamese ladies, but, given the law of supply and demand, I guessed that after another month or two the local Cambodian prostitutes would face serious competition. After dinner I printed out the data that we had gathered that day, and Sergei checked it late into the night. When we finally made it to bed, the air-conditioned room felt wonderful. But it was too good to be true: halfway through the night the electricity went off and we woke up wet with sweat in our hot, stuffy room. Undaunted, my cheerful leader noted that at least our truck was air-conditioned, and early in the morning Sergei, one cartographer, our driver, and I traveled 60 kilometers north to the provincial capital of Banteay Meanchey, Sisophon (*See-so-pone*).

As we drove I noticed that the countryside seemed lusher, more tropical than what I had seen around Phnom Penh. I remarked to Sergei that many people seemed to be, for farmers in Cambodia, doing just fine. He agreed, adding that, with its large fields and adequate rainfall, the Cambodians considered this corner to be the rice basket of their country. Even in the dry season many people still had a small irrigation pond on their land.

The road was the usual mess of potholes and ditches, but not for long. The United Nations was working to improve it from Battambang to Sisophon, while the Royal Thai Army Engineers were working on the road from Sisophon to the Thai border town of Aranyaprathet (*A-rhan-ya-pra-thet*). For thirteen years Aranyaprathet had been the center of Thai/Cambodian border relief operations. Almost every vehicle we saw had "UN" written in big black letters on it, as did our own. Huge dump trucks and road grading machines passed us, stirring up clouds of dust that forced the drivers to drive with their lights on. We passed some of the temporary camps that had been set up for the returnees—sturdy wooden barracks that, no doubt, had made some contractor rich.

By the time we reached Sisophon, we felt as if we had spent three hours inside a cement mixer. But, professional as always, my Russian leader presented us to the provincial authorities as if we had just stepped down from the American presidential jet. This time the governor, Mr. Ith Loeur, turned out to be an old friend of Sergei's who had studied in Russia and had known Sergei there. Like the last governor, he had been swamped by foreign aid workers, but he was warm and friendly. He impressed me as a man who would have chosen to be an artist if fate had not intervened to make him governor. He assigned his chief of police to help us.

As we sat outside his office talking in the shade of a large mango tree, a convoy of buses drove by. The buses were filled with returnees from Thailand, and behind the buses trailed a few trucks filled with the passengers' belongings. Sisophon, we learned, just 50 kilometers from the Thai border and Aranyaprathet, had become the returnees' gateway back into Cambodia.

Our introduction over, it was time for lunch. The chief of police and his lieutenant rode ahead on the chief's motorcycle, somehow ignoring the dust, and led us to the best restaurant in town, the Chung Hua. We had chicken with lunch; that is, there was a live full-grown squawking chicken under and around our table throughout the meal.

With the chief in tow, the service was excellent. The police ordered beer for themselves and what I thought was an unusually large lunch. I had fried fish with vegetables. At the end of the meal the waitress handed the bill to the chief, who grinned sheepishly and handed it to us. Lunch was our treat, as would be dinner. The bill came to almost five dollars apiece.

The chief took us to the best and only hotel in town, the government guesthouse. Our room was a long hall with eight narrow metal beds that spanned the top floor of a run-down two-story concrete building. Downstairs stood a tank for bailing water to bathe with and the lone water-seal toilet. There were no fans and it was 36 degrees centigrade (96 degrees Fahrenheit) in the shade. In the room next to ours were UN soldiers from Malaysia and Indonesia. After they said it was hot, I felt better.

Both that night and the next were, according to Sergei, far too hot to sleep. Baking in our concrete oven, we stayed up long past the time the electricity went off and even after the BBC had finished the 10 P.M. news. We talked until we were sure that we had exhausted every known topic of human conversation, including a recital in Russian of one of Pushkin's poems so that I could more easily grasp the "intangible soul of Russia." Finally, with nothing more to say, Sergei blurted out, "You don't know how much I hate this."

"Hate what?" I was surprised. Was my affable Russian leader complaining?

The room was dark. We were both stretched out on our cots.

"Hate this traveling around, this heat, the car sickness, the food, this room."

He was complaining.

"Come on," I said, "This is our adventure, our tour of duty to the front lines."

"I hate it. I can't tell you how much I hate it."

"Then why are you here?"

"Right now things are rather difficult in Russia. Here my salary is quite good, and you know, after thirteen years, Cambodia is my second motherland."

"So you like it a little?"

"Sometimes it's bearable, but my son is six years old now, and we have a cottage in the country with apple trees."

Sergei thought for a moment, "And you, you could have a comfortable life in America. How can you say that you *like* this?"

"For me, America was boring. Here things aren't boring."

At 39, I still had nothing to lose by leaving the U.S.A.

"I miss my wife."

"I miss whole wheat bread and my mountain bike, but here life is on the edge and we are too. Here, comrade, life is razor sharp."

"You like it that much?"

"Hey, the frill is gone and the thrill is here to stay."

"So, it's just an adventure?"

"Here I'm doing something that makes a difference."

"Really?"

"We'll see."

With that settled, we called it a day.

The next morning we drove back to Battambang and a few hours later flew back to Phnom Penh.

HOTEL LIFE AND FOREIGN WOMEN

I was still living in Le Royal Hotel. In the grounds of the hotel was an open air restaurant with about twenty large round concrete tables and a beach umbrella above each one for shade. Every night there was a disco there for Vietnamese prostitutes and horny foreign men. I went once. The ladies in their skintight dresses and high heels, like professionals everywhere, could be beautiful and exotic. They sat together at tables and waited for drunken, but well-behaved, UN soldiers and civilians to ask them to dance and, they hoped, to take them home. I realized that if I were ever going to drink enough to feel comfortable there, I'd have to give up my liver and all my money. I never went back again. Almost every day, though, one of the men who worked in the hotel urged me to take a Vietnamese girl. I never did.

I met other foreign women who were not prostitutes—secretaries and low-level administrators for the United Nations (all senior positions were held by men). Soon I had the feeling that every pushing-forty woman who still had not found that "someone special" had come to Cambodia, so we had some things in common. They wanted to tell me about their careers or other interesting things—like what it was like to work in UN headquarters in New York City. One of them asked if I wanted to go touring with her. I said yes, and that Sunday she drove me to a few places in a UN truck. I told her that I'd get back in touch with her, but somehow never found the time.

Every day I took a motorcycle taxi to work. At first I had to explain to the crowd of motorcycle taxi drivers who waited at the gate outside Le Royal where my office was, but after a few days they all knew. I could hurry out of the hotel, get on any motorcycle, and away we would go. It was a strange kind of terror to be on one of a throng of motorcycles in the jammed roads—an ant in a huge stream of ants. Occasionally I would touch the arm of a passenger on another motorcycle to remind him or her that their kick starter was about to make contact with the spokes of my motorcycle. At other times I would push us away from a car that was about to cut us off. By the time I got to work, I felt I could do anything.

I kept eating with the rickshaw drivers—men who got quality for a reasonable price. The usual sidewalk restaurant consisted of five or six big aluminum pots on a low table. One pot contained white rice, the rest soups flavored with vegetables, fish, meat, and the ever-present pig fat. From the benches the drivers could keep an eye on their rickshaws while enjoying lunch. The cooks and the drivers were always warm and friendly. They did their best to make me feel comfortable and occasionally had long philosophical conversations with me that included squeezing my knee or laughing at their own jokes, not one of which I understood.

Two weeks after Battambang, I went on one last field trip.

Mission impossible to Siem Reap and Preah Vihear

This would be, we were told, the Mission Impossible of all field trips: we would be going out of radio contact, where no UN people had gone before, to the distant, remote, and virtually unknown province of Preah Vihear (*Pree-ah-wee-hee-a).* "Gosh Superman," I said to Sergei, "really?" "Yes, really."

The first leg of the journey was a flight to Siem Reap (*See-im Ree-ap).* As we strapped ourselves into our canvas seats on the plane, it felt wonderful to be out of the office and on the road again with Sergei, the cartographers, and the interpreters in a C160 with a French crew. I set my watch to see if it took the same amount of time to fly to Siem Reap as it did to Battambang—on the map Siem Reap looked just a little closer. I was right, and we landed in just forty minutes instead of forty-five. There was only one problem: we were not in Siem Reap; we were in Battambang. But never mind, the French crew told us, in an hour we would be flying to Siem Reap. As we waited to get back on the plane, the Australian soldiers, "peacekeepers" who had been on the plane with us, unpacked their gear. They had high-tech plastic rifles with scopes they claimed could put a bullet "between a bloke's eyebrows at four hundred meters." The soldiers from Malaysia and Indonesia all wanted to pick up the guns and sight them. According to one of the Australian soldiers, the United Nations was willing to "risk substantial casualties" to keep the peace, and it looked as if they meant business. After an hour, just as we started to lose that I'm-almost-airsick feeling, we climbed back on the plane and flew to Siem Reap.

The UN believed that 20 percent of the countryside of Cambodia remained under Khmer Rouge control and that most of that area was here in northern Cambodia. Perhaps this explains why we flew very low—just above the tree tops. We enjoyed the trip. Because the seven of us were the only people on the plane, the crew let us stand up, put our heads in the portholes, and look down at the rice fields and forests below. A few times beautiful flocks of white birds swarmed up beneath us. This time we landed in Siem Reap.

Siem Reap is the spiritual center of Cambodia and home of one of the biggest religious monuments in the world, Angkor Wat. Although many don't quite make it, all Cambodians claim that they plan to visit Angkor Wat before they die. The place is regarded as so sacred that even the Khmer Rouge left it alone. It is also Cambodia's main tourist attraction, so the airport had a large waiting room.

The British Military Liaison Officer, Major Lewis, was waiting for us at the airport. He said he had been trying to make arrangements for us to reach our final destination—the provincial capital of Preah Vihear, Tbeng Meanchey, but so far no one could even tell him where Preah Vihear was, or how to get in touch with the people there. "Never mind," Sergei told him, "those are just details, we'll go tomorrow."

As we were standing in the shade of the waiting room, trying to figure out a way into town, I noticed a sprightly Cambodian man squatting down on his heels the way people do in Asia. He had turned his body in the direction of the plane, and yet I felt he was staring directly at us: who were we?—what did we want?—could we be of use to him? He was trim, in his mid-thirties, wore wire-rimmed glasses, and seemed to be intently studying the plane while sizing us up. Major Lewis, who lacked only a monocle to keep himself from looking like an officer from the British Raj, indicated that we should keep our mouths shut, and told us that this gentleman was a Khmer Rouge general with whom the foreign military liaison had secretly made contact. We all gave him another glance, which he seemed not to notice.

Siem Reap was pleasant. Many of the streets were shaded; there was a muddy river flowing slowly through town and a palatial hotel that was appropriately named "Grand Hotel d'Angkor." Angkor Wat was just six kilometers down the road through a beautiful forest that was, unfortunately, mined. The Grand had rooms for $46 a night. So when a second military liaison officer, Major Wu from the People's Republic of China, showed up, we asked him if he could find us a cheaper place. Major Wu, who suavely dismissed his fluent English as a product of the Chinese educational system, said that he would be happy to. He put us up in a small guesthouse run by an industrious family who kept a crocodile farm out back. Air-conditioned double rooms were $25. The family raised the crocodiles to ship them to Thailand where they were made into handbags. All the rooms, which smelled of freshly poured concrete, had running water and balconies that overlooked the walled crocodile enclosure below. The hotel was a pleasant surprise—and it was clean.

After we had settled in, Sergei called us together, ordered ice-water, and announced the plan.

Three members of the team—a secretary, a cartographer, and a translator—would stay in Siem Reap to gather data for the election, while he, a cartographer, another translator, and I flew by UN helicopter to Preah Vihear, a place that only existed on the map, as far as anyone in Siem Reap knew.

Early that afternoon Sergei appealed to the governor of Siem Reap province to try to contact Preah Vihear for us. We went back to see him later in the day. The governor said that contact with Preah Vihear was impossible.

A look at a map showed that Tbeng Meanchey was about as far from Siem Reap as Siem Reap was from Battambang. The problem was that to get there it was necessary to fly over territory that some people described as "contested" and others said was controlled by the Khmer Rouge. I talked to Sergei about it that night.

"Have you written your will?" he asked me seriously.

"Yes, and I sent some letters home just before I came here. But you're the man with a wife and son."

"I know."

"So?"

"So I'm reasonably sure that nothing too bad will happen."

I left well enough alone and didn't ask what made him so sure.

We were back at the airport at seven the next morning. The two military liaison officers came to see us off as if they wanted to note our departure for some future report or investigation. Major Lewis kindly offered us his helmet and flak jacket. Since there was only one of each, Sergei declined. If it came to that, we would all go down together. We watched the chopper come into view from Battambang and land. It was a white "Puma," with "UN" painted in huge black letters on the sides. It could seat eight—six on the fold-up canvas benches that were bolted to the floor of the main cabin, and two just inside the door near the cockpit.

The three-man French crew stepped out, said "Bonjour," and shook hands with the four of us. Sergei showed them on a map where he thought we would find Tbeng Meanchey.

We climbed in, fastened our seat belts, put on the hearing protectors, and waited for them to close the doors. But it was too hot to close the doors. And anyway, why block the view? Yes, I thought, let's be cool, and fly with the doors open.

The blades rotated, the chopper shook, and even with the hearing protectors on, the sound rose to an earsplitting whirring roar. After a long taxi down the runway, we took off.

One of the military liaison officers had asked the pilot to fly us over Angkor Wat, which he was only too happy to do. We flew over thick forest, the moat that surrounds the wat, and then Angkor Wat came into center view. From the air it looked like a mud fairy castle, with the large surrounding wall, the long walkway that leads to the main shrine, and the three steeples that crown the temple. It looked too mystical, too dreamlike, to be the largest religious structure on earth.

My watch had an altimeter—we were flying at exactly one thousand meters, about three thousand feet. The countryside—forest and rice fields—did not look much different from what we had seen the day before, only now there were no paved roads below us. The rice fields ended when we crossed a forested mountain range scarred by large patches of fallen trees—cuttings made by local non-Khmer minorities who still practiced "slash and burn" agriculture.

Supposedly, large parts of Preah Vihear were controlled by the Khmer Rouge. I kept waiting for some idiot kid with an automatic rifle to open up on us, the first UN helicopter to fly into Preah Vihear.

At that moment—sitting in the helicopter's doorway, looking down at the top of the jungle, and waiting for some silent, invisible messenger of death to come racing up faster than I could see it from an encampment hidden under the green canopy below—I felt the same terror that everyone who flew in the Vietnam War must have felt. In my terror, in what could have been the last moments of my life, it also occurred to me that flying in a helicopter with the doors open while sitting on your hat and occasionally grabbing onto the person sitting next to you when you felt your stomach moving up to your throat, was about the most fun a person could have anywhere. I could now understand why, to helicopter pilots, the thrill of flying like this made everything else seem pretty dull.

After about an hour the pilot somehow determined that we were close to Tbeng Meanchey. He circled around a few times, wondering where to land. People below had come out of their houses and were looking up at us as if we were extraterrestrials. We waved down at them, and many waved back at the strangers from outer space.

The pilot decided to land at the local soccer field. As we came down, a crowd of people, including the entire nearby primary school, swarmed to meet us with the children running on ahead. Who, everyone wondered, were we? What did we want? What could we do for them? I had questions of my own. Who are they? What do they want? Haven't they ever seen a helicopter landing in their soccer field? The rotors were creating a dust storm below. Everyone except the pilot, who was wearing a helmet and goggles, cupped his hands over his eyes. I waited for the rotor to stop spinning, uncovered my eyes, and noticed that I was covered with dust. The Eagle had landed on Mars.

I peered out. A crowd had surrounded us just beyond the sweep of the blades, and it looked friendly. The interpreter jumped out, followed by one of the crew. Together they signaled the crowd to keep back. The children, however, could not resist coming up close to the space ship. I jumped out and enlisted the help of some local men to keep the children away. Sergei moved into the crowd to find out who was in charge.

We did not have to wait long. A Russian-made jeep drove up, and men in uniforms stepped out. They told us that we had landed in the wrong place. Sergei apologized for the rude touchdown and told them who we were. They told us who they were—officials of the local government, not Khmer Rouge. With that settled, they said that we were welcome and volunteered to take us in their jeep to the governor's office.

Meanwhile, the helicopter crew had set up a radio antenna to inform headquarters that we were still alive and had made it this far. A moment later, Sergei explained to the helicopter pilot where the government officials wanted him to land next time, in forty-eight hours, and they took off.

Provincial headquarters, like everything else in Tbeng Meanchey, was not very far away. The town seemed relaxed. Just a few Japanese motorcycles and Russian jeeps traveled on the dark red dirt roads of downtown. The square wooden and thatched houses were widely spaced with stick fences around them. Maybe in the rainy season Tbeng Meanchey would be beautiful. But now, in the dry season, everything was brown, and there were not enough trees to make things lush or cool. It was just hot and dry.

We drove into the courtyard of the government compound, and, even though we were unannounced, the officials were waiting for us. We were ushered into the conference room, sat down, and promptly served Chinese tea followed by Seven-Up with ice. Provincial authorities had tried to solve their heating and cooling problems by placing their conference table outside, with just a roof for shade and lattice walls to let in a stray breeze.

Sergei introduced us as usual. They nodded politely. Yes, one of them began, they had heard that the UN was in Cambodia, but we were the first representatives of the United Nations to visit their province. They then told us the same thing that almost everyone we would meet over the next two days would tell us. It went about like this:

We are sick of this war, tired of all the fighting, the terror, the death. Can you help us stop this war? We want to live in peace, to be able to visit our relatives, to be secure at night. Can you do anything to stop the fighting? Why do the Khmer Rouge keep fighting? Will the United Nations make them stop? Why don't you go talk to the Khmer Rouge and ask them why the fighting continues? When will there be peace?

We had read the Paris Peace Agreement, so we could tell them some of the things that should be happening during the peace process, but we could not give them specific answers or speak on behalf of the entire United Nations. Mostly, we could just listen.

One comforting tidbit we told them, having just heard it from the Australians, was that the head of the United Nations military operation in Cambodia, General Sanderson, had said that if the Khmer Rouge, or anyone else, did not eventually surrender their arms, they would be hunted as outlaws. So there was, we believed, a very good chance that peace was coming.

As usual, everyone was hospitable. In preparation for the eventual arrival of UNTAC, they had appointed a special committee, to whose chairman we were now talking. He promised to do everything he could for us. He could have all the statistics ready for us by the next day, and our cartographer could begin work that afternoon using maps prepared by the local military. But first, we could go to our hotel, which was their hotel. As usual, the only accommodation in town was the government guesthouse. The chairman told us that we could stay there for free and eat gratuitously as well. This was a first.

We climbed back into the jeep for another short ride.

The guesthouse was an airy two-story wooden building with big rooms and pleasant furnishing. The toilet and shower were out back; there was a separate kitchen/dining room. By the time we arrived, the cook and her helpers were already doing in some chickens.

The cook was a Cambodian-Vietnamese woman who told Sergei that she had watched the execution of her parents and had seen her brother gutted by the Khmer Rouge. Only in her mid-thirties, she had the perpetual look of terror that one saw on some of the faces in Cambodia, but she was an excellent cook. For the next two days I had to take back all of the terrible things I'd said about food in Cambodia, but then again she was Vietnamese. She treated us to lots of fresh bean sprouts, green leaves, and spicy (not outrageously hot) sauces to put on the rice, broiled fish and meat.

And somehow at every meal she managed to provide us with imported, and then smuggled, beer. Preah Vihear had been cut off by road from the rest of Cambodia for six weeks. The government officials told us that the Khmer Rouge had monitored their walkie-talkie conversations. Having learned that a large rice convoy was going to travel out of Preah Vihear to Phnom Penh south through Kampong Thom province on the only remaining open road, they had mined the road. When the convoy hit the mines, the Khmer Rouge killed one of the drivers, took the rice, and left another man with no legs. Since that time no one had tried to make it out. There had been helicopter flights to and from Phnom Penh, but they were irregular. Surprisingly, though, when we visited the market it was jammed with any consumer goods that the locals might desire—our cartographer even bought himself a golf shirt. How could that be? It could be because, after twenty years of war, the Cambodian people were capable of smuggling anything anywhere. A little risk was part of doing business.

The provincial authorities joined us for lunch, as they would join us for dinner and every meal after that. Sergei had said that he'd never met a Cambodian he didn't like, and I was beginning to see his point. People listened politely. I sensed that any kind of confrontational approach or hint of moral or intellectual superiority was not the style here. So we could talk. Two of the five men who ate with us had been shipped to Preah Vihear from Phnom Penh by Pol Pot's forces in the late 1970s. For some reason they had decided to stay; they said they preferred the quiet life. This was good: if they hadn't, I was sure they'd have gone crazy long ago.

These men, unlike our dear cook, did not have much bad to say about Pol Pot and life in the late seventies. There were not any killing fields here, and when the Vietnamese arrived in 1979 the Khmer Rouge soldiers fled for the jungle. Later, in 1980, when parts of Cambodia were starving during the famine that followed the Vietnamese invasion, Preah Vihear, perhaps because of its isolation, was able to feed itself. Their main complaint was with the continued fighting. Enough was enough. Yes, everyone was damn tired of the fighting, as they told us over and over again.

That afternoon we began the cartographic and statistical work. In the middle of the afternoon a government official informed us that the temperature was 42 degrees centigrade (108 F.), or hot enough for a Khmer military man to step outside the crowded office and unbutton his shirt

Two Cambodian militiamen, after investigating mysterious gunshots, pose with the author on the bank of the Tonlé Sap river in Kampong Chhnang province. The children of Vietnamese fishermen look on.

Dressed like a queen, Rita pauses for a moment on the morning of her wedding day. She has about six more costume changes to go before the big day is over..

for a minute. Yes, one of the officials told us, Preah Vihear was Cambodia's hottest and, because of its remoteness and lack of rainfall, poorest province.

On the second afternoon, with all our work done, the provincial authorities invited us on a field trip to the nearby village of an ethnic minority. It sounded interesting, so at three in the afternoon a convoy of three jeeps, the first carrying soldiers, headed off for the village.

"But Sergei," I said as we sat in the second jeep, "if the Khmer Rouge listen to the radios of the provincial authorities, they know we're coming, right?"

"Right, but don't worry. We aren't carrying any rice."

"Yes, of course." But I couldn't help but wonder if the soldiers in the lead vehicle knew how to use their ancient rifles.

The road, after we left town, was two parallel ungraded dirt tracks that wandered through the scrub. As we bounced along Sergei assured me that the Russian-made jeeps, which never wore out, could go anywhere. We drove through barren dry-season scrub and then through patches of green hardwood forests. After forty minutes, we came to a village that looked abandoned. As if the plague or a marauding army had recently swept through, things were a mess. Yards had not been swept, doors and windows were missing. The bush was about to reclaim the area. It was also, we learned, the village that was hosting us. We drove to the center of town. There the entire population of perhaps two hundred people was waiting for us under the shade of two large pipal trees.

The villagers were standing in a semicircle with the unmarried women at one end and the old men and village officials at the other. In the middle were three picnic tables placed end to end. We climbed out of the jeeps and everyone applauded. To the villagers, the United Nations and the possibility of peace had arrived!

We shook hands with everyone who wanted to shake hands, sat down, and proceeded to be stared at—everyone wanted to have a look at the foreigners. And we wanted to have a look at them. This "ethnic minority" looked and spoke Khmer like any other Cambodian people we had met. The only real difference was that here almost everyone had whooping cough. A constant hacking *whoop* accompanied the background of any conversation. Some of the children had the lifeless wiry hair that comes from vitamin deficiencies. Other people had serious eye and teeth problems, but everyone I saw had all four limbs, which was not always the case in Cambodia.

Our hosts provided us with the best they could find: Seven-Up, local tea, and coconut toddy. We opted for the toddy. Sergei explained our mission and everyone listened. Soon someone produced a huge portable tape player and began bombarding us with the screeching sound of Khmer rock and roll. Sergei asked for local music instead. Instantly, two young men dashed off and returned with the village band: a violin player and his drummer. They played music to accompany the *rom-voong*, the most popular dance in this part of Asia. For the *rom-voong* two circles are formed, with the women on the inside. Both circles, going in the same direction, walk slowly around to the beat of the music emanating, in this case, from a little hand-held drum. Hand movements are allowed, but if the dancers are too drunk or too hot, they can simply walk. No one ever touches his or her partner. After a few more glasses of coconut toddy, at everyone's request, we joined the rom-voong. My dancing partner was a chubby 14-year-old who said that, although I was basically okay, for a foreigner, she would wait until she was seventeen to get married. Yes, I said, it is better to wait.

I was almost forty and still waiting.

Back at the guesthouse, the government officials kept the electricity on until midnight, even though we had told them they could turn off the generator at ten o'clock. They said that our comfort and happiness were their greatest desire. After nine o'clock, however, I noticed that they did not want to talk to us and thus interrupt their card game that would, coincidentally, continue until midnight.

The next morning we assembled at the official helicopter landing site, and at exactly the right time our helicopter landed. We shook hands with everyone one last time and climbed on board. As we lifted off, the crew threw down chocolate bars and then, just for fun and to see who had fastened their seat belts and digested breakfast, the pilot performed a few crazy swoops and loops over the village.

That night we had a reunion with our team members who had stayed behind in Siem Reap. After a few beers, Sergei, in the tradition of Tolstoy and Solzhenitsyn, explained his version of our return journey. According to Sergei, on the way back our helicopter had been hit by a surface-to-air missile. He explained how, as the 'copter had slowly plummeted to earth, I had parachuted out to lighten the passenger load. Sergei said that the pilot was then able to regain control and land safely on an isolated mountain top where he could make emergency repairs. I met them there, Sergei continued, after slithering through Khmer Rouge small arms fire. A fierce battle ensued, with Sergei eventually wrestling a bazooka away from a Khmer Rouge soldier and blasting him and his buddies. Some of the details were a little sketchy, Sergei admitted, but never mind. As he would personally give a full detailed account to the United Nations Secretary-General, he did not have to elaborate right now.

2 Stop Making Sense
June - July 1992

That was the last of the field trips and the last time I worked with Sergei. He was relegated to some administrative post in the Electoral Component, and I was kept in what became known as the "Computer Room." Now the *real* census of Cambodia was beginning.

United Nations Volunteers who had just finished the language and culture classes would survey the eligible voters of Cambodia. There were about eleven thousand villages in the twenty-one provinces of Cambodia. Each volunteer would get a province or two, a team of interpreters, motorcycles, trucks, radios, and one "Village Description Form" for each village in his area. It sounded good so far. The "Village Description Form" was drawn up by a Frenchman who could not really read English. He made the form by copying the questions he read in a scholarly report that someone else had written to outline the need for an Advanced Electoral Planning Unit in Cambodia. No one field-tested the questionnaire, discussed it, or asked what kind of data the form would generate. Did it ask the questions that needed answering? No one knew. No one asked. I was asked several times to make modifications on the form because I could do the computer work. No one told me what it was for.

Anyone who studies history knows that people do not learn from history or from their mistakes, nor do they listen to anthropologists. What do they know? So the work began with everyone working in the dark and not knowing what they were doing.

Many of the UNV volunteers were from India and Nepal. They had a difficult time understanding my American English and a more difficult time following complex written English instructions, as I found out when I was asked to teach an introductory computer class. The UN was going to give each of them a laptop computer—laptop computers became the symbol of the UN in Cambodia—and felt that the volunteers should know how to use them. Fair enough.

I planned the class and posted a sign-up sheet. Anyone who wanted to take the class at ten the next morning could write his or her name on the sheet. I numbered the sheet from one to twenty.

These were the complex written English instructions that baffled my South Asian colleagues: "Write your name below if you want to take the class."

The next day, I found that most people had squashed their names in at number ten, because, as one of them told me, "We all want to study computers at ten o'clock."

This was an omen of things to come.

Thus, a few days later, when my colleagues left Phnom Penh in their air-conditioned trucks jammed with their personal possessions, eight hundred dollar walkie-talkies, and four thousand dollar laptop computers, they had only a vague idea of what they were supposed to do. No one had explained their job to them *in a way they could understand*, and as is the Asian way, they had not asked. Some of them were very bright people. One man from India had spent years working in Washington, D.C. juggling numbers in the Agency for International Development (A.I.D.). "Statistics," he said when I asked him if he was going to enjoy collecting data on Mars, "I enjoy working with statistics."

Work began. The main idea, I gleaned from reading the report that outlined the need for the electoral planning unit, was to find out where the villages were, how many potential voters lived in them, and how easy it would be for potential voters in village "A" to go to village "B" to vote. One of the questions on the form was, "Discuss the usual travel routine of the people." To me that meant that if everyone from villages A, B, and C went to the market in village D, then D would be the logical place for a polling station. But no one had explained this to the people making the survey. When the forms started coming back to the Computer Room, we learned that vast numbers of people all over Cambodia only went to the rice fields or never went anywhere. Another part of the form had an "Other comments" section. Other comments included, "The chief of the village asks that the UN build a hospital, school, and dig wells as water is the big problem." We also discovered that many of the volunteers or their assistants could not be bothered *actually to go* to the more isolated villages and had simply asked a government official in the district capital about them—exactly what Sergei and I had just done on our whirlwind tour of remote provinces.

The survey also called for a map of the area so that later people could find the village again, but no guidelines were given as to how a map was to be drawn. In many parts of the East, if you ask someone for directions, they will accompany you part way or say, "Go there and ask someone else." Not unexpectedly, then, map-making was not something most people knew much about. After a few weeks, when the maps started trickling back to the office, I noticed that direction indicators and scale remained mysteries to our newly commissioned cartographers. One man produced beautifully drawn maps with yellow and green highlighter pens that photocopied into perfectly blank pages.

Much of the data then, as they say in computer lingo, was GIGO—Garbage In Garbage Out.

WHY COMMUNISM FAILED

My boss, Hugo, was from the former Soviet satellite state of Bulgaria. He had some of that European charm that makes Americans feel as if they were raised in a barn. When we would meet European women I would say, "Hey, how ya doin'?" He would kiss them on both cheeks. When we went to a restaurant, which I would do if someone else was paying, he would ask for something like "chilled Chardonnay." I'd ask for a beer with ice. He had charm, no doubt about that—but everyone hated him. Everywhere he went he made enemies. So many people disliked him that I decided, just to be different, that I would try to like him. But it was impossible.

Sometimes he would tell the five Cambodians who worked in the office not to be shy, to speak up, and to practice their English more by speaking to him. But his hearing and their English were not the problem—the problem was, they hated him. The Cambodian people, even after twenty-two years of war, are about the most laid-back and polite people on earth. They are so polite that most of the time they don't even call people by name. Instead, everyone is "Brother," "Uncle," or "Older sister." Cambodians like to have a *personal* relationship with everyone; Hugo preferred a *mechanical* relationship with everyone. To him, people were like a hammer or a saw. If the tool didn't do the job the way you wanted it done, you yelled at it and threw it aside.

A public display of anger is not the way in Southeast Asia. There, when people are publicly subjected to your anger, they *never* forget it and they hate you forever. After a few weeks of working with Hugo, the Cambodians in the office told me that they would hate him forever. For me, Hugo came to symbolize what communist life in Bulgaria must have been like. He was, though, in his own way, a brilliant computer programmer.

He violated, however, the first rule of database design: never refer to anything by name—give it a number. Names can be misspelled, duplicated, reversed, and otherwise confused, which is why the U.S. Social Security system gives everyone a number. Not Hugo. So, as always and as expected, names were misspelled, duplicated, reversed, and otherwise confused.

To Hugo, everything was a problem and everything that anyone else did was wrong, unless they were his superiors, who were always right. As underlings, according to Hugo, we had only to do what our superiors told us and all would go well. Under his regime the Cambodians and I learned to play dumb. If you're just a useless tool, play cool. After a few weeks of working closely with Hugo, I had gained a clear understanding of the collapse of communism and had resolved never to visit Bulgaria.

There was one other United Nations Volunteer on the Computer Room team. Mohammed Ali was from Pakistan. Tall, rail-thin, and chain-smoking, he had been a database programmer in Pakistan and believed that he could do the same job in Cambodia. He did his best to work with Hugo on the database design, which meant that after a few weeks he and Hugo had stopped speaking to each other. I think that Mohammed Ali now understands the collapse of communism and never wants to visit Bulgaria either.

Driving Rules and Traffic Safety in Phnom Penh

I had been in Cambodia eight weeks when the UN decided to move the UN volunteers who had not gone to the provinces out of our beloved Le Royal Hotel and into a guesthouse. We all worked in the same place, but the guesthouse was located on the other side of Phnom Penh, so I continued to take a motorcycle taxi to work.

By now I had developed a level of motorcycle taxi expertise that was virtually unequaled in the expatriate community. Foreigners in Phnom Penh said that motorcycle taxi drivers drove with no concern for any rules whatsoever, but with my experience as a passenger and as a former university lecturer in anthropology, I discovered that motorcycle taxi drivers did indeed follow their own strict set of rules:

1) Never stop at an intersection. Somehow you will get through it. If you absolutely cannot get through, turn against the flow of traffic for a while, riding near the curbside. If you are obstructed by water or too many pedestrians along the curb, never mind; ride in the middle of the oncoming lane, against the flow of traffic.

    In the West we call this "playing chicken." In Cambodia it's the normal driving style.

2) Never wear a helmet. Helmets are for foreigners and sold in

the market for twelve dollars. It is true that most deaths in traffic accidents—and there are a lot of deaths in traffic accidents—are the result of head injuries. Nevertheless, if you watch where you are going, and even if you don't, it will happen to someone else. Also, helmets cause hair loss.

3) Disregard all traffic signs and what people in the West call "common sense." *"One way," "Look before entering a busy intersection," "Slower traffic to the curbside,"* and *"Move disabled vehicles to the side of the road"* have absolutely no meaning to the drivers of Phnom Penh.

It was rule number one that proved my undoing. My driver was zooming north up Monivong Boulevard—the major business street—toward the intersection where traffic converges on the busy New Market area. As usual, the cars and motorcycles were entering the intersection at full speed as if they were the only vehicles on the road. From the back of the motorcycle, I looked ahead and felt as though I were in some horrific full-color-graphics and sound-enhanced multimedia computer game—*Motorcycle Gauntlet.* Now, I thought, how is this guy going to sail through this without getting hit? But he did it. That is, an oncoming motorcycle missed him and hit me. A handle bar smashed into my stomach and whacked me off the bike. I landed on my hands and knees. After a minute, I stood up. My shirt was torn, my stomach was oozing blood, my knee was bleeding, and my hand was hurting. I was in a state of shock and confusion as were both drivers—they couldn't decide if they should fight each other or run away. They looked at each other menacingly for a minute and decided to leave well enough alone. My driver indicated to me that I should get back on his motorcycle.

Reaching the office, I stumbled inside and asked a Khmer interpreter to explain to the driver that, even though there was immense competition, he might very well be the worst driver in Phnom Penh. Furthermore, using body language, I showed the driver that my shirt was torn, my gut was oozing blood, my knee was bleeding, my hand still hurt, and that he should be thankful I did not report him to the police. My driver nodded and informed me that I was entitled to my own opinion, but, more importantly, he was entitled to his fare. I was entering the final stage of shock, so I paid him.

Inside the office, I found a quiet corner, lay down, and wondered what was going to happen. Death by internal bleeding, I realized, was one of the less messy ways to go. As the darkness descended, I...I fell asleep. Fifteen minutes later I woke up. I was alive, and all of my body's vital signs were active. I shortly discovered that, other than the exceedingly masculine imprint of a motorcycle handlebar on my stomach and some equally masculine blood on my clothes, I seemed to be, at least physically, intact.

More on Missing Body Parts and Dining in the Capital

That ended my motorcycle taxi days. I now had to find a new way to travel between home and work.

I decided to live in my office, UNTAC XIII, Electoral Headquarters. Why not? The UNV guesthouse would not be much of a loss.

I moved in, stored my clothes in a file cabinet, kept my toothbrush in my desk, and showered in the shower. Most Cambodian offices have showers: the landlords know that although business may be cyclical, the housing shortage is chronic. I slept on a mat on the floor. The office had hired a young man to act as the nighttime guard. His responsibility was to lock the front gate at ten o'clock each night. Other than that, he did not pay much attention to what went on around him. I let him play with the computers a few times, and we became friends. As I was discreet about it and no one seemed to care, living in the office worked out surprisingly well.

On most evenings I walked over to Monivong Boulevard, crossed it, and had dinner at a sidewalk food stall. Crossing Monivong could be a major adventure in itself. Frequently the street lights would be out, and many motorcyclists did not have lights on their motorcycles, a sense of a reasonable speed, or any understanding of what was the proper side of the road to drive on. They came at me from all angles like missiles in the computer game *Missile Command.*

Dinner was always exactly the same—a fruit shake of blended papaya with sweet condensed milk and sugar water, and a sandwich of French bread with cucumber, grated pickled green papaya, and fresh onion. After a few weeks I started to like it. I became friends with the street vendors after I took their pictures and gave them prints. They would see me coming and start making my dinner. A few of them worked there all day and most of the night. One woman told me that her husband, a wounded soldier, could not work; to support the family she stayed on the street from dawn until midnight.

I was the only UN person eating regularly in the street stalls of Phnom Penh. Everyone else ate in the old locally run French restaurants or in the new Western restaurants that were springing up around Phnom Penh. I couldn't stand the atmosphere or the price of the Western restaurants, and the French restaurants all had the sanitary standards of the street, but were more expensive.

Most people in the UN hierarchy still subscribed to the germ theory of disease transmission. But not me. By this time I had thrown away the memo from Headquarters that said something about cholera in Cambodia and that cautioned us about eating on the street. I chose to believe the Cambodian theory: the flies in Cambodia had been specially trained not to carry disease, and things could be "spiritually clean" while appearing to be physically dirty.

I seldom got diarrhea. Many foreigners complained about it all the time.

I went to the same roadside stalls for breakfast—a delicious glass of freshly squeezed sugarcane juice with ice, and a bowl of white rice-noodle curry with basil and mint leaves thrown in for flavor.

For lunch, I would have someone drop me off at the New Market or *Psah Thmay*. Built by the French in the 1930s in Art-Deco style, New Market was the Eiffel Tower of Cambodian markets. Four huge wings converged into a central dome big enough for the birds who lived there never to venture outside. Under the dome were the gold merchants, jewelers, and watch sellers. The wings were divided into electronics, new and used clothing, canned goods, meat and fish, fresh fruit and vegetables, and food stalls.

Monkeys and marijuana were for sale, plus the usual Asian delicacies of live frogs, eels, and live and fried insects. People who weren't vendors gained their livelihood by telling fortunes, reading palms, begging, or by sitting beside a scale on the floor hoping that people would pay one cent to weigh themselves. I would have lunch perched on a little stool in one of the food stalls. It was hot, noisy, smoky, and crowded, with Cambodia's specially trained flies everywhere and in abundance. Food was cooked on wood fires, and smoke rose through the holes in the low metal roof, leaving the roof beams black with soot. The foreigners I worked with told me that they felt nauseous just walking through the market, but to me it was exciting and exotic. Sitting there, always entertained by the passing crowd, I could easily imagine someone selling their virgin daughter to one of the UNTAC administrators (always a rumor), or selling a truckload of AK-47s to a foreign government (probably true). Often I would buy lunch for a beggar or two. They would ask for money and I would tell them to sit down. They were usually surprised by the invitation, and after eating they rarely expressed much thanks, but then again they didn't have to. What did I care?

Some of the beggars were missing fingers, limbs, or eyes, not to mention husbands, a bath, and clean clothes. One day I saw a blind man playing a guitar as he walked through the market. The guitar, like its owner, was on its last legs—what kept it from falling apart was the burlap case that had been permanently sewn around it. The musician held his guitar straight up in front of him so as not to hit other people with it as he walked through the crowded market. His wife, who looked to be in her late thirties, walked in front of him. She was blind as well. A short string, with which she pulled her husband along, was tied from behind her waist to the front of her husband's pants. Her tattered shirt was open, exposing her sagging breasts as she nursed a baby. She kept one hand on the shoulder of a little boy, apparently her son, who was walking in front of her and could see. One did not need to speak Khmer to know that her husband was singing a dirge about a man who was way down on his luck. He only knew a few chords. The market people were pretty tough, but even they gave this family a second look.

Another day my luncheon guest was an amputee who was only missing a leg below the knee, a minor injury when compared to the double amputees who parked themselves at the entrances to the market. He continued to wear his army uniform, as did many of the amputees, and maintained something of a military presence—perhaps he had been an officer. He saw that I was in a bad mood, was lonely, hung over, or all three. Still the leader, he caught me with a look in his eye that said, "Hey guy, cheer up, will ya?"

I looked away.

He had not given up. "The food's pretty good, eh?" He smiled.

"Not too bad." I said,

He offered me a cigarette.

I told him that I didn't smoke. He lit up, leaned back, and made a pantomime of a film star smoking a cigarette. In spite of everything, I had to smile.

One night months later, I saw him stumbling drunk on the street. The life of a beggar seemed to have gotten the better of him.

Once a rather good-looking teenage girl asked me for money. She looked like she had last washed her clothes before entering puberty—now she was bursting out of them. "Where are you from?" I asked her.

"I'm from Svay Rieng province, uncle," she said.

"So what are you doing here?"

"I'm looking for my brother."

"Have you found him yet?"

"No, not yet."

"Where do you think he is?"

"I don't know, uncle. I only know he is somewhere in Phnom Penh."

"I see." I gave her some money. "Good luck—I hope you find him."

I finished lunch. As I was leaving the market she saw me again. "Sir, sir," she said, "money for food."

"I just gave you some money. Don't you remember?"

"Sorry uncle, all foreigners look alike."

Another time, in front of the Calmette Hospital, I invited a mother and her young son to join me for noodles. The mother was hesitant, so the little boy, who looked about six years old, put his arms around her waist, and looked up into her eyes. His face had lit up as though I had just offered him a ticket to Disneyland. "Oh Mama," he whispered, "please let's have breakfast." He was incredibly cross-eyed. They sat down and I bought them breakfast.

OFFICE LIFE, ADULTERY, AND THE THAI LADY

In the office, crisis seemed to follow crisis. The big problem was that no one ever knew what was going on. We could not see or understand where things were leading. Were we collecting the right information? Were we organizing it in a way that would make sense to other people? Would it be useful to them? We didn't know. Hugo told us not to think about it.

By early July we started receiving thick folders filled with the village description forms from the provinces, but we had a very difficult time aggregating them into one database. If, for example, the province of Pursat had eight hundred villages and five districts, over a week typists A, B, and C could type in that data on three different computers while typists D, E, and F were typing the data from another province, Ratanak Kiri, which had six hundred villages in nine districts. Next, we had to combine the data from the six computers into one master database that would allow us to compare Pursat to Ratanak Kiri. That turned out to be the big problem. We needed, of course, to network, or link, the computers together, but Hugo, whose superiors were always right and not to be bothered, did not want to ask the UN bureaucratic system to put a network in place, although different UN systems in Cambodia would later become networked. So he tried his own solutions, none of which worked very well.

The Computer Room office staff consisted of two Cambodian men, two Cambodian women, one Thai woman, and me. Hugo and Mohammed Ali chain smoked in another room. Everyone in the Computer Room liked everyone else, so we went on a few picnics together, and soon a married man and a single woman were committing adultery together. But not me. I was checking out the Thai lady, Lok.

Lok, with her smallpox complexion, broken smile, and stick-figure body, could never be described as pretty, but she was sweet and fun-loving, two qualities that the Thais are famous for. I had lived in Thailand for three years and knew something about the Thais—they are okay. She was Chinese-Thai, and they're okay too. The Chinese are the business people in Thailand. Lok had a sister, Dim, who had worked as an accountant for the UN in Bangkok before being transferred to Cambodia. I guessed that Dim was now some kind of high-ranking UN official because every day she would come by the office in a chauffeur-driven UN car to pick up her sister.

I started to know and like Lok. She had charm. From the first she told me that she liked me because all women liked me, and all women liked me because I was so charming. It was hard to resist a line like that.

At the end of May Dim was transferred to Singapore, but the chauffeur-driven car did not stop coming for Lok, who continued to live in the same large house. Lok would occasionally invite me over for dinner. She was checking me out. The house by any standards was comfortable. Downstairs was a living room, kitchen, and one bedroom; upstairs were more bedrooms. There was a large yard outside and a live-in housekeeper who stayed downstairs. The housekeeper was an older matronly Chinese lady who seemed to think that if she spoke loudly enough I would start to understand Chinese. Her system never worked, but she never stopped trying. She did all the cleaning, cooking and shopping for Lok.

Thus relieved of the menial and mundane tasks of life, Lok, although she still complained, had it easy.

Lok and I spent a few Saturday afternoons walking around Phnom Penh. We always had something to talk about—work, her past, her family, life in Thailand.

Soon I was her best friend, and she told me as much. But not long after that, I came to see that she was as simple as a hot Cambodian dry-season day is long, and I completely lost interest in her.

But life is short, and she still sat at the desk next to mine in the office. She liked me, and we were friends. I had been in Cambodia three months. The UN was now flooding Cambodia with new offices, equipment, and people. There were no computer technicians, though, so people would sometimes drop by the office for help. Hugo, who could be very rude in telling everyone except his superiors that he could not help them, would, if we were not too busy, send them to me.

That was how I met Sari, from Pakistan, who worked as a secretary in another UN office. I helped her zap a computer virus, and she invited me to a party where I discovered that she was an extraordinary nonstop MTV rock-video dancer. I could follow along. As the party ended, at two in the morning, we shared a cramped motorcycle taxi ride to her house where she jumped off, and I continued on to the office. The next week, she invited me to another party. By the second party I was excited enough to tell a friend who was going to the same party that Sari would be there and easy to spot—she would be the most beautiful woman. And there she was with her skintight pants and halter top. We had a beer, and danced. But when we started talking, she gave me a surprise by saying those two dreaded words: "I'm married."

"That's good," I said.

"What's good about it?"

"I don't know, give me a minute to think about it."

Sari was married to "the only decent man in Pakistan" who had stayed in Pakistan to run his business. But never mind, she said, anyway, we could be friends. "Never mind," I thought, trying to show that worse things had happened to me, "anyway you are too sexy to be in your mid-twenties, to like me, and still be single." But, as she said, never mind.

After that, she decided that she would "mother" me, the blue-eyed American who slept on the office floor. She would invite me to her house for dinner and take me to some of the classier restaurants that were springing up around town. I couldn't say no, nor could I ever talk her into eating with me in New Market.

Sari had a Thai roommate, Nara. One day the two of them invited me on a picnic. "Can I invite the Thai lady who works in my office?" I asked.

"Who is she?"

I told her. Nara did not know Lok.

"Do you have a picture of her?" Nara asked.

By chance I did and I showed it to her. She looked at the picture for a second and said, "Oh, Dim's sister. We all know Dim."

Something was amiss.

Nara proceeded to tell me a long story about Dim.

Nara and Dim had worked together in the same United Nations office in Bangkok where Dim had worked in procurement with an older Indian man, Mr. Krishnadas. Nara claimed that Mr. Krishnadas had embezzled tens of thousands of dollars from the UN, and Dim was, the Thai community believed, his accomplice. Together they had a scheme whereby they would order things like fifty file cabinets and pay for sixty, pocketing the cost of ten. Nara did not explain the details. When Mr. Krishnadas was transferred to Cambodia, he had arranged to bring Dim along and to fix her up with the nice house complete with the live-in maid, car and driver. When Dim, with Mr. Krishnadas's blessing, was transferred to Singapore to do procurement, Mr. Krishnadas let Lok keep everything that he had provided for Dim.

"Do you know Lok well?" Nara asked me.

"Well, I'm with her all·day, and I've been to her house a few times."

"Then you know that she has no Thai friends."

"I see."

"You can see, but you can't say anything to Lok."

"Yes, of course."

Now I knew how the low-level secretary lived like a queen.

Here I was living on the office floor, and there was Lok coming to work in her chauffeur-driven car. What should I do? I thought about it for a long weekend. I decided to write an anonymous letter to the local UN personnel office.

A few day's later Lok started walking to work. It was pathetic, sort of, to see her trudging along the road. Although she was only in her late twenties, Lok had never walked much before and didn't like it.

Two weeks later Mr. Krishnadas was transferred out of Cambodia by the head of the UNTAC administration. Some people wondered why they did not arrest old Krishnadas, or even fire him, but they didn't. Nara told me that he was sent to Africa.

A day or so later, Lok found out that she was going to lose the house and the maid. She asked me if I knew of any cheap places to stay. By coincidence, I did, and told her about a curiously unused room in my UNV guesthouse where I was sure she could stay for free.

A few weeks later she lost her job. It turned out that old Krishnadas had used his connections to get her the secretarial job in the first place, but with him out of the picture no one could think of a good excuse to keep Lok around. Hugo tried to renew her contract, but without connections it was hopeless. She was, after all, no one special.

As her contract was finishing, she asked me if I could help her with her résumé. Sure, I said, no problem...helping you with your résumé is the least I can do.

Later, months after I had lost touch with Lok, a UNV from Nigeria told me in his melodious English accent that Lok had found a job with an NGO in Phnom Penh and that he was going to her house for lunch. "She says she likes me," he said happily, "but she says that is natural because all women like me."

Who could resist a line like that?

PEACE AND COCONUTS

In early July a late rainy season arrived—the streets would flash-flood, and water would be knee-deep around Wat Phnom. The rain cooled things down enough that sometimes we turned off the air conditioner and opened the windows to let the cool, sweet monsoon air into the office. Upstairs in the same building was a large balcony. I would occasionally sit up there and watch the rain pour down. During his experiment in communal living, Mr. Pot had instructed his gardeners to plant coconut trees everywhere in Phnom Penh. When people first came back to the city in 1980, they thought that their city looked like a jungle, but they left most of the coconut trees standing. Now the trees were about fifteen years old, which is a good age for coconut trees. A coconut tree frond looks a little like a double-sided comb with the long thin green leaves being the teeth of the comb. After a midday monsoon shower, the sun would glisten on the fronds, making them look like shiny green fingers waving up and down as they caught the slightest breeze.

As the rains began, the UN's holiday in Cambodia ended, and everyone knew that the peace process, as outlined in the Paris Peace Agreement, was in trouble. According to the agreement, on June 15 the warring parties were supposed to begin putting their troops into holding centers for vocational training. The NADK, or National Army of Democratic Kampuchea, better known as the Khmer Rouge, decided not to play. They said that there were still too many Vietnamese forces in Cambodia and that the old Phnom Penh government had not been sufficiently dismantled for the Supreme National Council to have complete control over Cambodia. The UN now had to decide what to do. Part of the UN Military Component in Cambodia wanted to go after the Khmer Rouge, but Mr. Yasushi Akashi, the head of the entire UNTAC operation, said no: just wait; maybe they will come back into the fold. Consequently, the deputy commander, a Frenchman, resigned. After that, the Khmer Rouge flexed their muscles a little bit more and moved into areas of Battambang and Siem Reap that Phnom Penh government troops had left open. Some civilians were killed.

As the rains began in Phnom Penh, the mosquitoes began to breed in immense numbers. At night, I slept with the office windows closed and the air conditioner turned on to keep them at bay.

In the office the clerks and I typed in data while Hugo and Mohammed Ali sat in the next room, argued with each other, chain smoked, and worked on the program design. The clerks worked hard and did a good job with answers to questions like "Possible voters in this village ____." But they were helpless with "Describe access to this village." They could not turn what had originally been written in an almost illegible scrawl, and in excruciatingly bad English, into English that anyone could understand. As the only native speaker on the team, I was put in charge of entering into the database all English "comments."

I took the job seriously, and before long I could finish the comments for one village in fifteen minutes. That meant—as I explained in a memo to the Frenchman who was supposedly in charge of the AEPU—that if I worked seven days a week, it would take me 343 days to enter the comments for the 11,000 villages of Cambodia. He took my memo seriously and found some more people to help me. New to Cambodia and fresh out of Mr. Til Ting's language and culture classes, they were part of the group of four hundred United Nations Volunteers who were waiting to be deployed to the provinces to begin setting up the infrastructure for voter registration. They were filled with life, enthusiasm, and a desire to succeed. I met them and felt ashamed of myself when I realized how cynical I had become. After a few days, though, most of them no longer trusted the data and found excuses to quit or not to come, and I felt better.

I could foresee that things were going to get very bad in the Computer Room.

One day in mid-July I was attending a reception for a visiting UN dignitary when the Chief Electoral Officer, Professor Reginald Austin, called me aside. My immediate thought was that he was going to ask me how bad things really were, or tell me that it was embarrassing to have a staff member living out of a file cabinet and sleeping on the office floor. Instead, he asked me if I would like to go to New York City for two weeks to learn how to run the huge computer that would be used to keep track of registered voters. Voter registration, he said, would run from October through January, and he expected that about four million people would register.

Was I interested? After he said "two weeks in New York City" he could have said, "to learn how to defuse rusting land mines," and I still would have been interested.

He continued: the Sequent Computer Company had been given a

contract to develop a system for putting all of Cambodia's soon-to-be-registered voters into a database. The system would run twenty-four hours a day with Cambodian data entry clerks in each shift typing in the voter names and related information. My job would be to serve as one of the four international supervisors, with Hugo as the manager. That rather soured the offer, but I figured that with a round-the-clock schedule the odds of my encountering Hugo on an eight-hour shift were three to one and not too bad.

I told Professor Austin that I would be happy to accept the offer, and we shook hands.

Three local men (two from the AEPU office) were asked to be "Cambodian supervisors" and would go to New York with me. Mohammed Ali opted to go back to Pakistan—he'd had enough of Hugo and of Cambodia. Naturally, the people in the office who were not chosen to go to New York wanted to poison the food of those who were. To the Cambodians, a trip to New York was like a free ride on the Space Shuttle.

Unusually Long Fingers

Hugo left for New York on July 20. The three Cambodians and I were scheduled to leave on July 29. We were all virtually sleepless with excitement as the time for departure grew nearer. We had heard that we would be receiving $135 per diem while in New York, which was almost as much as the Cambodian staff made in a month.

There was, however, still work to be done in the office. One of my duties was to interview potential data entry clerks to verify whether they could speak minimal English and type ten or twenty words a minute. Rather routinely, then, Mary Murphy, the head of office administration, swung by the Computer Room one morning and dropped off an applicant with a simple, "This is Miss Sovan."

Sovan was wearing a formal full-length green silk sarong and a long-sleeved white blouse, which were appropriate for an interview.

"Hey, how ya doing?" I said.

"Very well, and you?"

"Not too bad. Do you say it So-van or Sove-an?"

"So-van. It means 'gold' in Cambodian."

"Gold, I see. So So-van, can you type?"

I stood up to let her sit down at my computer and type something. By this time two things had become absolutely clear: she was taller and spoke English better than any Cambodian woman I had met before. So she had passed the English test, and there was no height limit.

I asked her to begin typing the form that happened to be on my desk. She did. There was something very unusual about the way she typed: she had unusually long fingers which she used to touch type with the effortless grace of an accomplished pianist playing a warm-up drill on a grand piano. After one line I told her to stop. She had passed the typing test as easily as she had passed the English test, and I saw no reason to continue the interview.

"I notice," I said, "that you studied at the Phnom Penh School of High-Speed Typing."

"No, actually I studied at Buri Ram Teacher's College."

"But that's in Thailand."

"I know, I studied Macintosh Computers there for three months."

"How was the weather in Thailand?"

"About the same as the weather in Cambodia."

"Hot?"

"No, not so hot."

She had a striking, self-confident poise.

Not wanting to waste her time, I asked her to come with me upstairs to Mary's office.

I nodded to Mary, and a second later Mary had signed her form and told her to go back to the UNTAC personnel office.

So everything was finished when Sovan said, "What about going to New York for more training?"

Mary and I were tired of hearing everyone ask us about "going to New York for more training." Here was one more, and this one had just walked in off the street.

I had fixed Mary's computer for her once, and after that, Mary liked me and would wink at me as we passed in the hall. Now she pulled me by the arm into the hallway for a conference. "Do you think," she whispered, "she should go to New York?"

How could I know if she should go to New York? But Hugo was already in New York and by chance all the upper-level management staff were out of town at an international conference, so I was the only person here who knew anything about the New York operation. The decision was up to me. I had known Sovan for less than ten minutes, had not seen a résumé or a letter of recommendation, and basically knew nothing about her. I took a deep breath, composed myself, and said: "Mary, yes, she *must* go to New York." Mary nodded. In an instant, she told her driver to take Sovan and me across town to the American Mission, where I was to help her begin the process of getting a visa for the U.S.

Lightning had struck.

As we waited in the hallway of the American Mission, I asked Sovan about her life. "From the border," she said, "my family and I just came from the border two weeks ago."

Part of the Paris Peace Agreement was that the 370,000 Cambodians who had been sitting on the Thai/Cambodian border for thirteen years were to return to Cambodia. Sovan and her family had decided to be among the first hundred thousand to return.

"The border! How romantic!" I said inanely.

"There wasn't anything romantic about it."

"Yes, but it sounds romantic."

"Only to you."

"Well, all right, maybe not so romantic. So where on the border?"

"Site Two."

"Site Two, of course. Beautiful, Site Two. I've been there."

Site Two was indeed beautiful in a frightening sort of way. The camp was just a few kilometers inside Thailand, and all around it were military bunkers and heavily armed Thai soldiers. From the last checkpoint the camp stretched out in an immense brown checkerboard of flat, treeless, low-lying blocks of bamboo and thatched huts. These had housed, from the mid-1980s onwards, some 218,000 people in a virtual prison whose inmates were brutalized by both Thai and Cambodian bandits. Along many of the roads inside the camp were huge ditches where the residents could take cover when the camp was shelled from Cambodia.

"I didn't see you there," she said.

"Actually, um, I was only there for two hours."

"When?"

I tried to make a joke. "When you were still a little kid playing naked in the rain..." In Cambodia until the age of five or six, modesty is on holiday, and children are allowed to play naked in the rain. She did not see the humor in it. Anyway Sovan looked to be about thirty, too old to be playing naked in the rain when I visited her camp.

"In 1987," I quickly added.

She made an embarrassed smile.

"So," I said, "if you lived on the border you must be a rice-Christian." Many Cambodians on the border had converted to Christianity with the hope that this would help make them eligible for Christian aid and resettlement in a "Christian" country.

She knew the phrase. "No, my family and I are Buddhists."

"Really? Good for you."

She told me that she knew why so many Cambodians had converted.

I continued the interview, "So how do you like Phnom Penh?"

"Phnom Penh is fine, but housing is a big problem. Right now we are staying with relatives, but we would like to find a better place." She was standing with her back to the wall and her hands behind her, gently bouncing herself off the wall with her finger tips as we talked.

"You don't have to tell me about housing problems! I know all about them. If you knew about my housing, you would know that I live like a dog, a bug, or a cockroach!"

I had finally shocked her.

Gesturing with her unusually long fingers she said, "I have just met you, and already I don't know what to think."

Soon it was lunch time and we were both hungry and tired of waiting for the Mission people. She said that she would go home for lunch and come back in the afternoon by herself. I wished her luck as we parted.

I was very impressed. After four months, I had finally met a woman in Cambodia whom I could talk to. She liked computers, too.

Two days later, the day after I moved out of the office and into a rooming house that the UNVs had rented, the three men and I left Cambodia for New York. I had not seen Sovan again.

The UN flew us business class to New York. The food was better than I had remembered.

3

Heating Up
August 1992 - January 1993

In New York I told Hugo I had hired another person. "What?" he said. It was true. What could he say? Sovan was on her way as Mary had secured a visa and ticket for her. On the afternoon of the first day of training, I went to the airport to meet her.

I caught her eye as she walked out of customs and asked her to come with me. She said she was sorry, but she had forgotten my name. I told her.

I checked her into my hotel—the YMCA on 48th Street where the Cambodians and I stayed. The other UN staff stayed in hotels for rich people. By this time it was after dark, the streets were quiet, and we were both hungry. I volunteered to help her find something to eat, and we walked up Second Avenue to a neighborhood deli. It was a hot summer night. I wore shorts and sandals. She wore what she had worn on the plane—a battered skirt and a blouse that most people, even in Cambodia, would have thrown out long ago. As we walked by a clothing store I told her that tomorrow I would help her buy some more clothes.

She was completely uninterested and dismissed my idea with, "They're too expensive."

We sat on a park bench and ate blueberry muffins. A homeless person was sleeping a few benches away.

I felt foolish. What did she need new clothes for? Fancy clothes were for women who needed them, and anyone with her intelligence and poise could dress any way she liked. She was as pretty as I had remembered. Besides the poise and the long tall body, she had thick jet-black shoulder-length hair, a high forehead, large inquisitive roaming eyes, and a wide charming smile.

The next day I introduced her to the team: the Australian man who had designed the computer program, the software engineers at Sequent Computers, the Cambodian-American computer consultant, the other international supervisors, the three Cambodian supervisors, the software engineer from India who would come with us to Cambodia, and Hugo. I was the only UNV.

The designer and software engineers had produced a slick system which we had been given two weeks to learn. Their system looked flawless and was, we were told, crucial to the election. UNTAC needed to register four million voters and give the different Cambodian political parties a way to question, and possibly de-register, people who were not qualified to vote—that is, Vietnamese. The idea was that the four million names would go into the system right off the voter registration card receipts and in the 56-letter Khmer script. At that point the political parties could question and, after a hearing on the provincial level, de-register, via the computer, anyone who was not Cambodian.

The system was also designed so that registered voters who had lost their voter registration cards could still vote. This part was easy—if a voter lost his card, he would simply give his name and address to the polling official as he voted, the Computer Center would verify that he had registered, and his vote would be counted.

Finally, UNTAC needed a way for people who had registered in one province to vote in another, which was crucial for the 370,000 returnees. Again, the answer was that the computer system would keep everyone honest.

If that wasn't enough, the system could transliterate the 56-letter Khmer alphabet to the 26-letter Roman alphabet so that people like me could type in a voter registration number and see to whom that card belonged. The first time I tried it, I was amazed—the computer seemed to hear Khmer and speak English.

At the heart of the system were three $200,000 computer "towers" that contained the software and the hardware for the system in 16 gigabytes of hard disk space and 256 megabytes of random access memory. The towers were tied to ninety terminals. Once in Cambodia, 240 data entry clerks would type in the data in three eighty-clerk shifts that would keep the Computer Center open twenty-four hours a day.

Wow.

Everyone thought that the two million dollar system was great. The Cambodian-American special-hire consultant thought that it was especially great. He was on holiday from his business of selling the computers he assembled in his office to Cambodians in the U.S. Judging from his tailored suits, I guessed that being a consultant for the UN was helping to balance the books in his business. Every day, he was consulted, dressed well, smiled, and said yes, until one day he confided to me that the system was too complicated to work in Cambodia. But what did he know?

The system was flawless—except for a few bugs. We would come into the office each morning, play with the machines for a while, and new bugs would appear. The Cambodians and I would then have the rest of the day off while the designer and the Sequent engineers worked, sometimes all night, fixing the bugs. Sometimes no bugs would appear; the system would simply lock up. Thus, training became, for the Cambodians and me, a holiday in the city.

For the Cambodians, New York City was not so much the financial and cultural capital of the free world as it was the place that sold cheap cameras. Actually, maybe not so cheap, but better because they were purchased, if not made, in America. New York was also a place that had tasteless, boring food and where they could easily become lost while walking through cavernous streets that all looked alike. To avoid getting lost, they said they needed a guide—me. As leader of "peasants in the city," I guided them to the New Market of New York City, 47th Street Photo. On the way, as we walked in the late afternoon sun of a delightful summer day, Sovan was the only person to ask a question: "Do people live in the buildings?"

"In some of them," I said. "Others are office buildings." No need to get too technical.

Early in our first week in New York, the three Cambodian men moved out to the suburbs of New York, where the local Cambodian community had agreed to host them and where they could save more money. From the suburbs their Cambodian hosts showed them some *real* culture—Atlantic City, the Las Vegas of the East Coast. Sovan had to miss the fun and stay in the YMCA: the man she referred to as "my adopted father," and her long lost Cambodian suitor were coming to see her. I saw her around the hotel with them. Her "adopted father" was a huge fat American in his late fifties. She called him "Daddy."

One day in 1988, Sovan had been sitting around Site Two when, by chance, she was interviewed by an American newspaper reporter. "Daddy," a businessman in Kentucky, read that article and promptly dedicated himself to getting this promising intellectual to the U.S.A. He spent thousands of dollars and wrote hundreds of letters, but after five years he concluded that he was no match for the U.S. government's Immigration and Naturalization Service, and gave up. Now he was seeing his long-distance adopted daughter for the first time.

Along with Daddy came Mr. Right. In the U.S.A. since the early 1980s, Mr. Right was a mechanical engineer in an aircraft factory and had somehow been fixed up as Sovan's long-distance fiancé. Only in his late twenties, he looked like someone who was losing his fight with depression, chronic tuberculosis, and bulimia. I met him and immediately felt sorry for him—life had been tough. He had flown in from California with flowers, a gold watch, and big plans.

Her adoptive father, and now chaperon, did not want his daughter to have any illusions about America: the first place he took the young couple was Times Square.

"Did you see the prostitutes?" I asked Sovan the next day.

"Yes."

"How did they look?"

"They looked fine."

"They know me."

"Really?"

"Sure, they like me too. They call me 'sailor.' 'Hey, sailor,' they say, 'where ya goin'?' "

"Hey sailor, where ya goin'?" she said, copying my accent.

"That's right, but you should only say that to me. Other people might get the wrong idea."

"Might get the wrong idea," she said, again mimicking and thoroughly enjoying mocking me.

The two visitors stayed a few days. Then it was my turn to take her around the city. I took her to the top of the World Trade Center, to Fifth Avenue, and across the Brooklyn Bridge. She said that everything was interesting, but that I walked too fast.

One night, as we were slowly walking up 47th Street to catch an uptown train to see a friend of mine who lived near Central Park, I asked her about her fiancé. It was raining. She carried an umbrella for both of us.

"I think he asked you to marry him," I said.

She raised her eyebrows, which in Cambodian means yes.

"And I think you said no."

She raised her eyebrows again.

"And then what?" I asked.

"And then just the same."

"You mean you're still engaged?"

"I mean I told him that I can't marry him now."

"When can you marry him?"

"Later."

"I see. Later." No need to get too personal.

After the training I planned to take two weeks off to see my family in Ohio. "You'll go back to Cambodia," I said to Sovan, "but you'll miss me a little."

"Not a little." She paused. "A lot."

We had become friends.

Tom Riddle

A street vendor in Phnom Penh prepares the author's morning glass of sugarcane juice.

John Westhrop

Making up the rules as they go, Cambodian drivers prepare for their next move on the main street of Phnom Penh

On the train to Ohio, I realized that something was different: I was in a good mood.

GETTING THINGS STARTED WITH A BANG

By the time I had returned to Cambodia, the UNTAC Computer Center was mostly set up, but the computers were not actually working. One of the three $200,000 towers had been lost in shipment, but all ninety terminals were on the desks on the bottom floor of a building that had been built to be a discotheque-hotel and was now Electoral Headquarters. The building was in the same ·compound as my former home-cum-office.

Most of our 240 data entry clerks had been hired directly from the border camps. Someone had decided that the people with the best computer skills were to be found in the camps where computer classes had been going on for years, and that giving them jobs would aid in their resettlement. Good idea. Most of the clerks were under thirty—half of them women.

It was Friday, September 4. Sovan was in the Computer Center when I walked in. She seemed glad to see me, so I asked her if she would go to a party with me that night. She said no: "We are not in New York now. We are in Cambodia and I am a Cambodian." But she did want me to teach her more about personal computers.

Yes, of course, I would. And yes, definitely, "The first class is tomorrow at 9 A.M., right here."

So instead, I took my Pakistani friend, Sari, to the party.

It was an unusually large party, held in the top two floors of a four-story rambling concrete palace of a house. But it was a typical UN party—people from everywhere on earth, except Cambodia, were there trying to impress each other and pick each other up. Sari knew almost everyone; I knew hardly anyone. Someone had spent a fortune on alcohol. The two of us started drinking and dancing. We danced for a while on the third floor and then walked up the stairs to the roof to talk and drink some more.

By this time, my mind was wandering.

It was a clear night. From the roof, in the distance, we could see the illuminated top of Wat Phnom, where Mrs. Penh's ashes were buried. It rose like a church steeple, just above the tree tops. There remained a few moments, I mused, when one could imagine that the city had once been very pleasant. Sovan had told me that when she was small, she could walk around the city without fear of getting hit by a car. She would walk up to the palace and hear the dancers and musicians practicing Khmer classical dance inside. A few of the old French mansions could still be seen around town with their high ceilings, tall windows, and nineteenth century iron work. It was easy to picture men in white suits in those mansions smoking cigars, drinking Singapore slings, flirting with high-class whores. Until the 1940s, caravans of elephants would still troop into town. I was, I decided, born too late.

Sari finished another cigarette.

"What," I asked, looking out over the city, "is your wish tonight?" I was in a sentimental mood.

"I wish that the mission lasts two years."

"You want to stay *here* two years?"

"I want to buy a house in Pakistan."

"So why not wish for a house?"

"I am."

For Sari, like so many UN staff, Cambodia was a place to make a lot of money and have a little fun. She was not the sentimental type.

We went back downstairs where two black women from the Caribbean were dancing the Lambada—holding each other very tightly, arms and legs entwined, as they whirled around the dance floor locked together. It was wild, frantic, passionate, and changed the mood of the party.

"That's incredible!" I said to Sari. "Like a scene from a James Bond movie."

Suddenly, Sari decided she wanted to Lambada with me. I gulped down the rest of my beer to forget my dignity and steady my coordination. The Lambada is a little like slow dancing except that it is fast and the woman puts one leg between the man's legs so that both torsos are locked together in passion and so that, at least in our case, no one falls down. It is not a dance for people who do not want to have sex later in the evening. We danced very close and very fast. It would have been embarrassing if we were not already so drunk and having so much fun. When we tired of the Lambada, we did our best to imitate the Africans at the party whose wild dancing began where the Lambada left off. Things began to go out of control.

At midnight we decided to get something to eat. There was a late night restaurant, Le Bar, near Independence Monument. Le Bar was between our two houses and Phnom Penh was quite safe, so why not go?

In the restaurant Sari and I had more to drink. She told me she wanted to see my pictures from New York.

"Now?"

"Now."

"Sure," I said. "Now."

We left the bar and walked down the main street of Norodom Boulevard, careful not to fall through the huge gaps in the sidewalk. From Norodom Boulevard, we walked across flooded cross streets to the UNV guesthouse where I was now living—House 26, Street 334. Across one flooded street someone had made a bridge of stepping stones. Sari danced over it. I fell off twice.

My house was surrounded by a high metal fence and, as the gate was locked, we climbed it. I opened the door to my one-room apartment. We left our shoes outside. The overhead light did not work, so I turned on the desk light. Sari noticed, but didn't comment on, the condition of the room. Rather than unpack my bags, I had turned them upside down in the corner. Mosquitoes came in through the open bathroom window. My bed was covered with books and computer magazines. Sari collapsed on a little mat in the middle of a clutter-free circle. I lay down beside her, reached into the pile where I had dumped my bags, and found the pictures. We were both lying on our stomachs. She rolled over onto her side, and, without touching, curled up beside me. She started to finger my hair, putting her face close to mine. She had forgotten about the pictures.

"I could fall asleep right here," she whispered.

"Married women don't do that."

I rolled over onto my back and put one leg over, but not on, her.

"What's marriage?" she asked, as she rubbed the nape of my neck.

"Marriage is a commitment that two people make to each other, you know, 'to have and to hold in sickness and in health until death do us part.'"

"We didn't have a Christian wedding."

"Yes, but you signed the papers."

"They were in my husband's native language that I can't read," she said as she combed my hair with her fingers.

"So?"

"So, there was no commitment."

Was she going to give me money to make the first move? Our faces were very close. It was too late.

...so this was married life in the UN.

At four in the morning the alarm clock went off. Outside the house, we climbed the fence again and walked through the dark, damp, hot tropical streets to Independence Monument where we split up.

I walked back home, slept for two hours, showered, and arrived at the office for Sovan's nine o'clock computer class. If Sovan knew I was hung over, she was too polite to say anything. She was also, now that we were back in Cambodia, too Khmer to have come alone. Her cousin Rita was there to act as chaperon.

Meeting Godzilla

After class, I thought about what my chances were of being murdered by Sari's husband—if Moslems cut off hands for stealing, what body part would they cut off for adultery? I also wondered about any potential relationship with Sovan.

A mind that is hung over is not blinded by rationality: I invited both women on a picnic.

A picnic in Phnom Penh meant driving at least thirty minutes east, out of the city. But the place we went to in our rented cars was Wat Ampe Phnom, one hour to the west. It was a park with a little muddy river running through it and a temple in the adjacent forest. The park's main attraction was a pedestrian suspension bridge across the river. The owners of the bridge felt that people would pay to walk across the only suspension bridge in Cambodia if they had nothing else to do. People had nothing else to do, so everyone, including the occasional bridal party, paid the equivalent of five cents to hold onto two guide wires and walk across, careful lest they fall off the creaking and swaying bridge into the shallow water below.

Along the river were thatch and bamboo platforms where picnickers could eat and drink what they had purchased from the vendors in the park. Cambodian men like to eat, quietly get drunk, and forget their suffering for a while, which may be why they go on picnics and have car accidents on the way home.

Americans and little children like more active pursuits. I talked Sovan into letting me take her two chaperons, her little niece and nephew, for a ride on an elephant. Sovan said that she did not like elephants. Sari came along to watch. People boarded the elephant by hopping from a second story balcony to the saddle. The two kids jumped on, more passengers climbed on, I climbed on, the mahout stood on the back, and away we went. I looked down: this was the Godzilla of elephants, and it was a very long way to the ground. The saddle was just a flat, square piece of wood mounted on the back of the elephant, but not mounted very well. The saddle began to tilt violently from one side of the elephant to the other as if we were on a giant seesaw. The mahout shouted and gestured wildly for the passengers to move this way and then that way to avoid tipping the saddle, and everyone on it, off the elephant. Things looked bad. One passenger made a lunge off the saddle and landed safely on the elephant's neck. I had to seem calm for the longest fifteen minutes of my life so as to not frighten the children. When we finally arrived back at the balcony, I realized that Sovan, who asked me why I was so pale, had the right idea all along and that maybe there was some merit in the Cambodian way of picnic celebration: passive drunken gluttony.

But it was worth the risk: my plan worked. The two women liked each other. Subtle messages were communicated, and everyone was happy, which was a relief, since Sovan and I would soon have much more to worry about.

Life during Registration

Things continued to go well in the Computer Center. Sovan, as she was a woman with ten years' teaching experience, had been given a secretarial job, while the three men, as they were men with no previous teaching experience, were each given shifts of 80 people to train. The international staff was busy as well. An old UN hand used his connections to round up miscellaneous equipment for the Computer Center. Patrick, a computer consultant from England, was sent around Asia to find the missing $200,00 computer. A female secretary from Kenya helped Hugo, and I was put in charge of training. Training was not so easy. Very few of the data entry clerks had ever typed in Khmer before, and no one had ever used the specially designed UNTAC Khmer keyboard. Once we went "on-line," we expected them to type into the database the potential voter's ten-digit voter registration card number twice (the second time to verify that the first one was correct), followed by the voter's full name, age, birth date (if known), place of registration, date of registration, place of birth, and parents' place of birth. Finally, they were to click with the mouse the abbreviation of one of the twenty-two provisionally registered political parties if that party's representative had questioned a potential voter's qualifications. All this was to be done in about four minutes. We told the clerks that, for security reasons, it would be impossible to edit an entry after they used the mouse to click the "Finished" button. They had to get it right the first time.

Meanwhile, up country, four hundred newly arrived UNVs were hiring and training the Cambodian teams to do the actual registration. The election was scheduled for the dry season, but now, in the middle of the rainy season, unpaved roads were becoming so soaked that old anti-tank land mines were rising to the surface. One such mine turned up in the driveway of a colleague who lived in the province of Kratie. When he drove over it on his way to work, his van flew ten meters. The driver, a young man from India, was concussed, but otherwise unhurt. Wow.

Voter registration began in Phnom Penh on October 5. Two days earlier, the Khmer Rouge had informed us that they were still out there by massacring fourteen Vietnamese fishermen. With their hands tied behind their backs, the Vietnamese were shot in the head. Things were getting ugly.

After registration began, every day as I came to work I saw long lines of people queuing outside the voter registration tents. Each voter was asked a few questions and given a laminated voter registration card with his or her picture on it. In Phnom Penh, seventy thousand people registered to vote in the first two weeks.

A few people would register and immediately have their voter registration cards cancelled. Perhaps the representative of a political party had challenged them to prove that they were not Vietnamese, they realized that they were too young, or they were caught trying to register twice. Whatever the reason, the registrar would write "canceled" on the card and confiscate it. He then stapled the card into a receipt book and sent it to the Computer Center. Looking at the pictures on those cards would later become one of the main amusements of my life.

After three weeks of training the data entry clerks, we decided to test them. We made up big batches of sample voter registration cards and forced everyone to type sixty cards into a dummy database. Some people did very well the first time and smirked with relief; some people did not do well and feared they were about to lose their high-pay, high-prestige jobs. I felt that a few people, through no fault of their own, did not have whatever it took to be data entry clerks and should do other work in UNTAC. But every day we tested, more people passed, and soon everyone passed. Even the man whom Sovan and I had thought was mentally slow, and with whom she had completely lost patience, passed. So that was that, and for better or worse, training was a complete success.

A few days after voter registration began, Hugo announced that we would go on-line in two days. Everyone was excited—the first shift would use just twenty-four data entry clerks, one of the Khmer trainers, and two of the international supervisors.

On Monday, October 11, the Computer Center went on-line. To everyone's relief, the system worked, but very slowly. Hugo, the software engineer, and the on-line supervisors worked a week of twelve- and eighteen-hour days. The data entry clerks had problems as well—they would forget to tell the database that a political party had challenged a certain voter or they would confuse voter registration card numbers. Hugo decided that if a clerk made ten mistakes he or she would be fired, but at the end of the week it seemed that everyone would have to be fired. So the supervisors just noted the mistakes and left them for the software engineer to correct. No one could alter the database except the software engineer.

ALL THIS TIME

All this time I had been trying to find out what had happened to the Advanced Electoral Planning Unit's report. I managed to piece together the story. After I had left for New York, someone suddenly believed everything I had written, or figured it out for themselves. They hired more people, made them work seven days a week and, by the beginning of September, finished the report. Over one meter thick, its twenty thousand pages contained information on every province, district, commune, and village in non-Khmer Rouge Cambodia. I asked around trying to find someone who had actually used the report; I never found anyone who had. My guess was that people in the field never used it because when the time came to set up polling stations, they just intuitively *knew* where the population centers were, how to find people, and where to put the polling stations. Also by this time the six UNV cartographers, who worked many twelve-hour days, had made detailed maps of every district in Cambodia. Those maps probably did more for the logistics of the election than the AEPU report.

The report was crucial, however, in one way. Its estimates of the number of voters in each of Cambodia's 170 districts determined how many sequentially numbered voter registration cards were allocated to each district. In the Computer Center, these same numbers corresponded to the range of numbers of voter registration cards that the database would accept from each district. If the report said that district X had ten thousand possible voters, the Computer Center made certain that ten thousand voter registration card numbers, in a certain and precise range, were allocated to the database for that district.

Things were beginning to get more technical.

SALT, RICE AND VIDEO TAPE

A week after we went on-line, I asked Sovan to invite me to her house for lunch. Since I was featured in some of the pictures she had taken in New York, I thought her mother would be curious to meet me. Moreover, I wanted to see where my best computer class student lived; I had little else to do; and I liked her.

She knew that I did not eat meat and liked to tease me about it.

"What do you want to eat?" she asked.

"I don't know—how about rice and salt?" I teased back.

"Rice and salt? Yes, I can cook that very well. Come about twelve o'clock, and I'll have a big plate of rice and salt ready for you."

"Wonderful. I'll look forward to it."

She wrote directions in Khmer that I could show to a motorcycle taxi driver. With her house just a kilometer or two from mine, I would chance a motorcycle taxi ride.

"Is your house air-conditioned?" I asked.

"Better than air-conditioned—heat-conditioned!"

"So I should bring a sweater."

"A jacket."

Before I went, she told me a little family history, which was similar to what I had heard from other pre-1975 residents of Phnom Penh. Once there had been a large family, and now the father and most of the children were dead. The survivors were Sovan, her mother, and her older brother, Setee. In early July, just three months ago, the three of them had stepped off the Sisophon-Phnom Penh train. Not having seen the capital for eighteen years, they looked for relatives who might help them. Some relatives acted as though they had never met, but an old aunt, who had done very well in the furniture business, found them a place to live with her daughter's family in a small apartment above the furniture factory.

I showed up on time. Behind a little muddy outdoor food market, the furniture factory was a large building with a dirt floor and a roof that peaked in a series of steep M's. Looking at it from the outside, I thought that perhaps I had the wrong place. People would not actually

Meaning a different kind of business, two Vietnamese prostitutes in Phnom Penh while away the time waiting for the evening's customers.

live up there, with the noise and the fumes from the factory engines blasting up to the roof, would they? Walking inside, I was surprised to find that what should have been storage lofts in each roof peak were indeed apartments.

I found her apartment. Directly beneath one end of the loft-cum-apartment, on a raised wooden platform, were the kitchen and shower. The kitchen stove was an earthen crock in which they burned scrap wood from the furniture factory; the shower was a large ceramic pot to one side. The toilet was in the house of a cousin a few buildings away.

As a guest I was immediately ushered up the ladder, through the open trap door at the top, and into the loft. The original occupants of the apartment, Pavee, her husband Pawn, and their child, Nop, now lived in one room. Sovan, her mother, and her brother had the rest—a hallway divided into a bedroom and a TV room by a curtain mounted on a metal frame. Sovan told me that her family had used their UN resettlement grant to buy the bed and bureau. The other furniture—two chairs, TV, video tape player, and food cabinet—belonged to Pavee and Pawn. The roof/ceiling was asbestos, which they seemed to think was fine; the floor was made from long hardwood boards. Any air that entered the apartment came from Pavee's end of the loft, which opened onto a tiny balcony.

All Cambodian houses, even if they are factory lofts, have a painting of Angkor Wat or an ancient Khmer god or goddess on the wall. This home had both. And, although this one didn't, most Cambodian living room walls also have a picture of a rock and roll or movie star, a baby boy urinating, or a cute painting of dogs posing as humans eating lunch.

Sovan completed the introductions. A nod sufficed for everyone except her mother, to whom I performed a "sompiah," the traditional greeting of bowing with the hands pressed together as if in prayer. Her mother, whom I called Om—elder lady—was sixty, diabetic and in ill-health. She smiled, and we all sat down. Sovan had been right about the heat-conditioning, but had failed to mention the noise-conditioning and fume-conditioning. I didn't care. I was happy to be there.

Lunch was fine—rice, vegetables and fish. We ate seated on the floor Cambodian style, helping ourselves to tiny portions of food from common dishes.

The two families who shared the apartment did not eat together. Instead, television and video movies were the bonding agent. Today's bond was an MTV video that Setee, a traveling translator for UNTAC, had purchased on a recent trip to the Thai border.

Lunchtime conversation, conducted to the background of the rock and roll video, centered around two recent neighborhood murders. One involved a married man who had brought a prostitute to live with him. Second wives are generally tolerated in Cambodia, but in this case the two wives were not compatible bedfellows: the prostitute had tried to wrest control of the family finances away from the first wife. This was too much, so the first wife's brother stepped in to try to talk some sense into the whore-crazed husband. Their conversation became heated, and where words could not prove the point, bullets could. The brother-in-law shot the husband and the husband shot the brother-in-law. The brother-in-law died; the husband was hospitalized.

"When?" I asked.

"Just this week."

"What did your mother think?"

Her mother, who could not speak English, had listened as her son translated the story.

"She got used to gunfire on the border."

"I see."

The second murder involved two teenage boys. The best of friends, they let a motorcycle come between them when they could not agree on who had sovereignty over the bike. Neither one had a gun, so to settle the argument one boy split the other's head open with an ax.

"With an ax?" I asked.

"With an ax."

"So what happened to the ax murderer?"

"He ran away."

"Did the police catch him?"

"Here the police don't catch anyone unless you pay them. Why should they risk their lives when they don't get paid?"

"Yes, of course."

Setee was watching his video. "I like the dancing," he concluded. He was just home for a few days, and next week he was off to another province. "Translating for UNTAC is a good job," he said, "but I want to work in the medical field." He had been a medic in Site Two. Now he was seeing his country for the first time and having the time of his life. A serious man, he was in his early thirties and still not married. Far from being the playboy, he was, I picked up, too tight with his money for whoring around.

BECOMING A MOVIE STAR

After two more weeks there were enough voter registration cards and enough trained clerks for the Computer Center to expand to two shifts and, a week later, to three shifts, twenty-four hours a day. The plan was that each of the three shifts would rotate, so that each would work the night shift once every third week .

The night shift. For the Cambodians the night was frightening, dangerous, and foreboding—time to lock the door, stay inside and sleep. The night, everyone knew, was the time for drunks, robbers, and prostitutes. After eight o'clock at night most of Phnom Penh's streets were deserted. The men, and especially the women, wanted to get out of working at night, but they had signed contracts and there was no going back. Only one woman quit.

But for once the UN bureaucracy was accommodating and agreed to send buses to pick up all the clerks near their homes. Many of the staff could not read a map to show us where they lived, while most of the bus drivers could not read a map either. But somehow people showed up and the first night shift began.

My first night shift was also the first one for Sovan and her crew. Everyone was worried. Would they be able to stay up all night? If they fell asleep, would they be fired? Could they stay up all night all week? I was worried too.

We started at 10 P.M., my usual bedtime, with a break scheduled for every two hours. The "lunch" break was at 2 A.M. Most people went outside. It was a cold night, so for me the air had a refreshing chill to it. Many of the Cambodians wore jackets. The neighborhood was dark, but the Computer Center's generator, which sounded like a huge ship's engine, powered the lights that illuminated the immediate area. A few of the men smoked while other people had snacks or soft drinks. I stood off in the shadows and did yoga stretches. I noticed Sovan. As always—perhaps because she was taller than anyone else or perhaps because she was the leader—a group of women stood around her with some men looking on. Someone played Cambodian music from a tape player. Sovan heard it, slightly shifted her stance to freeze into a stylized Khmer dance pose, and then for a moment flashed the intricate hand movements of classical Khmer dancing. She did it just long enough to tell everyone that, although the night was long, we did not have to take it too seriously. Everyone laughed and applauded.

At 4 A.M. I drank tea, ate oatmeal, and told myself that there were just two more hours to go—be tough. By this time some of the clerks were falling asleep at their terminals, were in a daze, or had collapsed in the hallways. Sovan, as a supervisor, had to keep walking around and stayed awake.

At 5:30, even inside the Computer Center, we could hear the birds waking up with the dawn. At six Patrick, the next shift's supervisor, pulled up in his UN truck, and three buses filled with data entry clerks drove in. Patrick took Sovan, who lived in a different part of the city than the rest of her shift, and me home. The roads were already crowded. When we dropped her off it was just 6:30 and the furniture factory was already pounding away full-blast. Patrick let me out at the end of my street. In my room, the air conditioner had been on all night; it was cool and peaceful. I took a shower, lay down, pulled a sheet over my head, and thought about living in Hollywood, California. If I had pursued a career in the movies, after every premier I would be staying up all night like this and coming home, after dropping off a beautiful babe at her house, just after sunrise. Yes, in a strange way, I reflected, I was now living the life of a movie star.

The rest of the week went well for me. It was a different story for the Cambodians. How could they sleep in their crowded, noisy, hot houses? The women, some of whom were mothers, were still expected to do the cooking and cleaning. The men hated it just as much and everyone complained. I was the only one who liked it—what a relief to get away from Hugo and have afternoons off! In the daytime the supervisors—mostly because Hugo was unorganized or in a bad mood—sometimes had to work twelve or fourteen hours. The nights were cool and quiet. The only person who ever came in to see what was going on was the Chief Electoral Officer, Professor Austin. He was in his late fifties, but only slept about four hours a night. Always the flamboyant professor, he would drop by to say a friendly hello and "Howz it?" I always told him how many cards we had entered into the database that night and said that things were fine.

At the end of the week I decided to continue living the life of a movie star and tried to talk a few of the locals into continuing with me. They thought I was crazy.

Sovan bought a motorcycle, a secondhand Honda, with the thousand dollars she had saved in New York. One of her relatives gave her a twenty-minute lesson and she was on her own. After I saw her driving around town, I decided to get a motorcycle too. If she could do it, so could I. I asked the United Nations Volunteers to give me one, and they did —a little thing with no clutch, a Honda "Dream."

Now that both of us had motorcycles, we could drive around town together and discuss motorcycle safety and why she refused to wear the motorcycle helmet I bought for her in the market. First the helmet was too hot, next it was too heavy, then she drove too carefully to need it, and finally it was fine to wear with pants, but not with a dress. In the end, though, it was the sight of someone's hair and blood on the road which finally convinced her and her brother to be the only Cambodians in Phnom Penh I ever saw wearing motorcycle helmets.

Driving around town on a motorcycle was much better than I had imagined. The Cambodian motorcycle drivers were not particularly skillful, but—as I learned after stalling the bike in the middle of a busy intersection—they were very polite. UN drivers were my main worry. Many had never driven before, or they were from countries whose citizens believed that one's driving speed should increase exponentially according to the amount of alcohol one had just consumed. Embarrassed, the UN started a driving school and a "don't-drink-and-drive" campaign, but those UN drivers remained people, as they say, to steer clear of.

After a couple of weeks I decided to drive my motorcycle to work at night. "People get shot for their motorcycles," Sovan told me.

"But no UN people have been shot," I said.

"Do you want to be the first?" she asked, pointing one of her unusually long fingers at me.

I didn't, but I knew that even in the dark my helmet would give me away as a UN person, and things would be all right.

It turned out that because most Cambodians were afraid to go out after eight at night, I had the roads to myself.

THE REPUBLIC OF UNTAC AND NGO LIFE

By mid-October it was clear to everyone that the United Nations had succeeded in setting up what one of the Khmer supervisors called "The Republic of UNTAC." By this time, with the election now vaguely scheduled for late March, we had our full contingent of 15,000 soldiers, nearly 3,000 civilian police, 1,300 civilian support people, 600 UNVs, and 6,000 locally hired Cambodians scattered around the country, headquartered in prefabricated air-conditioned office buildings in the provincial capitals. In Phnom Penh, UNTAC had set up and staffed, thanks to the Germans, a three-story field hospital open to any Cambodian who wanted medical treatment. Just outside of town UNTAC had built the biggest vehicle repair shop I had ever seen to maintain the eight thousand UN vehicles that were now in Cambodia. Clearly, there could be no doubt in any one's mind that the UN was now the big name in town. The morning traffic jam was mostly UN vehicles, UNTAC offices were everywhere, and UNTAC had even started a radio station, Radio UNTAC.

That shows what you can do with 2.8 billion dollars.

By this time, the Khmer Rouge had come to town as well. They did not like people calling them "Khmer Rouge" though. They preferred "Democratic Kampuchea." The DK, as many people called them, lived in a large walled compound and occasionally gave press conferences. Their president was Khieu Samphan, as Pol Pot had supposedly retired. Once I saw the white-haired Khieu at a UN ceremony. He was something of a disappointment. He had traded his Khmer Rouge uniform—black pajamas and a red-checkered neck scarf—for a gray pin-striped suit and looked more like an American corporate lawyer than the leader of an ill-fated experiment in communal living.

Outside the UN, the main employer remained the non-governmental organizations, or NGOs. It appeared that every NGO on earth—Redd Barna, Maryknoll, International Committee of the Red Cross, French Red Cross, Swiss Interchurch Aid, World Council of Churches, Lutheran World Service, Australian Save the Children, Catholic Relief Services, Jesuit Refugee Service, Australian Catholic Relief, American Rescue Committee, OXFAM and dozens more—now had an office in Phnom Penh. Entire neighborhoods seemed to be nothing but NGOs. Most of them scorned the uppity UN, who could afford to pay ridiculously high office rent and had a local base pay of US $120 a month, while the NGO base pay, good by Cambodian standards, was $70 a month.

Whenever I met an NGO person, I would say that I worked for the UN, "but I'm a UNV." To many people, being a UNV meant that I was not just another fabulously paid UN staff person on "one more damn mission" to a country for which I had no feeling or compassion. After I told the administrator of one NGO what I was doing, Roland offered me a job—teaching computers to his staff. Roland said that his office workers wanted to know how to use the computers that were collecting dust in his office and, well, so did he.

It was strictly forbidden for me, as a UN worker and a UNV, to take an outside paying job—even the UN had standards of professionalism. "Sure," I told him, "no problem."

That particular NGO, International Outreach Project*, helped people who had experienced negative encounters with land mines. Anyone who had lost a foot or two could go there and be fixed up with an aluminum and rubber leg or two for free.

The walls of the IOP office were plastered with pictures of the happy clientele walking around on their new prosthetic limbs. "Single amputee below the knee is no problem," Roland told me as I studied the pictures. "It's the double amputees, especially the above the knee jobs, that are a problem."

"I guess so."

IOP had been founded by, and was staffed mostly by, American men who had been wounded by land mines or booby traps in Vietnam and were missing limbs. One of the staff was a double above-the-knee amputee who walked.

I suggested that Roland hire Sovan to teach the Cambodian staff. He said fine. When I told Sovan the good news, she said no. "How can the ·blind lead the blind?" she asked.

I knew differently: for the past six weeks, we had spent at least part of every weekend studying computer programs.

"Wait a minute," I said. "These people are missing limbs, not eyes."

"Don't you see?" she pleaded. "How can I teach them when I myself don't know?"

"I hate it when people know something and say they don't know it," I said.

"I hate it when people say they hate people for not knowing something they really don't know!"

"Look, if they paid you three dollars an hour and I were there to help you, would you do it?"

"Sure."

"Good, they said they'll pay you five."

So, twice a week the two of us met at the International Outreach Project to have lunch and teach word processing. The amputees would be there hobbling around or dragging themselves along the floor. There is a prejudice in Cambodia against amputees. They are seen as inferior, and no one wants to marry one or give one a job. We found that working with them was much more pleasant than working in the Computer Center. We came to know and admire the American Vietnam War veterans as well. These were men who continued to live the 1970 Saigon life-style of marijuana, guns, and women. When they went out at night, it was to visit prostitutes, and if the establishment they were visiting asked them to leave their weapons at the front desk, they would take their business elsewhere. After all, you never knew when you might

need your eight millimeter Chinese-made pistol that you carried because
your AK-47 could not fit into your back pocket.

One day at lunch we learned that a French soldier had raped a Cambodian virgin, whereupon she tried suicide and the French military arranged a cover-up. During the investigation one of the UN lawyers was
sickened by the case and resigned. The woman's family had some con-
nection with the International Outreach Project and the veterans were
up in arms over the case. One suggested that "we take him out." Fortunately for everyone, the French flew their soldier back to France before
the veterans could decide if they really would kill him. Not the type to
worry too much about what the world thought of his organization, the
director of the IOP once drove his motorcycle onto the front steps of
the office of a Cambodian government official. They were, as everyone
who knew them agreed, a wild bunch, except for Roland, who hated
guns and had a family in the States.

Things went well in our computer class—the students liked Sovan, and I
helped Roland with a few technical problems. Always the leader, Roland
asked us if we could make ID cards for IOP. Yes, of course we could,
and a few days later we debuted our work. To the amusement of the
veterans and the pleasure of the locals, now the official IOP ID cards
bore a striking resemblance to my own UNTAC ID. The people at IOP
thought that these UN look-alikes would help them in their dealings
with the police in Phnom Penh and with the Khmer Rouge in the provinces. Their new baby blue ID cards were so flashy that soon other NGOs
asked us to make IDs for them too. We started a small business—I would
do the graphics and Sovan would type the Khmer text. In this way we
met more and more of the NGO people in town, many of whom were
women. Courageous and dedicated, they were different from the UN
women. They had more to worry about than what they were going to
wear to the next party.

I continued to live the life of a movie star who didn't know when to
slow down. From seven in the morning until eleven I would sleep. Then
I would wake up to a double whammy of *I'm-not-dead-yet* coffee. Later
I would meet Sovan at the International Outreach Project, or she would
visit my guesthouse to get help with her computer class lesson plans, or
just to see me. Sometimes she wanted a ride to work. When Cambodian
women sit on the back of a motorcycle, they sit, even if they are wearing pants, sidesaddle. To straddle the bike is known as "the Vietnamese
way" and is too *Vietnamese* and too sexually explicit for any Cambo-

dian woman, ever. Rather than risk her teetering off the back, I had Sovan drive, making me the only man in Phnom Penh with a female Cambodian motorcycle chauffeur. She felt embarrassed. "If anybody says anything," I told her, "tell them to go find their own foreigner." One day, as we pulled into the Computer Center, one of the young women who worked there looked at me and smiled. I knew what she was thinking: "Hey American guy, is it really that good?"

"Yes," I smiled back, "it is."

FALLING

In the Computer Center, morale among the other foreign supervisors was slipping as the day-to-day pressure wore them down and they started to quarrel with each other. Two of the supervisors stopped speaking to each other. One had put a sign on the wall: "Patrick messed things up again, as usual." I asked Hugo to intervene. He said that there was nothing wrong, did nothing, and the problems just got worse. After a few more weeks the other supervisors had stopped talking to each other, too, and no one knew what anyone else was doing. Everyone simply went off in their own directions. Patrick, always the gentleman, was still speaking to me. The two of us started writing memos to the people in the provinces, asking them about problems with their voter registration cards or telling them how to rectify a certain situation. The system was, after all, very complicated. We didn't know what Hugo and the other supervisors were doing.

More cracks in the system appeared. The system was set up so that, in province X, for example, the registration teams would have a certain and exact range of numbered voter registration cards, say from 1 to 50,000; these were divided among the districts of the province, whose population estimates we had garnered from the AEPU report. In the Computer Center, this meant that if an operator typed a wrong number for a certain district, say 50,010, the computer would not accept the card. This sounded perfect, but soon districts were running out of cards and having to borrow unused cards from other districts. The district officials then had to inform the Computer Center about the borrowed cards so that we could modify our database to allow the computer to accept them. People in the provinces tried sending radio messages and telegrams to let us know what they were doing, but the card numbers would get garbled in transmission, so we told them to send letters instead. As the system became more and more complicated, a few of the

Cambodian staff were given the responsibility of defining in the database what cards were borrowed from what district. Naturally, they made mistakes. By mid-November, as we typed in over half a million cards, the system had become extremely complex and Hugo was becoming harder and harder to work with. At times it seemed as if the entire Computer Center was going to slip into utter chaos and that Hugo was going crazy.

Some local staff could not stay awake all night, night after night, and early in the morning I would see them collapsed at their terminals or asleep in the hallways. At other times I saw them seemingly *typing and sleeping* at the same time, indicating to me that after five days with very little sleep a person could do just about anything. The supervisor from Kenya reported the sleepers on her shift to Hugo. He lined them up in front of the whole shift and threatened to fire them. One woman broke down and cried uncontrollably. Hugo did not know it, but he was lucky. If the people he had been intimidating had been Thai, he would have found his car windshield missing. God help him if they had been Vietnamese. But the Cambodians, after years in refugee camps, somehow put up with him and kept their rage to themselves.

Or perhaps they had their own subtle forms of revenge. The software engineer found that one man had entered Khmer obscenities for "new sub-district names." Others may have typed in garbage just for spite. They knew that the emphasis was on speed and that no one ever checked the data. The job was boring and thankless, so why not have some fun? Part of the garbage they typed in, according to one rumor that reached us, were the names of people whom different political parties had paid them ten dollars per name to enter into the database. But who could know for sure?

After weeks of working rotating shifts, most people started to waste away physically. Many clerks did not have much weight to lose in the first place, but they became thinner and thinner. Setee returned from a month in the provinces and told Sovan to quit. His sister was fading away, and he didn't think she would make it. But I told her to hang in there. I was pretty sure she would not be the first to completely waste away. One night I met an old friend who was now working for the American Red Cross. She didn't recognize me. Later she said she had some extra food in her house that I was welcome to any time. But how could I eat? Living the frantic movie star life, I didn't know breakfast from lunch from dinner. One day I read an article in a Bangkok newspaper that helped explain what was happening:

Doctors at the University of Chicago Sleep Research Laboratory put two rats into the same environment, but permitted only one to sleep. No striking differences emerged until the end of the second week, when the sleep-deprived rat began to gorge itself on food yet grew skinnier and skinnier without exercising more. After one more week the sleep-deprived rat lost the ability to regulate its body temperature and died.

The first rat to crack up in the Computer Center was the lady from Kenya. She lived on junk food, never exercised, and after two months of changing shifts and overwork went down with a bout of recurring malaria. I was thus promoted by default to "shift supervisor" in charge of one of the three shifts. Fortunately, very fortunately, it was Sovan's shift. By this time her talent had been recognized by the international staff, and she had been put in charge of the eighty data entry clerks of one shift, with more responsibility than any other Cambodian woman in UNTAC. Once Mr. Akashi had praised her in a speech to the foreign journalists, and when CNN (Cable News Network) came to town they interviewed her.

RISING

I was now called "Supervisor," but Sovan was, in fact, the supervisor. She told me what to do and I did it. She was one of those people who could, if asked in a nice way, plan the logistics for one of those techno-wars that Americans like to fight and the next day negotiate a cease-fire while cooking dinner. In the Computer Center she used a spreadsheet to keep track of how many voter registration cards each of the eighty people on her shift had typed, did the administrative chores, made certain that everyone was busy, solved problems that came up, translated for the internationals, and still found time to write letters to her friends in the U.S.A.

When bags of voter registration card receipts arrived at the Computer Center, one person would tell the computer the numerical ranges of cards within those bags. Next, those two thousand or so cards would be typed in on one terminal by two or three clerks over ten to twenty hours. Finally the international staff person on duty would tell the computer that those cards had been entered into the database and that the bag was now completed or "logged out." The problem was that the clerks would sometimes forget to type two or three or even thirty cards, so the supervisor could not log out the bag and the data entry clerk's terminal would be frozen. At this point the international supervisor had to ask the computer what the missing cards from the sequentially numbered ranges were. A Khmer supervisor would then have to search manually through the completed voter registration card receipts for those missing cards. At other times a sleepy clerk would see a number like 17 02 105765 as 19 02 105765, telling the computer that the voter lived in Stung Treng instead of Siem Reap. This meant that the real 19 02 105765 from Stung Treng would, if his card had not already been entered, now have a new name. And, later, when another operator tried to enter the data on the card that actually came from Stung Treng, he could not.

To put it simply: the system in Cambodia turned out to be much more complicated than the one we were taught in New York. If the international supervisor and the Khmer supervisor did not work together like a right and left hand, the system would bottleneck, and the problems would be left for the next shift. But Sovan could sing, dance and write letters with one hand while helping me with the other; so everything was under control.

She did everything so well that I decided to teach her how to do the computer searches and to let her use my unlimited access password. I trusted her. To her, because I had given her *real responsibility,* I was her "good boss."

There was, however, one thing that even I would never let her do, the thing that all the international supervisors believed was our sacred duty to perform in these "UN-supervised elections." We believed that, if CANCELED was written on a voter registration card, we were the only people whom God wanted to cancel it in the database. Supposedly we were neutral and would therefore not cancel people just because we didn't like them. Also, although I never told Sovan, if she started canceling cards, I would have nothing to do. This is why looking at the pictures on the canceled voter registration cards became one of the chief amusements of my life.

Now, for the first time, a feeling of teamwork had seeped into what had been a very intimidating atmosphere for the data entry clerks. Production increased dramatically. Soon they were typing over 6,000 cards in two hours or 24,000 cards a night. Morale became very high and work became a race. Every two hours I would write on the front door the number of cards they had typed, and they would work faster and faster. They broke all previous records, and even Hugo had to admit that things were going well.

As I came to know them I learned that they all hated the woman I had replaced. She had humiliated them by shouting angrily at them. She had told me that all Cambodians were lazy. I never felt the need to yell, and I knew, as they knew, that they weren't lazy. As the night wore on I would walk around, look for people sleeping, and rouse them by rubbing their shoulders, which would surprise them, especially the women.

After three weeks the Kenyan woman returned. A clerk I had worked closely with surprised me by saying, "Why couldn't she die?"

I became an underling again.

On November 24 a UNV from Fiji was shot in what the media called "the most serious attack on UN personnel in Cambodia to date." He was traveling down a dusty country road and sitting in the front passenger seat of a UN truck when bandits opened up with automatic rifle fire. Another bullet hit a Cambodian team member in the back seat. Both were hit in the right thigh and both lived.

Things like this made it very clear that there were worse things than working in the Computer Center and living the life of a movie star/laboratory rat.

GOING PLACES

One night, Hugo told me to get a driver's license. If there was an emergency in the Computer Center, he wanted someone there with a vehicle to drive to the software engineer's house and wake him up. I made an appointment at the UN transportation office, drove an air-conditioned five-on-the-floor 8-cylinder Toyota Land Cruiser around the block, and suddenly had a license.

"I can drive," I said to Sovan.

"Can you teach me how to drive?"

Teaching her how to drive would be against UN regulations, but what were UN regulations to me? I was, after all, *just a UNV*. Everyone knew that all international UN staff, from secretaries to supervisors, who were "on mission" in Cambodia, earned a "daily subsistence allowance" of $135 a day, or about $4,000 a month; added to that was their usual UN salary for doing exactly what I was doing. As "just a UNV" I was paid $729 per month and no per diem, which the Cambodians found hard to believe. To them I was either a liar or a fool. Hugo knew how much I was making, and to him I was a fool. Once when I was cleaning up some packaging and sweeping the floor, Hugo saw me and said, "If it was anyone else I would tell them not to do it, but since you are *just a UNV*, go ahead."

"Just a UNV" would begin driving class tomorrow night.

After a week of nightly driving classes, we were out of first gear and ready to practice driving in the country. On Sunday, our one day off, I decided that during our drive we would visit Phnom Penh's killing field, Choeung Ek (*Chueng Eighk*). Other provinces had their own killing fields.

I had been there twice before and did not mind going again. Choeung Ek was along a French-looking tree-lined country road. The killing field bordered a large swamp with Phnom Penh visible in the distance. My first visit there had been with some Cambodians who were all in their early twenties. They thought that Choeung Ek was great stuff.

The Khmer Rouge had a saying to summarize their feelings toward the people they did not like: "Alive no gain, dead no loss." Here it was easy to see what they meant. You walked around and looked into the excavated pits, each large enough to hold a small car, into which they had thrown the sixteen thousand people they had bludgeoned to death. Some of the pits had explanatory signs, "Mass grave of 160 victims without heads," "100 women with no clothes found here." There was also a memorial *stupa*. Stupas are usually stone bell-shaped domes that hold a relic of the Buddha. The center of this stupa was a glass display case that held eight thousand skulls on its shelves, including two or three labeled as "foreign." To some people, the stupa was a poignant testimony to the brutality of the Khmer Rouge. To others it was a frightening example of how far the Phnom Penh government would go to score a few propaganda points, while denying the relatives of those skulls whatever peace of mind it would give them to know that their relatives had been given a decent burial. The young Cambodians thought it was a good memorial; they wrote little messages in the guest book and had their pictures taken.

The second trip was with Sari and Nara. It was during the rainy season and the rain had eroded the pits a bit more, exposing bones, bits of cloth and teeth. I was carefully collecting a handful of teeth when Sari asked me if something dreadful hadn't happened to me in my childhood. I threw the teeth back into a pit that was filled with water.

Now the rainy season was just ending, and it was a cool and overcast day. Sovan and I drove out of Phnom Penh until I found some back roads where she could practice. After an hour she had mastered second gear and the basics of turning, so I had her drive down the road, which for Cambodia was in excellent condition, to Choeung Ek. As we drove in, I felt that if ever a place was eerie—haunted, if you will—this was it. All graveyards have their own aura, but Choeung Ek was not so much a graveyard as a human garbage dump—a place where human beings who had been treated like garbage had been dumped. How did the farmers who lived around it feel? Were they here then? Did ghosts haunt their dreams, as they did the dreams of people in other parts of Cambodia who slept where atrocities had taken place? Perhaps Sovan felt some of the same things.

As we pulled in, I mentally planned our tour of the open pits, the stupa and the explanatory signs. Sovan climbed out of the truck, walked to a small rise at the edge of the parking lot where the open pits began, sat down in the grass, and wouldn't move. For her, there was nothing interesting here and she did not need a tour guide.

I had never asked her about her past. When I worked in the refugee camps, I had heard enough stories, but now she wanted to talk and I was willing to listen.

"There were ten people in my family in 1975 when we left Phnom Penh," she began, staring off into the distant horizon.

The family left together, but after a few weeks they were separated by Angka, which was what the Khmer Rouge called themselves in those days. The children were sent to the nearby province of Kampong Speu, just east of Phnom Penh; the parents were sent to Takeo, the province of the mother's family. South of Phnom Penh, Takeo borders on Vietnam.

"My parents could have escaped to Vietnam then, but they didn't because of us."

That was in April. In October, Sovan and Setee were given permission to stay with their parents. "We rode a truck part way and walked the rest," Sovan continued. "When I saw my father, I didn't know who he was. My brother greeted him and said to me, 'Hey, why don't you pay your respects to him? He is your father.' But I didn't recognize him. His body was swelling up with starvation and in December he died."

She was thirteen.

Joined by their other brothers and sisters, they stayed in Takeo for over a year. Two of her younger brothers died from malnutrition. In 1977, the Angka sent the survivors to Battambang. The children were separated from their mother and sent to work in different "mobile brigades"—work groups of children and teenagers who traveled around Cambodia creating huge, poorly designed irrigation projects.

In 1978 the province of Battambang was one of the most brutal places in Cambodia. An insane paranoia swept the Angka, and many Cambodians disappeared. Cambodians do not share the American MIA (Missing in Action) hysteria. To them when a person is dead, that's it, and finding out the minute details or locating the body does not make a person any less dead. Sovan was with some of her brothers and sisters when they died, although she was too weak to bury her two older sisters without help from the neighbors. The deaths of the others she heard from her mother who heard the news from relatives and friends in different mobile brigades.

"In Battambang I fell sick with malaria. I told them that I was sick, but they said that I had to work anyway. Then I couldn't walk so they sent me to the hospital. In the hospital there wasn't any food or medicine. My mother came to see me and later told me that she thought I was going to be the next to die.

"In the hospital, every day I would try to escape, but how could I escape? I couldn't walk. The nurse would find me along the road and bring me back.

"Finally my mother was able to trade some gold for food and medicine, and I got better."

Her eyes had filled with tears.

"Every time I talk about it I cry."

We sat there for a long time. In the distance, just a few buildings and chimneys broke the horizon where Phnom Penh was. A few tourists walked around the stupa, but it was not the kind of place where anyone was going to ask you for directions or where you were from.

On the way home we took a detour to see where the family had lived before 1975. Squatters had ripped down the old house, near downtown Phnom Penh, and built a new one. Her old grade school was a short walk away, so we stopped by there too. It was now a museum and I had toured it before. After school closed in 1975, the Khmer Rouge had turned Toul Sleng School into Security Office 21—the Auschwitz of Cambodia. There they had tortured their enemies and, during a frantic series of internal purges, their friends, some of whom were women and children. The Khmer Rouge took their victims' pictures as they tortured them; now those pictures were on display along with some paintings made by a survivor. Sovan just peeked in. She said that it looked about the same.

She learned driving quickly, and in a few weeks we had a new hobby—going places. *Going places* was a popular weekend UN hobby in Cambodia, and why not? Fuel, vehicle maintenance, and indeed the air-conditioned over-powered four-wheel-drive vehicle were all absolutely free. Most gas stations around Phnom Penh had contracts with UNTAC. You drove in, they filled it up, they checked the oil, they smiled at you,

you signed the form, and away you went. What could be easier than
that? I called it legal stealing. Everyone did it. There was nothing else to
do. Every weekend one of the UNVs in my guesthouse would pick a
place and drive there or for half the day, whichever came first, and drive
back. It didn't matter if he reached his destination or not—he was just
driving around for fun. UN staff would drive three hours to the resort
of Sihanouk Ville, spend four hours on the beach, and drive back. A few
people would fly to Bangkok almost every weekend on the free UN-
TAC flights. Some people, when they grew tired of going places, bought
a VCR and passed the weekend watching videos. Until I had my license,
I used to rent vehicles or go with someone else, but now with my new
hobby, legal stealing, and a partner in crime, Sovan, life was much better. One of the nicest things about my accomplice was that not only
could she speak the language and drive, she had a near photographic
memory. This was useful since all the roads looked alike, were never
marked, and there were no maps.

One Sunday morning Sovan wanted to deliver a letter to her mother's
best friend from Site Two. The woman's son had sent his mother a letter in care of Sovan. "I will take it to his mother," she said, "but I hate
him."

"I hate him, too."

"You don't even know him."

"But I hate him."

"Because I hate him, you hate him?"

"That's right."

"I don't really hate him. I'm angry at him because he called me
'younger sister'."

"He called you 'younger sister'? Really? That's terrible."

Sovan showed me the letter he had sent her. There was the evidence
in black and white: "amom," younger sister.

"He thinks," she continued, "he can do that because he makes four
hundred dollars a month working for UNTAC in Siem Reap, but I am
older than he is."

"You are older, almost thirty. He's just a kid, a total air-head, and a
wimp. And it's just a hundred dollars more than you make anyway."

"I don't care. Let's just go."

She drove. The young man's mother lived about an hour from town,
off the paved highway to Vietnam, down a dirt road, through a maze of
dirt tracks, and finally along a very narrow lane with tiny houses on
both sides. It was a private housing project. The UN gave families return-

ing to Cambodia fifty dollars per adult and twenty-five dollars per child. This family had taken that money and their savings—$600—to buy a piece of land about the size of a one-car garage with a little thatched hut on it. There was no electricity or plumbing; the toilet was in the bushes. Every morning the residents bought water from a cart that a vendor pushed down the road. Until recently the land had been a forest, and a few trees remained.

We delivered the letter. The mother, whom we addressed as Om, asked us to come in. Her furniture consisted of two large nylon bags of rice labeled "United Nations." They were part of her 200-day UN food grant for a Phnom Penh returnee. Country returnees received a 400-day food grant.

A tiny, stout, lively woman in her fifties, Om did not have any babies around the house; instead she had a dog. "Hello Tricky, how are you?" Sovan greeted the dog in English, remembering him from Site Two. The mother gave us water, showed us some photos, and offered to show us around the neighborhood.

Some of the houses were pleasant two-story wooden bungalows, which, if you could live without electricity and plumbing, would have been bearable. On the tour, indeed any time I walked around a Cambodian neighborhood, I had the feeling that I was in Oz among the munchkins: children, like the flies in New Market, were everywhere. About half of the population of Cambodia was under fifteen and most seemed to be under ten. With no birth control, the population was skyrocketing at just under three percent a year.

"Sovan," I asked as we headed home, "do you think that those kids will have a better life than their parents?"

"No way."

I couldn't see any way, either. The population had nearly doubled during twenty-two years of war. Never, I read, would Cambodia be self-sufficient in food again. There were simply too many people for the country to feed itself. It was headed the way of the Philippines or Pakistan: an out-of-control population explosion which the economy could never sustain, and which in turn would spiral the people down into more poverty and despair.

"Don't think too much about things you cannot change," Sovan concluded.

"Yes, okay," I said, "but still, what a bozo—'amom!' How can you be his younger sister?"

After she learned to drive, I wanted Sovan to get her driver's license.

"What do I want a license for?" she asked.

"So you can drive legally."

"But I don't have a car."

"You have my car."

"What good is that?"

"Look," I said, "you're going to get your license. I'll pick you up at one this afternoon." That week, we were both working the night shift, and I was usually awake by noon. Sometimes a man has to take control.

"The office closes for lunch until two."

"I'll pick you up at two."

The Ministry of Transport was near Wat Phnom. Sovan did not want to be seen entering with a foreigner, so she had me wait outside. Five minutes later I wandered in. The Ministry of Transport consisted of clerks sitting in hot un-air-conditioned offices in front of ancient typewriters or no typewriters at all, and working for a tenth of what Sovan made. Many of them were her age. By two o'clock the dust and heat had made everyone grimy. The building, with its high ceilings, wooden floors and tall shuttered windows, was left over from the French and more recently from the Sihanouk era. After that, it had been abandoned for four years during Pol Pot's experiment in country living, and now no one had the money to fix it up. It could have been the movie set for a teenage horror film.

Sovan told the clerk that she wanted a driver's license. The clerk asked her a few questions and finished by asking her if she was a member of an opposition party. She had, after all, only recently come from the border. She said that she was not. Maybe, another clerk suggested, she was a spy. Again she said she was not. That settled, they explained to her that she could either "arrange" a license for a certain price, or pay the fifty dollar fee, take a test, and obtain a license legally. She had the confidence to take the test and told them so. Very good, they said, but first she must fill out the form.

She took the form, put it in her purse, and walked out. And that was the last I could ever get her to do with it. Who, she asked, would ever get a license if they were suspected of being a spy or a member of the traitorous opposition? Driving illegally was clearly better.

In late November Patrick went on vacation. His wife was coming from England and they were to spend the vacation in Thailand. During his five months in Cambodia his appearance had changed dramatically from that of a fat English Humpty Dumpty to that of a Cambodian scarecrow. He told me he was afraid his wife would not recognize him. I told him not to worry: she would get over it.

I took his place as supervisor. Again I gave the locals more responsibility and again production dramatically increased. One night a data entry clerk typed over seven hundred cards. She was a walking typing machine. We put her name up on the wall and took her picture. But I could never remember her name and always referred to her as "The Motorcycle Lady." The Motorcycle Lady, like a few of the other clerks, had had her face smashed up in a recent motorcycle accident. Anyway, names were not so important in a country where everyone called everyone else "uncle," "older brother," or "younger sister."

FIRST GOD CREATED CAMBODIANS

This may be a good time to explain how Cambodians feel about Westerners.

In the beginning, God created Cambodians, who would one day build Angkor Wat. He then created the other peoples of Asia, including, by mistake, the Vietnamese. Next he made chickens, dogs, and pigs. Some time later, one day, with nothing else to do, he created Westerners. The Westerners, God knew, would be good at making toys—AK-47s, rocket-propelled grenade launchers, land mines, videos, TVs, cars, cameras—and lots of money. They would be talented and rich toy makers, but they would remain a crude and insensitive people. In their crudeness, the Westerners would forget how desirable a virgin wife was and, as a consequence, not try very hard to avoid sex before marriage. Worse yet, after not-too-elaborate marriage ceremonies, they would often divorce. And God rested. Later, unfortunately, a few things went wrong in Cambodia, and some Cambodians decided to sacrifice almost everything to live in Western countries, but not like the Westerners. They felt they had to leave Cambodia not because they *really* wanted to, but rather to live safely, comfortably, and "be rich."

Understanding how Cambodians feel about Westerners may be useful in understanding why it was so hard for Sovan to tell me that her engagement to the Khmer-American man in the U.S.A. had fallen apart.

She asked me, "Do you want to see some pictures?"

"Yes, of course."

It was a hot Sunday morning and we were in the loft above the furniture factory. The diesel engines were not running, so I could breathe, but the air was filled with the earsplitting sound of nails being pounded into the hardwood lumber below.

She had a tall stack of pictures, all taken on the border, since everything that the family had owned before 1975 had been lost.

"Who is that beautiful woman?" I asked.

"You don't know her."

The woman in the picture was Sovan when her hair was down to her waist. She looked like Rapunzel or the girl on the Sunmaid Raisins box.

"I want to meet her. I've been waiting all of my life for a woman like that."

"Really?"

"Really. Why would I want anyone else?" I could feel my heart beating out of my chest. "But girls like that are usually engaged to men far away."

"That's true, but those long-distance romances don't often last," she said.

"No, I heard that a Cambodian woman could go to the U.S.A., become engaged to a guy there, and marry him six months or a year later."

"I think that would be hard to do. The man's family in the U.S.A. might have a misunderstanding and argue with the girl."

"Argue about what?" I asked.

"His family might think that she would want to bring her whole family with her to the U.S.A., which would put a big burden on them."

"I see."

"It would not be true, though. She would never think of taking anyone else, but anyway, that argument would stop everything."

"I see," I said. "So there might be some beautiful women left who are not engaged anymore."

"Maybe not so beautiful, but not engaged."

It was almost unbearably hot and stuffy in the loft. Why couldn't I find a Cambodian woman who lived along the river and fall for her?

REGISTRATION MADNESS

By late November registration madness had swept the nation. People lined up everywhere registration teams went, and registration teams went everywhere except areas controlled by the Khmer Rouge. Voter registration was now the Madonna, the Michael Jackson, and the super-lottery of Cambodia. Eight hundred and thirty-four five-person registration teams led by UNVs combed the country, occasionally competing with each other to see who could register the most voters in a single day—up to two hundred per team. Every day the Australian helicopter crew would drop off at least three huge duffle bags of registration card receipts at the Computer Center.

UN officials told the media that the rush to register was evidence of the Cambodian people's strong desire for democracy. Others said that a lot of people just wanted, for the first time in their lives, to have their picture taken. I saw Cambodians as survivors, and as survivors they knew that in different situations you did different things to survive. In this situation, you registered to vote.

In other ways things were not going so well. According to the Paris Peace Agreement, the warring armies were supposed to enter into holding areas where they would be trained in skills that a country not at war might need. Long ago the Khmer Rouge leadership had decided not to send their troops to the holding camps, and now the National Army of Democratic Kampuchea (NADK), as they liked to call themselves, decided to try something new.

In early December, some United Nations Military Observers, UNMOs (*un-moes*), were on patrol in what the Australians called "whoop-whoop land" in the northern province of Kampong Thom, when the NADK "invited" them to spend the night. No RSVP was necessary and they were not taking no for an answer. This was a new game—bush detention. They held the six men for three days without giving them a mosquito net at night, while UNTAC negotiated a letter from the Phnom Penh NADK commander that ordered the release of the UNMOs.

The UN's Final Legacy

Early in the morning of December 2, in Siem Reap, two UN Civilian Policemen from Africa were driving down a country road when they hit a land mine. One of the men lost a leg. Two hours later at the same place, with Indonesians driving this time, the same thing happened and another leg was lost. Things were heating up.

The man from Africa went to the International Outreach Project to get a new leg. He wanted to "walk" home, and no one could make a leg faster than the International Outreach Project. As my friends fitted him with his aluminum and rubber leg, he told them that during his stay in the hospital he had learned that he was HIV positive.

"Gosh," I said when Roland told me the story, "think of that—one day you wake up fondling some nice Vietnamese lady, and the next day you're missing a leg and you have AIDS!"

"That could be part of the problem," he said.

"What do you mean?"

"I mean the women he could have infected."

"Oh? Yes, I see." For me, prostitution was still glamorous and exotic. I had never considered its darker side.

Roland had teenage daughters in the U.S.A. He continued, "AIDS will be, I'm afraid, the UN's final legacy in Cambodia."

"You think so?"

"I think," he said from behind his bifocals, "that if you bring in men from all around the world, don't test them, and turn them loose with more money than they've ever seen in their lives, you are going to do some damage."

"Boys will be boys," I said, quoting Mr. Akashi's famous remark about UNTAC and prostitution.

Later, after a huge public uproar led by the NGOs, Mr. Akashi had tried to change his tune about the "boys," but by then whorehouses had popped up around Cambodia like frogs after a monsoon rain. Sex workers were everywhere in Phnom Penh—from the plush Thai Royal Massage Parlor, just outside the Prime Minister's compound, to the cheap and dirty sidewalk cafes just north of Electoral Headquarters. There the girls put their pancake makeup on outside before taking the customers into one of the curtained-off rooms in the back. Even my old barber shop had become a brothel. The town had gone whore-crazy with, if the women's groups were correct, some ten thousand prostitutes. A few of the locals decried the city's sex trade, but no one tried very hard to stop it. Most of the prostitutes were Vietnamese, and UNTAC soldiers were not their only customers. Indeed, many Khmer soldiers were, according to the clandestine Khmer Rouge radio, guilty of the horrendous sin of sleeping with the enemy.

The Civilian Policemen, or CivPol, were a strange bunch. The UN had decided that it needed people to handle some of the police work that comes with administering a country, so they had recruited over three thousand professional policemen from thirty-two countries around the world. But although the UN had remembered to give them more money

than most third world policemen ever dreamed of making, they forgot
to give them training, discipline, adequate leadership, a mutually intelli-
gible language, and a sense of mission. Around town, CivPol directed
traffic and documented UN traffic accidents, and some of them could
be very helpful. Still, most people saw them as men who wanted to
flaunt their newfound wealth by buying video cameras and visiting the
places that Mr. Akashi had halfheartedly declared off limits. In the provinces the UNVs never tired of complaining about CivPol.

LANDING THE SPACE SHUTTLE WITH COUNT DRACULA

By mid-December the system in the Computer Center had become at
least as complicated as the space shuttle. By this time over three million
people had registered to vote, and a thick notebook had filled up with a
backlog of letters from district electoral supervisors telling us which
voter registration card numbers they had borrowed from other districts.
Hugo had hired another international staff person to deal with the problem, but she hated the tediousness of the job and could not really handle
the technicalities of it. As a supervisor, I did not know what was going
on. How could I?

Early one night one of the local staff, who had trained to be a math-
ematician in Moscow and could speak Russian to Hugo, was trying to
assign a range of cards to a certain district and couldn't do it. She asked
Hugo for help and he sent her to me. I was, as always, running to keep
up with eighty data entry clerks, so I wrote a note about the problem
cards for the day shift technician. Hugo told me that I had to fix her
problem right now. Yes, I thought, and while I'm at it why don't I calculate the correct entry trajectory path for the space shuttle? I went
back to my work.

Hugo exploded, stopped everything, and even though it was difficult
for him to control himself, he spent the next two hours trying to teach
me how to land the space shuttle, which meant editing the guts of the
database. But even he could not quite figure out the correct flight path
and we quit, leaving it for the software engineer to sort out. Meanwhile,
back at the supervisor's desk, I had two hours of problems waiting for
me.

The next day I told the software engineer what had happened. Ravi
told me that our captain had gone off the deep end and that he, Ravi, did
not want anyone, even Hugo, messing with his database.

I agreed with Ravi. It was, I concluded, a good time for the low man
in the ranks—"just a UNV"—to jump ship. It is always better to walk

Children of families displaced by fighting rest on the sidewalks of Phnom Penh.

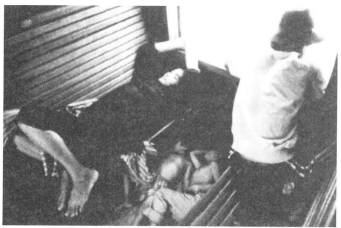

Returning to Cambodia after years in border camps, a family contemplates its future.

out than be carried out.

I told the director of the United Nations Volunteers that I wanted to transfer to another part of UNTAC. She had met Hugo, so I did not have to tell her why I wanted out. Hugo said he didn't care, but after he saw that I was actually going to leave, he remembered some of his old European charm, shook my hand, wished me well, and started calling me Mister R.

But what next?

By now I knew many people around UNTAC. A few had not forgotten that months ago I had skipped lunch or worked late to help them. I spread the word that I was looking for a job. No problem, they said, we can use you. I thought about it and opted for a new line of work: trainer. I would train the people who would, in five months, run the polling stations. My new boss, Judy Thompson, a Canadian, was one of the two women who were now in the higher ranks of UNTAC. Judy said that work would begin in mid-January, which was fine with me.

NEW HEIGHTS

Only four days had passed from the night Hugo and I attempted to land the space shuttle to the time I agreed to work with Judy. That weekend I borrowed a Toyota Land Cruiser, and with Setee in tow to run the tape player, Sovan and I made a pilgrimage to Phnom Chisor, one of the distant sister temples of Angkor Wat. Sovan told me that it was a four-hour drive, so we left at 8 A.M. and arrived at 10:30. "I said I knew the way," she said, "not how long it would take."

"Yes, dear."

I didn't care. Ninety percent of the solution to the dilemma of being human is having someone to tell your troubles to, and the two-and-a-half hour trip was long enough for me to tell her all of the details of the past week. I ended my monologue with, "So after that, he started calling me Mr. R, which means, if you want to get any respect around here—quit!"

She understood exactly how I felt. From the beginning, she and Hugo had gotten along well together and also from the beginning she had more or less pretended she couldn't speak English whenever he was around. That was the Asian way.

She and Setee knew the way to Phnom Chisor: it was near where the Khmer Rouge had let them reunite with their parents in late 1975, and

---

* Not its real name.

where her father had starved to death. Finding the way was easy—we drove south out of Phnom Penh until the road became an elephant track, kept going until we saw a mountain on the left, found the road that went to the mountain, and we were there.

The bottom of the mountain was like a scene from one of those old movies about slave life in ancient Rome. In a natural amphitheater families sat under thatched umbrellas and with little hammers smashed big rocks, which they had somehow pried out of the mountain, into little rocks that would later be used for construction in Phnom Penh. They did not use sledge hammers, just small tap hammers that filled the air with *tap, tap, tap* all day long. Walking through the quarry, I felt as if I were in an insane asylum. No one looked up at us, not wanting to risk pounding a finger, and everyone continued with the incessant *tap-tap-tap...tap-tap-tap-tap.*

We took a path up the hill. Little children seemed to be following us, but it was only a coincidence—they were on their way to scavenge firewood so that their parents could cook lunch. Halfway up the mountain, the children disappeared into the scrub. Now it was hot and quiet. We could not see the summit, but kept walking. Just as we thought we were lost, and as Sovan was starting to complain about the heat, we rounded a bend and saw the ancient temple that they had sliced the top off the mountain to build. We walked around to the main entrance. Here we felt a cool breeze and saw the ancient stairway that plunged straight down the steep mountain, leveled out on the plain below, and stretched straight through the rice fields to the horizon. Now we could sit in the shade of a large tree to have lunch, and I could open a warm beer, which was what I had been wanting to do for the last hour.

The astounding scale and artistry with which the ancient Cambodians built their temples eight hundred years ago remains the envy of the other Southeast Asian nations. This may help explain why looters sell the intricate temple carvings for fortunes on the international art market.

As we ate lunch and looked out at the fantastic view, Sovan and Setee, more proud than ever to be Khmer, promised each other that they would visit Angkor Wat before they died.

"I've already seen Angkor Wat, so can I die now?" I asked.

"Can you wait until we get home?" Sovan answered.

On the way back to Phnom Penh we stopped by their ancestral village and the house of an aunt who used to live in a big house in Phnom Penh. After the experiment and ensuing widowhood, she had retreated back to the old village. Now she and her children were existing in a thatched hut, wondering how to stay alive for another day.

I told Sovan that I was going to walk around while they were having their reunion. She checked with her aunt to find out if there were any land mines around. The aunt said the area was safe. Behind the house, two of her children were fishing. Fishing, as the dry season was just beginning, meant dragging a basket through the mud and picking up tiny crabs who had burrowed into the muck. This was dinner.

We had some fruit and bread in the truck. I gave it to the aunt to help spice up her dinner, and we left.

On the road again, Sovan summed up her visit: "Now some people's lives have gotten better, and some have gotten worse."

She drove the rest of the way back to Phnom Penh. As she and her brother talked, I fell asleep, thinking that my life had gotten better.

PURER THAN BREAST MILK

Christmas and a long break were coming up. I decided to go to Thailand and asked Sovan to come with me. She said that she wanted to, but that it would not look right when she had only recently returned from New York. In other words, if she were to remain, in the eyes of the world and her family, purer than breast milk, she would have to stay home. She said she would take her own vacation at the beach resort of Sihanouk Ville with the students of our recently graduated IOP computer class.

Her parting words to me were, "Don't bring AIDS back to Cambodia."

Bangkok was just a sixty minute C160 flight from Phnom Penh. I loved Thailand. For me Thailand was a place to go for great food, good movies, and beautiful women.

The Thais have their own myths about prostitution. They like to say that American soldiers popularized it during the Vietnam War. After that, they claim, they were helpless to stop it, and now prostitution is everywhere.

Bangkok never changed. As long as I could remember, there were always "new" solutions to the "problems" of traffic and prostitution. And the solutions were almost always the same: put them above the ground, or under the ground, or relegate them to special places, or pass a law to make the situation better. "Yes, it is bad, but this is not the real Thailand," Bangkok Thais liked to say. "To find the real Thailand you have to go to the Northeast." It was true that there was less traffic in the rural and poor Northeast Thailand, but the Bangkok Thais would forget to mention that over 5 percent of the military recruits from the

Northeast tested positive for HIV. All cultures have their myths.

I hated the whore scene in Phnom Penh. In Thailand though, it was more dignified. In Thailand a man can go into an air-conditioned bar, sit in a comfortable chair, have a cold beer, and watch twenty women dance naked on stage. Or at least you *used* to be able to. Recently, I had read, some new hotshot police commissioner had clamped down and stopped the nude dancing. It was the same old story—he wanted to improve Thailand's image.

I walked into my old haunt and saw that it was true. But the ladies on stage did not seem happy to be out of the buff and, rather than buy sequin bikinis or satin mini skirts, they had opted to wear their ratty old bras and panties. The waitresses and the girls who were not dancing wore street clothes. After a beer, I started to like it. Maybe the old police commissioner and I had attended the same high school. I sat alone in a corner and fantasized—this was secondary school heaven. Soon a young lady sat beside me and I started to live more of my old high school fantasies. She rubbed my shoulders, sat on my lap, whispered sweet nothings in my ear and, in a slight departure from my dream, asked me to do a short-time in the back room for five hundred baht—twenty dollars.

"Just five hundred baht?" I said in Thai. "You are very beautiful."

"Thank you." She was waiting for me to get up.

"Aren't you afraid of AIDS?" I asked.

"Okay, we can have oral sex."

She said she was eighteen, but looked fifteen. She wore a floor length skirt, and now, in the shadows, removed her brassiere. Her small firm breasts stood straight out from her chest. She wrapped my hands around them. She had a touch of baby fat.

"I heard that you can get AIDS that way too."

"I'll put a condom on it and blow you through the condom."

For someone who looked fifteen, she knew the business like the best of them.

"That wouldn't be any fun."

"Don't you like me?" she asked. Now she was pulling the heart strings.

"Yes, of course I like you. How can I not like you?" I was serious. "But my wife is afraid of AIDS."

"Is wife here?"

"She's waiting for me at home."

"Can you buy me a Coke?"

"Sure."

The old wife trick still worked.

As the night progressed I came to see that the bras and panties on stage were just a cheap cover-up. As soon as the manager signaled that the roaming police officers had retired for the night, the girls brought things out in the open again. Ah, I thought, now this is the Thailand I love.

But my heart was in Cambodia. As soon as the plane touched down at Phnom Penh's Pochentong airport, I raced to Sovan's house. Just at dusk I rode up on my motorcycle. It was too late to go out, but I was welcome to stay for dinner. After her vacation in Sihanouk Ville, she and Setee had taken an UNTAC flight to Siem Reap to see Angkor Wat—all UNTAC staff were allowed to ride the UNTAC flights for free. I told her that after seeing Angkor Wat she could die any day now. She said that she had missed me.

She had been right about not going to Thailand. Sometimes it is better to remain purer than breast milk.

MAJOR THOM

My last day in the Computer Center was January 14, two weeks before voter registration officially came to an end. Patrick left two weeks later. He had refused to renew his contract. One of his final comments was, "I've never met so many people that I disliked."

He had a knack for summaries.

My new office, Training, Education and Communications, or UNTAC XX, was across Monivong Boulevard, about a half hour's walk from the New Market toward the airport. I was to be one of seventeen trainers who would travel around Cambodia teaching people how to conduct the election, now re-scheduled for sometime in May. We had three weeks to prepare our teaching material. I took the job seriously and worked hard to prepare, but everyone kept coming to me with their computer problems. I was happy to help them, but I was supposed to be a trainer.

"This isn't working," I said to Judy after the first two weeks. The trainers complained that Judy had a bad temper and would not listen to them. To me, after Hugo, she was the Mother Teresa of bosses.

"I think we can use you in different ways," she said

"I think so too."

She decided that I would be the "Computer Liaison Officer."

As such, I used my computer skills to produce posters, charts, fliers, handouts, and booklets for the trainers, and helped secretaries with their computer problems. I had never been an officer before, and now I was, by my own declaration, "Major Thom."

I could have been a General.

On January 25, the Phnom Penh government attacked the Khmer Rouge near their Pailin headquarters. It was their biggest military move since the arrival of UNTAC. UNTAC said that they didn't like it, but what could UNTAC do? UNTAC was supposedly a peace-*keeping* and not a peace-*making* organization. Anyone's ideas about a cease-fire now went completely to hell. I saw pictures of the fighting on the television at Sovan's house, but from Phnom Penh the fighting was still far away.

Registration ended on January 31, on schedule, with about 4.7 million people registered. There were 38 percent more voters than predicted in the AEPU report for Phnom Penh; in some of the provinces, 25 percent more. UNTAC blamed the discrepancies on the returnees. The President of the Khmer Rouge, Khieu Samphan, knew better. He thought that the AEPU people had done a good job and declared that the extra voters were Vietnamese. To me, the discrepancies helped illustrate why people earned masters' degrees in demography—there was more to it than turning untrained internationals loose with motorcycles and a form they did not understand. But still, hey, thanks, Khieu.

I spent the weekends with Sovan and her family. It was winter now, so it was actually pleasant to be outside—walking in town, taking a cruise on the river, or going on a picnic. During the week we would find excuses to visit each other: she wanted to use my computer, I wanted to see someone in the Computer Center, she wanted me to take her somewhere for lunch. Life was good.

People from other parts of UNTAC sometimes would ask me for help with computer projects: fix that, show me how to do this, make me this. Judy hated it. She had hired me to work for her, but I never minded much. One day, I received an unusual request that would put me in the front of the election process and come close to making the whole Electoral effort look foolish. The story began simply enough, like a fairy tale...

4 Into the Fire
February - late May 1993

ONCE UPON A TIME

Once upon a time, there was a high United Nations electoral official in Cambodia. He was from a country filled with deserts, kangaroos, and wide open spaces. It was famous for the huge amounts of alcohol that the people who lived there could drink. Those people loved their favorite alcohol, beer, so much that they called it "piss." That country was also known as a place where people spoke English in a way that no one else could understand. That country was Australia and that official was Michael Maley, the Senior Deputy Chief Electoral Officer for Operations and Computerization, who lived on Coca-Cola and whose English very few people could understand.

And once upon a time there was a woman who had an aptitude for computers and languages. She was from a country that should have been known for its ancient architecture and the delicacy of its culture. Instead, it was widely known as a country whose most famous citizen had masterminded the death of about a million people. That country was Cambodia, that citizen was Pol Pot, and that woman was Sovan.

And finally, there was once a computer graphics artist. He was from a country that should have been famous for bombing the shit out of people in places like Cambodia, Vietnam, and Iraq, but instead was widely known as the birthplace of Michael Jackson. That country was the United States and that man was me.

One day the high electoral official asked the artist to make the ballot for the election that UNTAC was sponsoring. Michael Maley said, "You're an expert on scanning and all the party logos have to be scanned onto the ballot."

"Okay."

This overweight, balding and cheerful man explained that the idea was to make the ballot in Cambodia on an IBM personal computer and send that file over a telephone line to Canada where an outfit called "Elections Canada" would print it eight million times.

"But there are only four million voters in Cambodia."

"We don't want to run short of ballots."

"I see."

All of Cambodia would use one ballot, and on that ballot the voters would choose the one party that they wanted to lead their country. Each province would send representatives from the winning parties, based on the number of voters in the province, to Phnom Penh. The 120-member constituent assembly would then have three months to write a new constitution.

That was the plan.

The artist asked his friend, the woman with an aptitude for computers and languages, to help. "Yes I will," she said. "Why not?"

"It sounds like fun," they said to each other.

At least more fun than teaching secretaries word-processing, he thought. At least more fun than working in the Computer Center, she thought. She continued to work in the Computer Center, but said, "I want to work in a place where the people smile at each other." That was her way, being from a country that should have been famous for the delicacy of its culture, of saying she wanted to quit, but both she and the artist knew she never would.

PLASTIC SURGERY

Step one in making the ballot was obtaining the party logos. UNTAC had hired a lawyer, Frank Eppert, to liaise with the parties. One of his duties was to collect the official party logos, names, and abbreviations as the parties wanted them to appear on the ballot. He gave copies to me. Some of the logos were very crisp and clear. Others were pathetic and looked like they had been hastily drawn in pencil before being copied on a malfunctioning photocopy machine. Two of the twenty-two parties produced beautiful color logos that, reduced to black and white, turned into gray blobs.

Some logos were filled with goddesses, animals, or even different parts of the United Nations symbol. None were the kind of thing you could spray-paint on the wall of your neighbor's house or scribble on a bathroom wall: these were works of art. One party's logo bore a striking resemblance to an American twenty-five cent coin. Another party managed to put into their logo something for every conceivable voter:

Hun Sen, the darling of the Western media and the kind face of the Phnom Penh government, woos a crowd of would-be voters before the 1993 election.

Khieu Samphan, who wrote his Ph.D. thesis on the reformation of the Khmer economy, is bombarded by the press. As the official president of the Khmer Rouge's Democratic Kampuchea, he presents a more respectable version of the guerrilla group than did his predecessor, Pol Pot.

the Brooklyn Bridge, a dove carrying
an olive branch, two fishermen, seven
palm trees, a jet airplane, two hands
shaking, the Queen Mary being
towed into New York Harbor,
assorted rice fields, a satellite dish
antenna, nine shade trees, the sun,
three tourists sitting under beach
umbrellas, one tractor, two water
buffalos, a water wheel, a wind
generator, and what looked like New
York's World Trade Center. These
people were definitely not taking any
chances.

A party's symbol was, as far as the parties were concerned, the secret
of success in a country where at least 60 percent of the electorate could
not read. Uncle UNTAC, appreciating the symbol's significance, ap-
proved them one by one. Rule number one was that no party symbol
could have a picture of Angkor Wat or Prince Sihanouk in it. Rule number two was that no two logos could look very much alike. So when
two parties submitted elephants in their logos, the UN decided that one
of the parties had to find another animal—only one elephant per ballot,
thank you. The losing party swapped its elephant for a flattering picture
of the party leader decked out in a military uniform with a full suit of
medals pinned to his chest. That picture had been, as was the custom in
Cambodia, taken twenty years ago when the general was still young.
Two party officials gave me the picture of "his excellency" with a certain ceremonial flair. I looked at it and thought that, after twenty years
in someone's wallet, it wasn't too bad. It looked like an old ID card
picture. But who was I to judge? I came from a country that had put a
painting of Elvis Presley on a postage stamp.

To scan the logos into a computer image, Michael wanted me to use a
flatbed scanner, which looks and works a little like a photocopy machine, but instead of transferring the image to another piece of paper,
the image is changed into computer code that can later be edited. Scan-
ners were scattered around different UN offices, but almost no one knew
how to use them. I checked out the scanner that the military had. The
people there were nice to me, hoping that I would show them how to
use it, but the scanner's glass was cracked so there was a line across everything it scanned. I told Michael about it.

"That's typical of the UN for ya, mate," he said. UN bashing was a kind of hobby for non-UN people—Michael had just been hired for the Cambodia mission.

I opted to use a little hand scanner that was in my office.

UNTAC still did not know exactly how many political parties would be on the ballot, or in what order they would appear. Everything was up in the air, including, with the renewed fighting, the election. We kept working.

In order for a party to appear on the ballot, the *Electoral Law* said that by January 27 the party had to submit a petition with the signatures of five thousand party members who were registered voters. Those signatures would then be checked against the Computer Center's list of registered voters. Twenty parties submitted petitions. But something was wrong with their lists. Either the parties were submitting bogus names or the Computer Center was not functioning properly. I didn't trust either one. I heard that the Computer Center found an instance of six hundred people living in one house and a total of eighteen new provinces. I also heard that some of the parties had gone to great lengths to find more than five thousand registered voters to sign their lists and that they were sure that the names were valid. But how could the names be valid? Who would sign a petition if for the last few months they had heard stories like these?

> An opposition party member was shot to death in his home in Prey Veng province. His mother was shot and killed as she rushed to help him. UNTAC investigators determined that the shooting was "very likely to be politically-motivated."—from the Electoral newsletter, *Free Choice*

> The body of a SOC (State of Cambodia or Phnom Penh government) employee who was an active member of the FUNCINPEC party (headed by the son-of-Sihanouk, Prince Ranariddh) was found in a well in Kampong Cham province. The victim had been badly beaten and tortured.—*Free Choice*

> Four opposition party workers were injured when unidentified attackers fired a B-40 rocket at their office

in Chi Kreng district, 50 kilometers east of Siem Reap provincial town.—*Free Choice*

Six FUNCINPEC party members were abducted in broad daylight; two were released the next day.. The other four remain missing.—*Free Choice*

...the (non-government) party's secretary-general said, "We can't open party offices because we don't want to be killed or harassed."—*Free Choice*

Two data entry clerks came to me scared out of their wits. The night before two secret police had come to their house and accused them of being members of opposition political parties, which they denied. They asked me what they should do. I told them to calm down and not to do anything.—*told to me by one of the Khmer supervisors in the Computer Center*

and,

I ran into two people from the human rights group Asia Watch. They had spent a month riding motorcycle taxis in the provinces. They believed that political intimidation and murder were much more widespread than the media or the UN had reported. People were too scared to report that their neighbors had been assassinated.—*me*

There is not a tradition of martyrdom in Cambodia, and although plastic surgery was available, I do not think that it would induce anyone to sign a petition that many people viewed as certifying a death wish. If each party had really obtained 5,000 signatures, that would have meant that at least 100,000 people, or 20 percent of the voters of Phnom Penh, had signed petitions. Many parties did not have offices outside the capital.

Michael guessed that between ten and fifteen of the twenty "provisionally registered" parties would make it onto the six by thirteen inch (fifteen by thirty-three centimeter) ballot paper.

By this time, early March, data on every voter in Cambodia, or 4,755,580 registration cards, had been typed into the Computer Center's database. The rotating shifts had ended. Also at about this time, the repatriation of all the Cambodian people in the border camps was nearing completion. It was being hailed as a great humanitarian success and a shining example of voluntary repatriation. The volunteers had been given the choice of coming back to Cambodia or going to jail. Not all of them were willing volunteers. From Thailand one recalcitrant refugee explained to the media that the fighting was continuing in Cambodia—which some people thought nullified the Paris Agreement—and that the country was strewn with land mines. It would be crazy, he claimed, to go back. But no one cared about him, and in the end he went crazy and returned to Cambodia.

The returnee I knew best, who was not crazy, was Sovan. She too, I slowly learned, had been exceedingly depressed about returning to Cambodia. Right up to the end, she had hoped that the American Immigration and Naturalization Service would change its mind and allow her and her family to go to the U.S.A. so that her mother could get proper medical treatment for her diabetes. In her hopelessness, and for the first few months I knew her, she wore no makeup, no jewelry, and only her oldest clothes. There was, she felt, no reason to polish a stone that had been cast off. After we started "going places," however, she had perked up, and although she still asked me about ways to go to the U.S.A., she started buying clothes again and wearing bright red lipstick and jewelry. Part of her jewelry was the necklace that her mother had bought for her so that she, in her mother's words, wouldn't look like a water buffalo with no collar.

The War Continued with a Wife for the Night

The war continued, but I lived in a world of seemingly carefree market people, air-conditioned offices, and weekends spent with Sovan and her family.

Weekends were picnics. People would go just about anywhere to get out of Phnom Penh. I went to all the ancient temples around Phnom Penh and to all the picnic sites, Kien Svay (*Kee-an Svay*) being my favorite. To reach Kien Svay, you drove east out of the city, across the Monivong Bridge, and kept going on a paved but narrow road. This was the major highway to Vietnam, the one the Vietnamese used when they blitzed into Phnom Penh in 1979. You kept going past the market on the other side of the bridge and into the countryside where one could imagine, for a few minutes, that all of Cambodia lived in sturdy little wooden houses on stilts at the edge of lush rice fields and mango orchards. Forty minutes later a temple gate on the left marked the entrance to Kien Svay. Here cozy thatch and bamboo huts sat above a lazy tributary of the Mekong. Inside the huts it was cool and shady—how soothing to sit there, dangle your feet in the almost clear water, and look across the 75 meters of barely flowing river to more green fields and picturesque thatched farm houses. Young girls paddled up in canoes to sell fruit, shrimp, peanuts, and rice dishes. Cold beer was sold by the people who rented the hut. Someone always played music from a tape player to help the cold beer go down. There were shaded canoes for rent if you wanted to take a slow cruise on the river with your honey. It was not glamorous or exciting, but for an afternoon, after paying off the beggars, one could forget that this was a country that had not known peace for twenty-three years.

The war continued. On the night of Wednesday, January 27, in a village in Siem Reap province, two women who worked for UNTAC were sleeping in a tent used to conduct voter registration. After 11 P.M., between thirty and fifty armed men attacked the village with rocket-propelled grenades. They entered the house where a CivPol from Africa lived, and asked to meet his wife for the night; when he hesitated to introduce her they shot him in both arms. They also shot up the voter registration tent where the two women were sleeping. They died, as did a seven-year-old girl in a nearby house.

Professor Austin wanted pictures of the two women displayed in Electoral Headquarters. He asked me to artistically arrange the text that explained how they had died. I took the pictures to my office to do the text layout. One picture was of Ty Sary. In her late thirties, she was a two-time widow with two children. The other picture was of Sary's partner, Hang Vicheth. She was just twenty and had supported a large extended family with her salary. Her picture had been professionally done—to make her look prettier, the photographer had painted extra long eyelashes onto her face. Their families' wish was that their daughter or mother or sister did not die in vain. This was the first time I remember crying.

In other parts of the country, the Khmer Rouge continued to play the bush detention game. They would grab some UNTAC people, preferably soldiers, and hold them for a few hours or days before letting them go. Other times, the KR would take potshots at UN aircraft, causing some emergency landings but no deaths.

By this time, the original idea as outlined in the Paris Peace Agreement had long since gone to hell after the Khmer Rouge and, in response, the Phnom Penh government had dropped out of the demobilization process—the process that was supposed to bring about a "neutral environment" before the election. With the renewed fighting, it looked as if the election would be conducted in the middle of a civil war. The head of UNTAC, Mr. Akashi, said that he wondered if the conditions for free and fair elections could now be met. Good thinking, Mr. Akashi.

Judy talked about quitting: "I don't want my name associated with an election that is forced upon people."

A lot of other people were having second thoughts about the Paris Peace Agreement. Some political commentators and members of the NGO community felt that the UN should quit, for they had been hoodwinked by the Khmer Rouge—the KR had signed the Paris Agreement not to achieve peace, but to stall for more time to reorganize and rearm, and indeed they were stronger now and controlled more territory than they had a year ago. The UN could only play on a level playing field, so it should get out. Others, including some in the military, said "Go after the bloody bastards." The Khmer Rouge had signed the Paris Agreement, and now, like it or not, they were going to live with it. Another option, of course, was simply to have the election without the Khmer Rouge. If they didn't want to come to the party, well, have the party without them. And why not? This was the almost three billion-dollar Rolls Royce of UN operations, and if Mr. United Nations, Boutros Boutros-Ghali, wanted to use it to put the UN at the front of the new world order, then that was what was going to happen. Prince Sihanouk agreed it was going to happen and added, in an interview published in the *Far Eastern Economic Review*, that UNTAC was going ahead "despite the fact none of the conditions for the election have been met. None. It is a hideous comedy." To him it looked as if UNTAC was dividing his country even further by allowing an election that would not include a "state within a state," that is, the Khmer Rouge. He blamed UNTAC for not forcing everyone to disarm and enter holding centers.

I thought that UNTAC was going ahead with the election in the same way that the Americans had gone ahead with the dropping of the atomic bomb on Hiroshima and Nagasaki. In the end, after so much preparation, no one thought much about right and wrong or original intentions; they thought that, since they had come this far, they should go ahead with it. Bombs away!

Who were the Khmer Rouge anyway? They occupied just 15 or 20 percent of Cambodian territory, had an army of maybe just ten thousand men, and controlled only about five percent of the population. Five percent of the population, what's that? Sovan told me that when she fled to the border in 1979, she didn't know where she was going. Someone had said there was food there, so she made a run for it. She didn't know anything about politics, having never even heard of Pol Pot. When her run ended, she was in a friendly camp. Just as easily, she said, she could have ended up in a Khmer Rouge camp and now be one of those five percent.

Usually, I think, people are just details in these things.

Anyway, details aside, the idea was that now, instead of using the 15,000 UN soldiers and 3,500 civilian police to manage the demobilization, they would help insure a "free and fair" election, while keeping Phnom Penh's ten thousand prostitutes in business. General Sanderson, UNTAC's soldier number one, said that on election day the soldiers would be *in the vicinity* of the polling stations to keep an eye on things. He said they would provide a "reassuring presence," whatever that was.

I asked one of the Khmer men in the office which party he was going to vote for. He did not hesitate to tell me: "UNTAC."

A More Perfect Model and a Silly Law

Every day, I sat in my air-conditioned office, pushed buttons, and moved the mouse. Soon I had a prototype of the ballot. I wanted to make the party logos as large as possible so I spaced them vertically down the page in irregular rows. My model was beautiful. Sovan said that it was beautiful too, but, she continued, if we were going to use it, we might as well write it in Chinese because no Cambodians would understand it anyway. So I compromised and spaced the logos across the page in three horizontal columns with five parties in each column.

That became the model.

I knew that the parties would want to see their party logo on the ballot before we sent the file to Canada, so I took a free hand in cleaning up and editing their party symbols. One party had forgotten to put periods in their abbreviation—I stuck them in. In others, I leveled out skewed text, straightened broken lines or made their circles perfectly round. I darkened some and lightened others; I made some grays white, and other grays black. Sovan typed all the Cambodian script for the party names and abbreviations, and I showed her how to use a computer program to clean up the Khmer writing in the party logos. I could easily spend a few hours on one logo. She spent one afternoon redoing dot-by-dot the logo of a party that had submitted dark green text on a black background that had scanned to a basic black-on-black.

"If they win the election," I said as I looked at her day's work, "they should give us some money."

"Twenty thousand dollars," she concluded.

As we worked, the big problem continued to be that we did not know how many of the twenty parties would be on the ballot or in what order they would be. Two of the logos were in such bad shape that I could not do anything with them. I asked Frank if he could have the parties give me another copy. He said that he could get one of them, but as for the other, "Don't worry about them, they'll never make it onto the ballot."

He was sharp. He had assumed that I would be showing my work to the parties, so he wrote up a legal form that said something like, "I, the representative of _____, do hereby certify that the text and logo of my party are acceptable." We were not going to take any chances.

The Computer Center continued to struggle with the lists of registered voters. Someone in the Computer Center told me that only the Phnom Penh government party, known as CPP—Cambodian People's Party— had submitted a valid list of registered voters, but that the UN was going to let fourteen other parties slide under the table and onto the ballot. After all, how could you have a multi-party election with just one party? That made sense to me. In the name of democracy, who cared about that silly *Electoral Law* anyway?

In the provinces, after UNTAC had finished voter registration, the government and the Khmer Rouge began voter de-registration. To deregister someone, they asked to see his voter registration card "for statistical purposes" and then destroyed it. UNTAC claimed, after admitting that card confiscation was widespread throughout Cambodia, that it would have the last laugh. As UNTAC explained in a huge voter education campaign, on election day the voters who had had their cards stolen could write their name on an envelope that they would put their ballot into. Later, the international staff of the Computer Center would do a search to see if those voters were indeed registered, and if they were, count the vote. It sounded too good to be true, but that was the plan. High-tech would save the day.

The Meaning of Low Tech and the
One Chance to Get it Right

Our big day was to be Sunday, February 20—Professor Austin and Frank
Eppert would announce which parties had acceptable petitions and draw
the party names out of a Khmer basket to determine their order on the
ballot. Sovan and I were psyched up. We spent all day Saturday making
final changes in the logos and proofreading. One party, FUNCINPEC,
the party of Sihanouk's son, had submitted a new party symbol the day
before. Their submission was in the form of a huge full-color poster that
was, of course, impossible to scan.

"Now what are you gonna do?" Sovan asked.

"I know a trick. We call it low-tech."

"Low-tech?"

"When high-tech can't, low-tech can."

"Excuse me?"

I just drew the damn thing.

The government party had submitted a new party logo as well. "It looks
just like the old one," I said to Frank.

"Redo it anyway. If you don't," he paused, "they'll know it." I believed him and redid it.

We had done the scanning on a desk top computer, but I kept the
ballot on my own notebook computer that had about twice the speed
and memory of the UN computers. I powered my computer with illegal—if one considered the U.S. copyright law legal—software that I had
purchased for twenty dollars in Bangkok. Legal software, as far as the
UN in Cambodia was concerned, was a bothersome detail. The AEPU
report as well, with the exception of the work done on one computer,
had been written and distributed with illegal software. No one cared,
but a lot of the election material was produced illegally. Might is right.

Late Saturday afternoon Michael asked me how we were doing. I told
him that I was ready with nineteen party logos.

"What about the other one?"

"Frank said that I didn't have to worry about them—they'll never
make it onto the ballot."

"That doesn't matter," Michael grumbled. He was not the type to get
angry. "Tomorrow every party will want to see their logo."

"I see."

For the rest of the day, Sovan and I scanned, edited, typed, and did
the layout for the other horribly produced logo while I introduced Sovan

to American obscenities and in the end just "low-teched" it. We quit at 8 P.M., vowing to finish in the morning just before the big meeting.

As he drove us home, Michael was hesitating about whether we should let the parties see what we had done, and if they didn't like it, demand changes.

"Do you know," I remarked, "that you are talking to someone who in four years of college never submitted a paper that didn't have a misspelled word in it?"

"...that didn't have a misspelled word *on* it," Michael repeated slowly.

"That didn't have a misspelled word on it."

I had confided to Sovan that I had probably confused some of the party logos. Over the last month, several parties had submitted different versions of their logo to Frank, and I was fairly sure that I had gotten a couple, well, confused. Moreover, I had taken great liberty in "improving" many of the party symbols, not to mention "low-teching" a few. How could I be sure the political parties would approve of my improvements to their all-important party symbols?

"All right mate, ya talked me into it," Michael said. He was a reasonable kind of guy.

On Sunday morning Sovan and I dressed up to meet the party representatives, which meant she looked like a queen and I looked like someone about to go in front of a parole board.

Just as we were ready to show our work to the party representatives, Michael changed his mind again.

"No, that's it!" he declared. "They're not gonna see them! You see," he told me in his best father-to-son voice, "no matter how good of a job you do, some of those parties are still gonna want you to change something. We could be doing this another week!" He wanted to send the ballot to Canada that night.

So that was it. This is it, I thought, the excrement is going to hit the fan.

To narrow our margin of error, Michael had his own translator, Charuen, proofread Sovan's Khmer typing on the ballot. Charuen found one or two typing mistakes; after that Michael felt better.

By 10:30 Sunday morning, the big meeting with the party representatives, which Sovan and I had not attended, was over. It was now a simple matter of arranging the fifteen chosen party symbols on the ballot in the order that they had come out of the basket. That took eleven hours.

As Sovan and I were working, Michael stood behind us and never stopped fretting, "Shouldn't that be moved up a tweak?" "Are you sure it's spelled right, Sove-van?" "Are you sure that will print?"

We printed out a few drafts to be sure. By this time, Charuen had long ago gone home. So Michael, who could not speak, read, or write a word of Khmer, did the proofreading. "I can tell one squiggle from another," he announced as he meticulously compared our ballot to the party names and abbreviations in Frank Eppert's notebook.

He noticed that we were amazed at his sudden Khmer literacy. "You see," he declared, "there's one thing about elections—you only get one chance to get it right, so it has to be right the first time."

At ten that night, the technician, who was going to hook up the computer to the phone line to send the ballot to Canada, came in with his equipment and cigarettes, and Sovan and I went home.

On Monday morning Judy wanted to know how things had gone. "I wash my hands of it," I said. "We have never met. If anyone asks—I don't work here." I explained what had happened. She was amazed.

But at least I was done with it.

On Tuesday morning I destroyed all the draft copies of the ballot on various computers around the office and zapped the old party symbols, including those of the five dropped parties. Just as I finished, Michael telephoned me. "G'day. How are ya, mate?"

"Fine," I said. Why did he always call me mate? Something was wrong.

"Hey listen, Mr. Akashi decided that we need twenty parties on the ballot."

"Huh?"

"Yeah, we have to redo it."

"When?"

"I just called Canada and told them to stop work on the old ballot. I told them that we would send them a new ballot tonight."

He waited for me to say something. I didn't.

"Can you get right on it?" he asked.

"Wait a minute. Here, talk to Judy."

The story was that one of the five parties I had just zapped had heard that possibly fourteen of the parties on the ballot did not technically belong there. That party complained, and as a result, Mr. Akashi decided to simply let everyone who had submitted any kind of petition onto the ballot. He was always one to give people the benefit of the doubt. He called it the "Softly, softly policy."

That afternoon, I scanned and quickly edited the five new party logos. At five o'clock, I borrowed a UN truck to find Sovan. She wasn't home. Just as I was leaving, she drove in on her motorcycle. She had taken her mother to the beauty parlor.

"What's cooking?" she asked.

I told her that something had come up and Michael wanted her to type some Khmer. "You'll be home by 9 P.M., don't worry."

She was home by 4 A.M. Fitting five more parties onto the ballot meant shrinking fifteen others. Michael and the technician stayed up until seven in the morning trying to get the continuously failing phone line to Canada to stay up for a few minutes.

Everyone wanted to see the ballot. I printed out an extra copy for myself. Sovan gave a copy to one of the people she worked with. Michael might have given a copy to someone. The trainers wanted a copy as well, but they couldn't have one. It was high security—the administration was afraid that the parties would get a copy and reproduce fake ballots. A week later a friend of mine was in a photocopy shop when she saw a man get off a motorcycle, make a few copies of the ballot, and speed off. It had gotten out. Soon it was all over Cambodia. The trainers told me that the ballot was even on the wall of the distant district electoral offices.

After the ballot leaked out, UNTAC reproduced it as a poster. Soon my ballot was splattered everywhere around town, even if the government party defaced it on their posters by blotting out all of the parties except theirs.

Only the FUNCINPEC party complained. They liked my drawing, but said that I had botched their party symbol by not enclosing it in an outer circle. I told them that they could live with it. I kept waiting for other parties to complain and possibly make everyone (me) look foolish, but no one ever did, or if they did, I didn't hear about it.

The actual ballots were shipped to Cambodia a month or so before the election and kept in a warehouse. Michael showed me one. It was beautiful—like a hundred-dollar bill. It had been printed at six hundred dots per inch so that if it was photocopied anyone with a magnifying glass could tell that the border, which said UNTAC in microscopic lettering, was now illegible. It was also color-tinted and had a watermark. Sovan and I had truly created the Mona Lisa of all ballots.

OH, LOOK AT THAT

After I left the Computer Center, I started getting up at five in the morning. Sometimes, though, if out of sheer boredom I had gone to bed at nine o'clock the night before, I would get up even earlier.

One day I found that I was awake at 3 A.M. Later my neighbor told me that he had heard machine gun fire at about that time, but I can't be sure what it was that woke me up and, anyway, there was nothing so unusual about machine gun fire. People just liked to fire machine guns. Machine guns were good for shooting down coconuts, scaring stray dogs, stopping thunder, and helping you to wake up in the morning. Or maybe the guy who fired it just wanted to see if the thing was working.

Anyway, I was up and comfortably reading a computer magazine over a cup of coffee when the electricity went off. It's always the little things.

It was suddenly very dark, and I was still very awake. I decided to go jogging. Outside, all the street lights were out, but since a few houses had night lights on, I could see where the road was. As I jogged, I carefully avoided the missing manhole covers and stray dogs until I reached the Central Park of Phnom Penh, Independence Monument. Independence Monument was built to celebrate the independence of Cambodia from France (1954) and the dependence of Cambodia on Vietnam (1979 – 1989). In other words, the Cambodians built one part of the park in the early 1950s, and in the early 1980s the Vietnamese made an addition.

The park was a kilometer or so away from the main business section of town where, now that the UNTAC economic boom was in full swing, things had become rather glittery, with video-game arcade parlors, pizza places, big hotels, car dealerships, airline offices, fast food restaurants, cellular phone outlets and massage parlors. And it was there that many people slept side by side on the sidewalk. But not too many people slept in the park. Maybe Independence Monument was too dangerous or maybe the police patrolled it. For whatever reason, at five in the morning there weren't many people around. Two people were sweeping the paths, and a few more people squatted on the wall of the broken fountain. A couple of bicycle rickshaw drivers were sleeping, crumpled up in their carriages with just a rag covering them.

Later in the day things would pick up. By midmorning the park would fill up with food sellers who would watch the wedding parties that filed through to be photographed in the flower gardens. After sunset lovers would sit in the grass behind the bushes to talk and buy peanuts from the child vendors who would seek them out. But at five in the morning it was too early for other foreign joggers, and Cambodians don't jog.

I enjoyed the run. They say that jogging helps prevent heart attacks and, well, usually it gives me pleasant fantasies. On that morning I was Rambo. With just a knife in my hand, I snuck deep into Khmer Rouge territory and killed the punks who had murdered the two UNTAC women and the little girl. I cut their heads off, which is how Khmer soldiers usually take prisoners, and placed them on the fountain in the park, so that other Khmer Rouge would know that if they killed UN-TAC people again, they would have to deal with Rambo.

I only jogged for thirty minutes. Sometimes the fantasies weren't so pleasant.

Back at the house it was still dark and the gate was locked. The house-keeper heard me jingling the lock and let me in. Earlier, I had hopped the fence.

After a few minutes she turned on the generator, and now that I could see, I typed a letter. By the time I had finished, it was light and just 6:30. Maybe it was the run, or the fact that Rambo had just gotten his revenge, but anyway, suddenly I had the rare urge to clean my room. The urge lasted until I reached the closet.

There on the floor of the closet was a picture of Sovan. It was an old ID-photo from her refugee camp, Site Two. Now, eight months after she had left the camp, she felt that she no longer needed the picture and, at my request, had given it to me. The picture must have been taken shortly after her arrival in the camp. Waist-length hair frames her face and highlights an expression of innocence and terror. Strangely, except for the terror and the hints of malnutrition, it's a picture you might find of your grandmother when she was a little girl. Here was the face of someone so innocent she looked as if she had never done anything wrong or spent one unhappy moment. She had the eyes of a child, and you could easily get lost in them. I looked at the picture for a long time. Here was my best friend—the girl whose mother had once given her up for dead, the intellectual with a surprising knack for computers, and one of the funniest people I had ever met.

It was time, I decided, to move the picture from the floor of the closet to the wall above the desk where I had her other pictures:

- Sovan and what is left of her extended family.

- Sovan in the park where I had been jogging.

- Sovan and me at a wedding.

- Sovan and me at the most exclusive hotel in Phnom Penh.

In this last picture I looked frightening. The picture was taken in my Computer Center / movie star days when the veins of my neck were sticking out and my face was sallow, and yet I am smiling. She is beaming. She told me that it's natural to beam like that; but then she was raised in the sea of warmth and affection that I've seen in so many Cambodian families.

Yes, above my desk was a small gallery of pictures.

As the first man she had ever gone out with—even if it was always with a chaperon or two because as she said "more people mean more fun"—one might have thought I had made an impression. Yet she said we were just friends.

With the picture securely taped on the wall, I made breakfast. I could not really cook without a kitchen, but I could boil water. I made some instant noodles mixed with peanut butter and raisins, and read the local papers. As usual, the news was bad. The Cambodians were disappointed that UNTAC hadn't saved them, that the soldiers who came here to protect them were (surprise!) screwing their women, that the violence wasn't over, the government corruption was continuing, and that things probably would not improve.

Before I came to Cambodia I thought that the Khmer Rouge were the devil in the flesh. But by now it was clear that things were not that simple and that the main strategy of political campaigning, for all the major parties, was to murder the opposition and blame someone else. This made for bloody politics, with supposedly the worst to come just before the election, which may be why UNTAC issued a decree forbidding public campaigning until April 7. With just six weeks of campaigning, UNTAC hoped that only a few people would get killed. Already, though, some parties were getting a head start—a jump on the gun, as they say.

I would usually read both English-language newspapers—*The Cambodia Times* and the *Phnom Penh Post*. They only came out every other week, but that was enough. How much gloom did anyone need for breakfast?

After breakfast I packed my computer into my shoulder bag; I'd be using it all day.

The traffic situation had not improved, thanks to the UNTAC buildup and to the Cambodian drivers who drove like they operated politically, which was why I did not take my motorcycle to work if I could help it. This morning I waited outside for the office minibus to pick me up.

But the minibus was late. I set the computer down and wandered across the dusty street. Someone had put up a flier on the neighbor's wall. It was advertising prostitutes under the guise of an invitation to the "BK International Disco and Massage Parlor." In the picture, two young women were kissing. Hmm, I thought, that sounds interesting. I tore it off the wall.

I put the flier in my pocket, picked up the computer, and climbed into the minibus.

On the way to work the trainers and I played a game, the same one we played every morning—the *Oh, look at that.* game. "Oh, look at that, there are five men on a motorcycle." "Oh, look at that, our driver almost hit a man driving on the wrong side of the street." "No, our driver is driving on the wrong side of the street." "Yes, you're right." "Look, there's a bicycle rickshaw carrying a broken motorcycle." "That's nothing. Look at that! An accident! Do you think he's dead?" "I don't know, but he isn't moving." It was always hard to tell if the person hit was dead because, after an accident, a crowd instantly formed around the body. You could just barely see a body stretched out on the pavement as you looked through the legs.

Naturally it was rude for foreigners to play the *oh look at that* game with the Cambodians, but they knew that a lot of what we saw shocked us. Early one morning I was driving Sovan up Monivong Boulevard, past the business district, toward Electoral Headquarters, when we found ourselves behind a speeding motorcycle taxi whose passengers were two Vietnamese prostitutes. They'd had a long night and were still in uniform—thigh-high skirts. The two of them were sitting sidesaddle behind the crunched-forward driver. "Oh look! Isn't she pretty?" Sovan said. She said that whenever she saw me looking at another woman.

"Yes." I was looking at the woman in the back. Her skirt was climbing higher and higher up her thigh as she shifted to keep from falling off. We were getting quite a show. I didn't think that she was teasing me when she suddenly flashed her bright red panties at me.

It's always hard to be a man. "Sovan," I said to break the tension, "is it better to fall off a motorcycle or to show the color of your underwear?"

"It's better not to look."

"I'm watching out for her." If she fell off, I would have to slam on the brakes.

"Then let her worry about it."

"Oh...yes, you're right."

THE ODD BUNCH AND BIG TROUBLE IN SIEM REAP

I had a good job. The sixteen trainers—soon to travel around Cambodia teaching polling officials how to run the election—would come to me with their ideas about training material, and I would develop those ideas on the computer.

Often they would want me to take one of the many forms that polling officials had to fill out and make it into a poster. Other times, I would produce handouts to make their teaching easier. The trainers were, like everyone else in the UN, an odd bunch. We had two Khmer-speaking Thais—Porn (my affable office mate) and a woman with another Thai name, Bum. We had one woman from France. Other women were from Haiti, Sierra Leone, England, Romania, and Kenya, plus one Khmer-Australian lady. One man was from England, two from Bangladesh, and four from America—including a Khmer-American. Naturally there was some infighting, and some people did not speak to each other. But I had it easy—everyone had to be good to me if they wanted help with their computer work. I never knew if they liked me or not.

Fortunately, though, Sovan came to the office to work on the ballot or just to see me, and everyone liked her. The Khmer-American trainer liked her enough to invite the two of us over to his house for dinner one night. He had a big house with two housekeepers, a yard, an American wife and a two-year-old son. I made atomic screwdrivers from orange juice and gin, and the housekeepers cooked up a good feast. I didn't know if it was the screwdrivers or the company, maybe both, but we had lots of laughter with dinner. At ten I took Sovan, who was a little drunk, home to her loft. I went home and lay in bed. I was a little drunk too. Life is good, I thought. It is especially good if you find someone who is charming and likable—that's enough, no need to get too technical or ask for too much. I fell asleep. It was Wednesday, March 10.

In another part of Cambodia on that same night, at that same time, in Siem Reap province, on the Tonlé Sap Lake that has some of the best fishing grounds in the world, in one of the little fishing villages that nestle around the lake, some Vietnamese were doing the same thing we were—drinking and talking. Cambodia was to most of the 200,000 Vietnamese who the UN estimated lived there what California is to Mexicans: a place where you might not be particularly welcome, but a place where you could make a lot of money doing what other people did not want to do. In California most Mexicans picked fruits and vegetables; in Cambodia most Vietnamese fished. Others, like the carpenters in the furniture factory, did skilled jobs.

I was asleep in my air-conditioned room by 10:30, about the same time that the Khmer Rouge began emptying their machine guns and automatic rifles into the room where the Vietnamese in Siem Reap were talking, drinking, and watching a video. The Khmer Rouge killed 23 adults and 10 children.

Within a few days, flotillas of boats started moving down the Mekong towards Vietnam. For the Vietnamese, the party was over.

'Imagine a Polling Station

The big problem for the trainers was that they did not have a complete polling manual. All of them were teachers by profession, but still they needed to know how to run a polling station if they were going to teach other people how to run one. Judy had told Michael that she needed the polling manual no later than December 31 so that her trainers could read it, prepare their teaching materials and begin training in February for the election in May.

Every day the trainers waited for the manual, and every day Michael somehow did not get around to finishing it. Soon it was February and time to teach the four hundred UNV district electoral supervisors how to run a polling station. With no manual, the trainers taught in generalities. One trainer, not knowing what a polling station would look like, asked his audience to break into groups and *imagine* what a polling station would look like.

Finally, on March 19, we received the 39-page manual and saw what a "simple ordinary" polling station was supposed to look like.

It looked simple enough, but was not something that any of the trainers were comfortable *imagining.* Now they knew what was supposed to happen. A UN CivPol and a Cambodian queue controller would maintain order outside; inside, another queue controller would help people move to the line; the identifiers would check their records and each voter's registration card; the ink applicator would stick the voter's pointer finger in indelible ink to prevent him from voting twice; the voter would be given a ballot, mark it, and put it in the ballot box. The Assistant Presiding Officer would answer questions and fill out the forms. The political party agents were allowed to sit in to make sure that everything was fair. If the room was big enough, more than one team could be in it.

Things were shaping up.

FLYING BY NIGHT AND STAKING OUT THE COUNT

I had one more special project. It was a strange assignment that I had no business doing. Michael had asked his translator, Charuen, to translate some huge document or other from English into Khmer. Charuen translated it by writing it out in longhand before beginning to slowly type it on a computer, a device he had not previously encountered. After he realized that it would take him at least six months to finish, he asked Sovan to type it. But Sovan was too busy, and it was not her job, so she asked Teavi, a data entry clerk, to do it. Teavi proceeded to accidentally erase everything that Charuen had painstakingly typed on his computer. But human communication being what it is, Michael had assumed that everything was finished, and for reasons I never understood, searched *my* computer for the completed translation one afternoon when I wasn't there. Naturally, he couldn't find it, and naturally, when he eventually found me, *I knew nothing about the Khmer translation of the polling manual.*

The next day his assistant phoned to ask me to take charge of translating the polling manual into Khmer. I handed the phone to Judy. Judy, who was fifty but still trim and athletic, took the phone, shook her head and listened. By now I knew her well enough to know what she was thinking, "Were people getting paid to work for the UN? If they were, why was everything so damn unorganized and fly-by-night? Why did everyone wait until the last minute to do anything? And why the hell should we get involved with translating the polling manual?" She blamed her temper on her Irish genes. But, on the other hand, she knew that her trainers needed the manual in Khmer *next week.* She nodded into the phone and said yes.

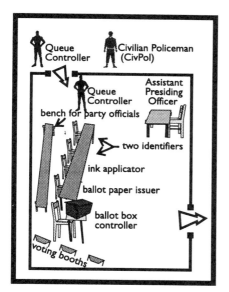

Now I was the head of the *Emergency Fly-by-Night UNTAC Translation Unit.* This was going to be fun.

Item number one was reaching over Hugo's head to pull Sovan and her friend,

Teavi, out of the Computer Center for a week. Hugo did not like it. He turned red, started shaking, and assumed his full Count Dracula demeanor, but for once my magic was stronger than his and he had to do what I said: "And one more thing—" This, item number two, was a dream come true. Now I was holding a wooden stake above the trembling Count Dracula, and I was going to pound it in. I continued, "We need one more notebook computer."

What could he do? Yes, I thought, it is these small moments of revenge that make life worth living. I gleefully toted the notebook computer back to my office.

Item number three was working as a mediator between Sovan and Charuen—they had stopped speaking to each other after Charuen's computer file had disappeared. Charuen let me search his computer for any remnants of what he had typed.

After that everything was easy. Sovan and Teavi typed Charuen's longhand text on two computers, which I had illegally loaded with the Khmer script program, and I formatted what they typed on a third computer.

They worked hard, and by late Thursday afternoon we were ready to present our masterpiece to the *official* UNTAC translators, the same people who had translated the 57-page *Electoral Law* into Khmer. The official translators were Cambodians who had been living in the U.S.A. until they realized they could make much more money in Cambodia. They were authorized to be the final legal translators of the most important UNTAC documents.

Their office was across town in UNTAC XII, "Information." Sovan and I waltzed in at five o'clock to make our grand presentation. With due respect the receptionist took us upstairs to where the translators were jammed into little cubicles with desktop computers. We introduced ourselves to one of the official translators, a woman about Sovan's age. She was rather glamorous—slightly taller even than Sovan, very fair, with wire-rimmed glasses, and long, straight, light-brown hair. "Are you really Khmer?" I asked.

"Yes, I am," she said with the crisp accent of the American East Coast, "but I don't always admit it. Most people, you know, think all Cambodians are kind of stupid."

"I see."

Sovan did not say anything.

I explained why we needed the translation of the polling manual checked in a hurry, to which she said, "Everyone always wants everything yesterday." To her, we were just another headache.

We left, but not before Sovan had formed an instant dislike of her. "No matter what," she fumed, "even if I lived in America for twenty years, I would never ever pretend that I was not Cambodian!"

"Don't worry," I told her, "she just said that because she's fat and you're beautiful."

The next afternoon Judy told me that the official translators had studied Charuen's translation and realized that they would have to do most of it over. This meant that the training of the Khmer polling officials would begin without the benefit of a manual in Khmer.

Someone once said that the election proceeded not *because of*, but *in spite of* the UN.

That Wednesday, March 26, the Khmer Rouge massacred another eight Vietnamese. This time it happened in Kampong Chhnang and they did it by shooting six in the back, spearing one woman in the chest, and axing a man in the neck.

DOWN AND OUT IN THE JUNGLE

Just as we were finishing the translation work, I accidentally stepped on an antipersonnel land mine. Not literally, but figuratively.

I *said* to Sovan: "I wish you liked to read more."

Sovan *heard* that as the supremely unforgivable and unforgettable slur from hell that went: "I wish you weren't a jungle girl."

I had just given her *Mastering Disk Operating Systems Six*, another of the many books that she said was not interesting. And kaboom!

I had accidentally discovered her Achilles heel. Being called "jungle girl," her expression for everything that could be wrong with a person, was to her the ultimate insult. She had spent ten years co-teaching an English class with an American Catholic priest. This had left her with educated-sounding American English, but with only a sixth-grade formal education, which meant, in Asia, and especially to her, that she was a jungle girl. I tried to calm her down, but she was beyond my ability to charm. She sulked, she cancelled our "post-translation" dinner, and she was too busy to do anything else, ever. I was now, suddenly and overwhelmingly, an outcast, a nothing.

Some anthropologists believe that friendships in Southeast Asia are "plagued by an element of tenuousness."* Traditionally, Southeast Asian villagers center their lives around their large extended families and see relations to others, outsiders, as tenuous. And just as family ties can never be cut, non-family ties can, in an instant, slip away. Some anthropologists claim that there is a relationship between this non-family tenuousness and the instability of governments in Southeast Asia.

Now *I* had instantly slipped away; I was *tenuous*, nothing. Now the two-day weekends were going to seem like two months.

Looking back over the last twenty-three years of Cambodian history, I could see clearly now that nothing ever worked the way it was planned— foreign interventions, coups d'état, carpet bombings, refugees, phony peace plans, phony liberations, evacuations, experiments in communal living, malaria, foreign invasions, border camps, border runs, more phony peace plans, demobilizations, prosthetics, begging, prostitution, AIDS, AK-47s, motorcycle taxi drivers, adultery, job transfers, failing peace plans, stealing, legal stealing, alienation, personal relations, mechanical relations, personal infighting, professional infighting, ethnic mix, ethnic hatred, ethnic massacres, special projects, misunderstandings, antipersonnel mines, and taking some petty pleasure in pounding a wooden stake into the trembling heart of Count Dracula before alienating my best friend, *the self-confessed jungle girl*.

But what to do?

The next evening, Saturday, March 27, as I sat in my air-conditioned room and wondered about my next solution to the human dilemma, the Khmer Rouge were pounding the shit out of the camp of the Bangladeshi Battalion in a village in Siem Reap. In their three-hour attack, the NADK lobbed sixty mortar rounds and fired a thousand rounds of ammunition at the Bangladeshis, killing one man. The first United Nations victim of hostile fire in Cambodia was twenty-five-year-old Mohammed Yusef.

Nothing ever went as planned.

ACT INTERNATIONAL

After my two-month weekend, I went back to work on Monday. I was still wondering what to do. We had just received a memo from Professor Austin saying that now, more than ever, everyone should rise above petty differences and give 100 percent to the team effort: no more time off, no more leaves. That sounded very noble, but suddenly I wanted to go to Thailand for a month.

I asked Judy. Judy said fine—go to Thailand! By coincidence, for better or worse, the trainers were about to go to the provinces full-time to train the Khmer polling officials for the election-in-wartime; there would be very little for me to do in the office. So, go!

Okay, I would go. I felt better immediately.

As I cleaned my desk to leave, I noticed an invitation to be an IPSO. I asked a reporter from Radio UNTAC, Niwit, what an IPSO was.

"International Polling Station something," he said. "You sit in a polling station during the election and act international." Niwit had been a newspaper reporter in Bangkok before he worked for the UN. I met him when he came to the office to visit Porn, my office mate.

"Are we going to get paid?" I asked.

"No."

"Then why do it?"

"Where do you want to be on election day?" he asked.

"I don't know. I haven't thought about it."

"You want to be in a polling station! Come on, man!" He was trying to cheer me up.

I had always wanted to act international. So why not? I filled out a form and now, on election day, I would be an IPSO, which rhymes with "if so."

That week we received a notice to plan for an emergency evacuation. The Civilian Police component wanted to know where everyone lived, and they wanted everyone to know where the nearest CivPol station was, where the common meeting points were, all that stuff. The plan was that if the Khmer Rouge attacked, the foreigners in UNTAC would be immediately evacuated to Thailand. My vacation in Thailand would then be a one-way trip.

The rest of the week I spent neatening up my things so that if anyone went inside my room they wouldn't think they had entered an insane asylum. My flight was on Friday morning. On Thursday night I decided, having not seen her all week, to say good-bye to Sovan.

I rode my motorcycle to her house at 8 P.M.

Earlier that week, on Monday, March 29, unidentified terrorists had played the hand-grenade game in Phnom Penh. They threw grenades into Vietnamese tea houses and video parlors in, as UNTAC reported, "a synchronized and military fashion," killing two Vietnamese and wounding twenty-seven. On Wednesday, the night before, another video parlor had been shot up; this one was in Kampong Thom. The Khmer Rouge had used B-40 rockets along with the standard AK-47s, and twenty-nine people died. Naturally, many of the Vietnamese carpenters in the furniture factory had fled back to Vietnam. The few that stayed behind tried to remain in the shadows. Now, for the first time, the local video parlor was closed, and the Vietnamese had posted a guard with a rifle at the gate. When I drove into the factory, it was quiet, spooky.

Sovan and her family were, as usual, watching television. I told her that I was leaving for a month and maybe forever. I explained the evacuation plan. She seemed genuinely sad. If I did not come back, I said, her brother, who was about my size, could have my clothes. I gave her the key to my room and told her that, when the order to evacuate came, she should at least grab my computer before looters or the UN found it. Sometime I would come back to get it, and if not, well, as the French say, *c'est la vie.*

I said good-bye to her family and climbed down the ladder. Sovan followed me and walked me through the shadows to my motorcycle. She said again how sorry she was that I was leaving, but it was too late, and the mosquitoes were eating both of us alive.

SORE KNEES

I left for Bangkok on schedule in the cattle car of the air, a C160.

Sentimental good-bye or not, I resolved that this time, for once, I was not going to get lost in the bars of Bangkok. Instead, I decided I would enter a monastery and practice meditation as taught by the Perfect One, the Buddha.

I arrived in Bangkok on Friday, April 2. That night, just west of Phnom Penh, in Kampong Speu Province, the Bulgarian Battalion, with their European charm, invited a local Khmer Rouge officer and two of his men for dinner, which they had done before. After dinner, the KR officer stepped out for a moment and returned with ten armed men. Sensing trouble, the Bulgarian sergeant ordered some of his men to get their own guns. Suddenly, the soldiers of the National Army of Democratic Kampuchea shot and killed three of their Bulgarian hosts.

I spent most of April in a Buddhist temple on an isolated spit of land surrounded by the Gulf of Thailand. The temple, or *wat*, turned out to be the same place the Supreme Patriarch of Thai Buddhism used for his retreats—it was the Hilton of monasteries. The abbot gave me my own little cottage and I was on my own. From four in the morning until ten at night, I did one hour of sitting meditation followed by one hour of walking meditation. No food was permitted after noon, and there was

Dressed for the beach, the first official UNTAC delegation to the remote province of Preah Vihear departs. From left to right, Fernando Pililao, a cartographer from Mozambique; the author; Im Serei Khut, our translator; and Sergei Ajadjanov, a Russian UNTAC administrator.

A British soldier teaches a Cambodian the delicate task of de-mining. Many de-miners were frustrated that as they risked their lives to clear mines, the warring factions continued to plant even more.

no talking, ever. The only sound was that of the waves breaking on the shore. Meditation is hard to understand in that, when doing it, one may not realize that the mind is healing. Only after leaving the temple does it become clear, for a while at least, that life has more meaning than one may have thought.

The meditation was good, but by the end of April my knees felt as if they had been struck by lightning. I complained about my sore knees to the former monk who had helped me find the temple. "What you need, my friend," he said, "is a good traditional Thai massage."

"Yeah?"

"Yeah."

Although he had never been there, he guaranteed me good results and gave me the address of a place to go to in Bangkok. In Bangkok I learned that the UN was still in Cambodia, and found the place the former monk had recommended.

I walked in. "Yes, I would like a massage."

The woman at the front desk nodded. She said that before the massage I was welcome to use the spa.

This was a lot to handle after a month of silent meditation.

"Thank you."

I took off my shoes and walked to a locker room. I took off my clothes, put them in a locker, wrapped a towel around my waist, and. left the key at the front desk.

The spa consisted of a tub of very hot water, a tub of very cold water, and a sauna. I sat in the tub of very hot water, in the tub of very cold water, which had a small waterfall pouring into it and, finally, in the sauna. It was very pleasant. After about an hour I was beginning to wonder if life could get any more pleasant when a young man told me that I could have my massage now.

He gave me a clean towel, which I wrapped around my waist, and led me upstairs. Along one side of a large room was a bed about twenty meters long. A woman smiled at me and led me to the bed. She told me to lie down on my back. I did. She drew the curtains around a section of the huge bed to form a cozy compartment about the size of a king-size bed. She wore loose Chinese pajamas.

She said that her name was Mr. Lot. No, I corrected her, Miss, not Mister, Lot.

"Miss Lot?" she asked.

"*Chai kap, Miss Lot.*" From here on, everything was in Thai.

Miss Lot asked me how long I wanted the massage to last.

"One hour."

"Oh, no," she said. "If it is only an hour, it won't be any good. It should be two hours."

She had positioned me on my back, with the towel still around my waist. I was relaxed after the sauna, the bed was soft, and Miss Lot seemed pleasant enough. She had talked me into it.

"No problem, two hours," I told her.

She explained that she would spend about half an hour on each leg and do the arms, shoulders and back in the next hour.

She said that she was thirty-five. "Is that too old?"

"No, not too old. Still young."

As she bent my foot in all directions and pulled my toes, she told me about her life. She enjoyed dancing, going to discos and drinking whiskey. She asked about me.

"Oh, just the same, only I like beer."

"Are you married?"

I said that I was not but that I would probably get married next year.

"Good, otherwise you'll be too old."

"Yes, I know that. Thank you."

She told me that she had been married and had a fifteen-year old son to support. He was in high school in the provinces.

"That's good," I said. "An education is the secret of success."

"Very true," she agreed.

She asked politely what I was doing in Thailand.

I explained to her that I worked in Cambodia, and that I had just done some meditation, which was, I knew now, the road to peace.

"Were you a monk?" she asked.

"No, but I lived like a monk."

"Monks don't like sex, so you must not like sex."

"No, I think that there is nothing wrong with sex."

By this time she had worked up both legs, so that when she said *sex* she was able to indicate with her hands which part of my body she meant. I sensed that few women understood the male anatomy as well as Miss Lot.

"If sex is okay," she said, "let's have sex."

"You mean you and me?" I asked.

"I mean you and me."

I thought that possibly she wanted to meet me later so that I could take her out on the town, "Where?"

"Here."

"When?"

"Now."

"Oh..."

She was big breasted for a Thai and, for a small woman, she had big hips. She looked younger than thirty-five. She continued, "Yes, right now, for just one thousand baht."

A thousand baht is about fifty dollars. "That's a lot of money."

"No, it's quite cheap, and anyway, you can afford it."

"Yeah, but still..."

"I wouldn't ask you for money, but you see my son's school fees are coming due and I really need it."

"I understand, yes, of course. But still, a thousand baht."

"Okay, for you, eight hundred."

"You are quite pretty, but I thought I was just coming for a massage—I didn't bring that much money." A gentleman should always try to be tactful.

"So please, the next time you come, bring eight hundred baht."

"Yes, of course. I'll be back to Bangkok in a few months."

That settled, she continued to bend, twist, rub, pound and massage me until, just fifteen minutes short of two hours, she said I was done. I reckoned that the missing fifteen minutes must have been for the sex that I wasn't getting.

As I walked out, I had to admit that my knees felt much better after the massage.

I flew back to Cambodia the next day, Monday, May 3.

EVERY MOTHER'S WORST NIGHTMARE

While I was meditating and being massaged in Thailand, every mother's worst nightmare had happened to a UNV man and his Cambodian interpreter. I read about it in the electoral newsletter, *Free Choice*:

> At the...press briefing, UNTAC Spokesman Eric Falt presented the findings of a Civilian Police (CivPol) investigation into the April 8 murders of Atsuhito Nakata and Lay Sok Phiep in Kampong Thom. According to the CivPol report, both men had left their office in Prasat Sambo district at approximately 7:30 A.M. to attend a meeting at the UNTAC provincial headquarters in Kampong Thom to discuss safety concerns.
> ...
> Between 7:45 and 7:50 A.M. the two UNTAC members were attacked as they drove on the road, about 8 km from Prasat Sambo and 16 km from the provincial capital.

The investigators based their findings on evidence and the statement of one witness. Their report concluded that one individual, wearing a green uniform with no cap, fired a shot from an AK-47 rifle from the bushes as the UNTAC vehicle approached. The bullet went through the windshield and exited through the front window without injuring anyone. The gunman is then believed to have rushed to the road as the vehicle drove past, firing again at the back of the vehicle. One bullet hit the passenger, Lay Sok Phiep, in the abdomen, arm and chest.

It is thought that Nakata, the driver, then brought the vehicle to a halt. The investigators said that the gunman then probably went to the passenger side of the vehicle, hit the window with the butt of his rifle and opened the door. Seeing that the interpreter was severely injured, the gunman had then probably gone to the other side of the vehicle and forced Nakata out. It is believed that Nakata was taken a few meters away from the car, which enabled Lay Sok Phiep to radio for help.

"The duty officer in Kampong Thom immediately endeavored to send a patrol team and an ambulance," Falt said. While Lay was sending his radio call, it is believed that Nakata tried to escape, possibly by trying to hide underneath the vehicle. At that point, he was killed by two shots at close range, one through the side of the head and one through the shoulder.

...

"The most likely motive was an act of revenge against UNTAC personnel, as a result of the recruitment of polling officers for the elections," Falt said. "The DESs had been facing intimidation and threats from the local population, including from CPAF (Cambodian People's Armed Forces) personnel. The disposition of the Cambodians in that area, which had been very friendly, appeared to have changed after some of them had been rejected."

I did not know Atsuhito, or "Atsu" as he was known to his friends. Everyone said that he was a good guy. After he died, his father quit his job in Japan to "work for peace." Phiep had just come back to Cambodia from a refugee camp in Malaysia to "work for peace" or, depending on how cynical you were, because no country would accept him for resettlement. Again, their pictures were placed in Electoral Headquarters, and again Professor Austin had me artistically arrange the text for them. Both men were in their twenties.

At first people believed that the Khmer Rouge had killed them. Khieu Samphan, however, said that a sloppy roadside ambush wasn't the Khmer Rouge style of murder and that turned out to be true. The killer, everyone believed, was a disgruntled kid who had not been hired by UNTAC. Not being hired, and not receiving the accompanying salary, was more than he could handle. So two men were murdered. The kid was never apprehended.

The Khmer Rouge closed their office in Phnom Penh on April 13, a few days after Atsu and Phiep were killed. As Khieu Samphan left town on a plane to Thailand, he made a promise to disrupt the election. "We can foresee," he told the *Phnom Penh Post*, "that the situation will get more unstable, more insecure, more confusing." He added that he was leaving because UNTAC could no longer guarantee his security. One of the UNTAC military said that what Khieu meant was that *he* could no longer guarantee *our* security. Rumor had it that old Paris-educated Khieu had a soft spot in his heart for us UN types that the boys in the jungle didn't share. His leaving, the total collapse of even a mockery of a peace process, renewed fighting, and Atsu's death, shook everyone up. The UN military promised to do a better job; CivPol promised to do a better job. The UNV office brought in a specialist in security. UNTAC offices began to look like military outposts as barricades, sandbagged machine gun positions and barbed wire fences went up in front of the UNTAC headquarters and the Electoral Headquarters/Computer Center. At the same time, UN soldiers with machine guns appeared in front of those and other UNTAC buildings around town. Security checks became the order of the day.

Meanwhile, UNTAC intelligence reported that the Khmer Rouge were regrouping into larger units and putting hard-line commanders on the front lines. A UNV told the media, "We are conscious of the fact that we are a target." Another UNV said that he was surprised he was still alive, but no, he was not going to quit and, no, his parents did not know his current situation. In Siem Reap, some of my colleagues were sleeping in the bunkers the military had built. There was shelling every night and on the morning of May 3, the day I came back to Phnom Penh, 250 Khmer Rouge troops attacked government soldiers near the Siem Reap airport. Nine people died. Two days later the KR attacked a train fifty kilometers from Battambang with rockets and small arms after they had blown up the tracks. Thirteen people were killed. Just sixty kilometers from Phnom Penh, in the province of Kampong Speu, the Khmer Rouge used rockets and mortars to blast the UNTAC District

Headquarters, which they then looted. During the attack, a soldier from Bulgaria was killed when his vehicle was hit with an antitank grenade. The same thing happened in at least two other places in the north, but without any UNTAC people becoming ghosts. This was, UNTAC reported to the media, a "fairly nonviolent" time.

Huh?

The election was less than three weeks away.

MORE ON DEATH, SEX, AND SCANDAL

Everyone at the office acted glad to see me, and why not? Unlike each other, they didn't know me well enough to dislike me. They had been sent out in teams of two to different provinces for weeks at a time. Porn had loved the adventure of traveling around to remote places; it was his partner he disliked. He told me how he had solved that problem the Thai way: after a few days, he had renewed eight of the ten precepts of a Buddhist monk. This meant, he was sorry to tell his partner, that he could no longer have the pleasure of her company for the evening meal as monks were forbidden to eat after noon. He filled me in on the rest of the news. One of our trainers was in a remote province, and as her team was preparing to leave, the Provincial Electoral Officer (PEO) announced that a $4,000 notebook computer was missing. He asked if he could search everyone's bags. Annie, our trainer from Romania, said no, and the team drove away. As soon as they were on the road, the PEO called CivPol and told them to stop and search the trainers' car. CivPol did, and there, in Annie's bag, was the notebook computer. It was worth the equivalent of three weeks of Annie's salary and the equivalent of three years' salary for the Khmer person who would have taken the blame had not the PEO been such a sleuth. After a formal investigation, Annie was ushered straight out of the Electoral Component and sent directly to the procurement section, perhaps to take old Krishnadas' place. The word was that, as UN staff, she might keep working for years before the bureaucracy dealt with her. Legal stealing was, we concluded, the way things worked in the UN.

The other scandal and office gossip, according to Porn, was that a grandmotherly international staffer had seduced a UNV who was less than half her age. She had told a trainer that this was the greatest thing since the Paris Peace Agreement and her UN salary. By chance, later that day, her lover dropped by the office. I could immediately understand why our grandma was so proud of herself: her lover was a walking definition of *androgynous*—with his pony tail, long legs and baby face, her cute little hunk was gorgeous.

The other trainers came back from the provinces with lots of stories as well. In some provinces they heard shelling every night and said that the resident UN staffs could tell by the sound who was firing the artillery and if it was "incoming" or "outgoing." One trainer was in a restaurant when it was shot up. After hearing the shots, everyone dived under the tables and waited. The local UN staff said not to worry—the Khmer Rouge were not trying to hurt anyone, they just wanted everyone to know they were out there. A reporter from *Free Choice* had also gone out to the provinces. She asked a villager near the Thai border what security was like there. "There are all these people running wild with guns," the villager said, "If they catch a bandit, they tie his hands behind his back and take him into the woods. Finished."

That day, May 4, in Banteay Meanchey province, Japan suffered its second casualty—a Japanese civilian policeman died when his convoy was hit by a B-40 rocket and small arms fire. Finished.

We Were Okay

In and out of the office, all anyone talked about was saving their neck. Most people stopped going out at night. Everyone was worried. We were worried, but we were okay. Then the UN decided to evacuate every expatriate dependent from all the UN organizations in town to a luxury hotel in Bangkok.

We were still worried.

Forty UNVs quit. They quit because they thought that they could be the next Atsu, a few having received personal death threats from the local Khmer Rouge. Some quit because the idea of conducting a "free and fair" election with a flak jacket on and an armed soldier beside them seemed absurd. As they left, the UN said that they understood and sympathized, but the people in New York and Geneva realized that if we all quit the election would have to be cancelled. So we were each given a $600 monthly bonus. It worked pretty well—people stopped quitting. Now I was making about 80 percent more than before and just 25 percent as much as the UN staff secretaries in my office whom I tutored in word-processing.

Every night I listened to the BBC to hear if anyone else had been killed.

SOON SEX WAS GOING TO BE IMPOSSIBLE

Sovan forgave me. She had the confidence, and had been around me long enough, to know that a formal education did not mean that you were smart. Besides, there is nothing like an impending civil war to warm a woman's heart. Anyway, we were friends again and suddenly it was wedding season. People were getting married as if God had decreed that sex was going to be impossible in another month. All day, every day, women, dressed in elaborate rented Western wedding dresses, and men, in rented tuxedos, posed for video cameras in front of Phnom Penh's only public flower gardens—Independence Monument.

"What's wrong with those people?" I asked Sovan.

"They want to get married."

"I know they want to get married, but why does everyone want to get married now?"

"They want to get married before the election."

"Before *the election*?"

"No one knows what will happen after the election. They want to do it now."

"What do they *think* will happen after the election?"

"Maybe war."

"So everyone should get married if there is going to be war?"

"That's what they say."

By now, after seeing Sovan almost every day for eight months, I had learned at least as much about courtship and dating in Cambodia as I had about motorcycle driving rules.

Basically, Cambodian women do not court or date. Why should they do that? Their mothers do the work for them, negotiating with another mother the details of a prospective marriage. What could be easier and more efficient? Things work especially well if the mothers are related by blood or marriage—everyone knows that you can trust relatives more than you can trust non-relatives. The system works very well. Divorce does not happen much in Cambodia. If a man gets tired of his wife, he gets another and then he has two; if the woman gets tired of the man, she, like women everywhere, gets tired of the man. What's the problem?

"The American people always want to do something romantic before the wedding," Sovan explained to me. "Cambodian people wait until after the wedding."

"What about Miss Watana?" Watana, Sovan's best friend in the Computer Center, lived with a UN staff person from Africa. His wife was in

Japanese civilian policemen carry the picture of a colleague who was killed when his convoy was fired upon by unidentified assailants.

England.

"Don't ask me about Watana."

"What about Miss Ratha?" Ratha lived with a Cambodian-Australian UN staff person who worked in Electoral Headquarters with Sovan. Ratha worked with me in UNTAC XX.

"I don't know anything about Ratha."

"What about behind the railway station?" The place where rickshaw drivers could go to heaven for fifteen minutes and two dollars. The fancier places started at ten dollars.

"Let's talk about something else."

"Yes, but," I pleaded, "you're the one who told me that your best friend from the camp has two wives."

"He can afford it, and it's his business!"

Sovan's brother was on my side. Thirty-three-year-old Setee believed that the Cambodian system was outmoded, old-fashioned, and a relic of the days when marriage meant a new team of farmers for the village. It was not for him. He had worked closely with the Western doctors in Site Two for ten years. Apparently, some Western culture had rubbed off on him.

One day, though, the day I came back from Thailand, Setee told me he was engaged.

"Engaged?" I asked.

"Engaged to be married."

"Yes?"

"Yes."

"To who?"

"A girl that my Aunt found for me."

"But I thought you weren't going to do that?"

"So did I, but you know, it is too hard to meet women in this country. So when my Aunt asked me if I wanted to get married, I said yes."

"Do you know the girl?"

"I've talked to her five times already."

"Oh, that's good."

The woman was eighteen. "Too young," he said.

"No, not too young," I said, "but..." I was surprised. So much for Western sophistication rubbing off on Setee.

"When is the marriage?" I asked.

"We haven't decided yet, but the engagement ceremony will be in two weeks."

"In two weeks?...engagement?"

"We went to the astrologer and he said that the match was right."

"The astrologer?"

Setee was embarrassed. "The astrologer hasn't missed yet."

Sovan told me later that, in fact, her brother had never talked to the young woman. He had seen her, as she was a distant relative, but that was so long ago that Sovan believed he did not remember what she looked like. But what difference did that make? If the relatives and the astrologer said that it was right, it was right. And the engagement was going to be in just two weeks because they, like everyone else, did not know what was going to happen after the election.

I was the only non-relative invited to the engagement. It was held at the house of the future bride's grandmother, across the Bassac River, just over the Monivong Bridge, past the market, in a pleasant shaded neighborhood of narrow streets and large yards. The idea of an engagement, Sovan explained to me as we traveled there in a small convoy of cars, is that two families come together, share food, exchange jewelry, and therefore bond. As soon as we arrived, just after seven in the morning, the bonding began with Setee's family forming a long procession and carrying in the food, mainly fruit, on rented silver platters up the lane to the grandmother's house. There the food was arranged in neat rows by the family matriarchs. When everything was in order, amidst much picture taking, but with no monks present because this was only an engagement, the couple, sitting properly next to each other on the floor, having scarcely spoken to each other, exchanged gifts. She gave him a gold ring, and he gave her a gold bracelet. Both gifts, it was understood, could be cashed in later if hard times came.

About a hundred people then sat down to a breakfast of rice soup. More pictures were taken, and by noon, most guests had left. Now everyone was in a good mood, and Sovan and her brother had pulled the engagement off for a mere four hundred dollars.

"Four hundred dollars!" I shouted. We were back at the furniture factory, dividing fruit left over from the ceremony.

"The bracelet was $250 and the fruit and platters another $150," Sovan said.

"And the bride's family?"

"They bought the food and the ring, and rented the tables and chairs for breakfast."

"So it might have cost eight hundred dollars total?"

"We tried to economize," Setee interrupted.

"Economize—for eight hundred dollars?"

"In the real way," Setee continued, "we should have had twenty-one kinds of fruit, but to save money we just had a few."

"So this was a big thing?" I asked seriously.

Sovan and Setee agreed that it was. Some family members had come from the Thai border, where they ran a business, and now, everyone felt, the two families were tied closer together.

"How much does it cost in America?" Setee asked.

"I don't know. Maybe fifty cents."

"Fifty cents?"

"Fifty cents if you want to call both parents and tell them that you're gonna get married. Twenty-five cents if you split the cost with the girl."

"That's why you're not married," Sovan commented dryly.

"Here, we can say," I said slowly, pointing at Sovan, "that the pot is calling the kettle black."

ROMANTIC GOOD-BYE

The *Electoral Law* stated that, on election day, polling stations were to be set up in North America, Europe, and Australia. In them, Cambodians who had registered to vote, which they could do only in Cambodia, could vote. That sounds ridiculous, but that was the deal. Michael Maley chose three people to go overseas to run the polling stations—in New York City, Paris, and Sydney. Michael gave Sydney to Sovan. All three "Presiding Officers" were trained by my office and left a week before the election. I took Sovan to the airport.

Her brother, aunt, and cousins came to see her off, but they were too shy to go into the passenger waiting lounge. After she said good-bye to them, she invited me to wait with her inside the air-conditioned lounge.

We walked over to the large picture window and looked out at the lone airplane on the wet runway.

"Sovan," I said, still looking out the window, "are you going to worry about me if the Khmer Rouge start shooting?"

"I have to worry about myself."

"But you'll think about me on election day?"

"I think about you every day."

"I think about you, too. You know, seriously, be careful of the Australian men. They drink too much beer and don't respect women the way American men do."

"How do you know?"

"I read it in a magazine."

"I think we should sit down."

We sat down.

I had been to Sydney and, as the passenger lounge filled up, I told her again how beautiful it was and what to see there. I finished with, "So after the election, try to come back to Cambodia, okay?"

"If I can, I will." She told me that if full-scale civil war erupted, she would not come back.

The outside door of the waiting lounge opened, and the passengers walked through the misty rain to the waiting plane.

NIGHT LIFE

She had left on the noon flight. It was Saturday, May 15. The election was a week and a day away. That night Niwit, the Radio UNTAC reporter in my office, took me out on the town with a friend of his. Porn couldn't come as his wife had flown in from Bangkok for a few days and was leaving the next morning.

Earlier in the week she had come to the office. I had met her once before and quite liked her. Relaxed, down-to-earth, not the dreamy type, she had come from a farming family and was now a nurse. Porn had met her when he went to her clinic for an injection, where, according to him, "She took one look at my behind and liked me."

She was still concerned about Porn's behind and had flown to Phnom Penh to take her husband back to Thailand—more than anything in the world, she did not want him to be an IPSO.

"I'm looking on the positive side," I assured her. "A violent death is quick, and now in the West you can live so long that death has become horrible. They fill you up with drugs and you hang on for years looking like boiled cabbage."

That was not what she was hoping to hear.

"I'm not making this up," I continued, "I've watched my old relatives die."

"Yes, but," she said, trying not to forget her Thai politeness, "I just think that since he has a wife and daughter he should think more about coming back to Thailand."

They have a four-year-old daughter.

I let the subject drop before she completely lost her Thai politeness. Anyway, I understood why Porn couldn't come with us for our night on the town.

Thais are the cultural cousins of Cambodians. The two seem to get along with each other and they frequently intermarry. Nevertheless, the Thais always complained to me that the Cambodians were not any fun. They should know—on a Thai picnic, the Thais pound drums, sing, dance, play guitars, stage mock fist fights, and otherwise act as if they are auditioning for a TV variety show or a circus. To the Thais, a Khmer picnic, not to mention a Cambodian nightclub, is pretty dull. We would therefore, my Thai hosts told me, go to the "BK International Disco and Massage Parlor," BK standing for Bangkok. The local Thai business community had imported some Thai culture to Phnom Penh, and tonight we would celebrate this fact.

Admission, beer, and potato chips all were two dollars. The place was packed with UN men who had parked their vehicles outside, everyone having forgotten that UN vehicles were not supposed to be parked in front of brothels or massage parlors. In attendance were also a few Cambodian men who stared agape at the two bikini-clad Thai dancers on stage.

Niwit thought it was great. Always the curious reporter, he interviewed one of the dancers during her break. I listened in as she sat in her housecoat at our table. She was from the Northeast of Thailand and had come to Cambodia via the BK's sister bar in Bangkok. Phnom Penh, she explained, was *na bua*, a Thai word that translates as boring and something to be avoided at almost all costs. But her salary was good, she said, so she stayed. After she heard that I could speak a little Thai, she interviewed me and ended the interview by shaking my hand and urging me to find a Thai wife. She was charming and a little lonely. We had another beer and Niwit told me more about the visit of Porn's wife.

Last night, she had totally lost her Thai politeness when she told her husband to get his *ass* safely back to Thailand *now*. But Porn wouldn't budge, surrender, or abandon Phnom Penh and now, Niwit concluded, she was not a little unhappy about flying back to Thailand without him.

I knew that Bum, the Thai woman who worked with us in the office, would side with Porn's wife. "What good," Bum once asked me, "is four thousand dollars a month when I'm dead?" She had quit UNTAC and had flown back to Thailand and her fiancé the week before.

But not me. I knew that it probably wouldn't matter much if I became a ghost. So what was I hanging on to? I told Niwit a story:

Phnom Penh's New Market was designed after the Pantheon in Rome. Around the domed market the traffic circles in two or three crowded, confused, and disorderly lanes. Once, in the middle of the day—the sun beating down hot enough to fry noodles on the sidewalk—I saw a man who looked about thirty crawling across the road. He wore jogging shoes on his hands, and his knees, which had developed large calluses, served as his feet. He was not an amputee. He had polio, I think. He held his head up and vainly hoped that the crowd of cars, trucks, and motor-cycles would move out of his way as he went to his work: begging in New Market. I had seen him there a few times before and had given him the name Four, as in "4-on-the-floor." It was easy to imagine Mr. Four being rolled over and flattened like a bug by one of the big trucks that circled the market. How could the driver see him? After the accident, the harried driver would fork over a few dollars to one of the relatives, and in a country where life is dirt cheap, that would be that. Squashed like a bug and who would care? But in his last second, would not Mr. Four, like any other living creature, squirm to get out of the way, as if to say that life crawling around on the ground, as bad as it might be, was still worth hanging onto?

"And me too," I said, "no matter what happens and no matter how rationally I can say that my life isn't worth a spit, I'm going to squirm to hang on to it. That's the human condition."

Niwit agreed and added that he had his own condition and his own marital problems. His highly educated Thai wife, whom he had met in the UN, had told him, "I can only ever have one mother, but I can always find another husband." It was the old mother-in-law story. Poor Niwit...it had been one hell of a sentimental day and it was great to be drinking with him.

The "show," what everyone was waiting for, was at midnight.

The show began with the dancers, in formal Thai clothing, staging a traditional rice harvest dance. This cultural highlight was immediately followed by a theatrical performance starring my new friend, the dancing marriage counselor. It was a complicated drama, and I'm not sure that I understood all of its subtleties and twists. The waiter put on a cap that made him either an airline pilot or a hotel bellboy/pimp. The dancer, who never looked at Niwit and me, put on a Thai schoolgirl's uniform that made her either a Thai schoolgirl or a prostitute. Anyway, at the end of the drama, the waiter still had his cap on while the charming dancer was naked and pulling a string knotted with razor blades out of her vagina.

I had seen these "erotic, exotic, and sexotic" shows in Bangkok and wondered if their subtle purpose was to encourage Thai men to become monks. I suspected that our next performance would be the shooting banana trick, followed by the ping-pong ball special. I decided to walk home.

A few weeks before, at the same time of night, a Bangladeshi Civilian Policeman had been shot and killed in Phnom Penh by local soldiers as he inadvertently drove through a checkpoint. The night before, a soldier from Uruguay had been shot and killed on his motorcycle just a few streets up. Those guys had been sober. I was drunk, so I knew I would be okay.

MAY 16, 1993: MORE ON THE ELECTION AND SECURITY

A few days before our cultural night out, Porn was having lunch in a restaurant in Kampong Cham, a provincial capital just two hours' drive from Phnom Penh. As he was eating, a car pulled up with six bodies in it. Robbers had attacked a taxi outside of town and killed everyone in it. The story did not make the news; only political violence made the news. On that day, ten or so people died in political violence. I cannot remember how they died—too many people were dying. Only UNTAC could keep a body count. UNTAC's Human Rights Component said that, since the beginning of March, two hundred people had died in documented political violence and that many more had been murdered in what Human Rights called "arbitrary killing."

Things were pretty bad.

I went to IPSO training. I had thought that IPSO meant International Polling Station Observer; during the training, however, I learned that it meant International Polling Station *Officer*. This meant that I would be in charge of a polling station and would help make sure that people had voter registration cards, that they only voted once, and that no one stuffed the ballot boxes—everything that needed to be done to direct a polling station. The job sounded interesting, but everyone in the training was worried about saving his or her neck.

Up to that point the UN had not told us exactly how it would protect us, which may have been why so many UN staff refused to be IPSOs. Earlier General Sanderson had said that because he had a "moral problem" with putting armed men inside a polling station, his men would be standing outside. But now Uncle UNTAC had changed tunes. After all, who cared about moral problems? During the training we were told that the plan now was for every polling station to have at least two highly paid and armed UN soldiers inside. There would also be one or two unarmed UN civilian police, CivPol, in every station. What about metal detectors? What about flak jackets and helmets? Would the entrances be sandbagged? No one knew. Someone told us that we would sleep in the polling station with the ballots for two nights so that the ballots were not molested. What if someone molested my neck?

That someone would probably be a Khmer Rouge. The KR believed, or at least they said they believed, that the UN supported "the puppet government," their name for the State of Cambodia. Their claim was that, if the SOC stayed in power, the Vietnamese would take over and Cambodia would cease to exist. The Khmer Rouge added that they, *Democratic Kampuchea*, were the true Cambodians, the living heirs of the builders of Angkor Wat, the real protectors of the culture and the territorial integrity of Cambodia. That song was, of course, a familiar tune to all Americans—we call it flag-waving patriotism and a good thing. Americans love nationalism. We know, as Khièu Samphan and Pol Pot know, that nationalism, ethnic hatred and an element of terror can help produce an effective fighting man. During the Vietnam War those principles enabled us to sprinkle the helpless Vietnamese with Amazing Birth Defect Dust, the defoliant we code-named Agent Orange.

I thought about being killed and wondered if I would call my assailant guilty or just someone who had been brainwashed and then terrorized into doing something that anyone else would do under the same circumstances. UNTAC had a man in jail who had massacred a Vietnamese family, and for the life of him, he couldn't figure out why he was in the slammer. His superiors had told him to kill someone: he was the gun and his superiors had pulled the trigger. He had followed orders. If he had not, he would be dead. It was simple, frighteningly simple.

In the weeks before the election, New Market had half its usual customers—no one wanted to spend money. Families had stocked up on rice and dried fish. An old Cambodia hand told me that this was 1975 all over again. I stocked up on beer and instant noodles.

The Phnom Penh government told the media that somehow eight hundred Khmer Rouge agents had sneaked into the city. Many people believed that on election day the local KR would use their Chinese high-tech weapons to rocket a few polling stations. They would not have to kill many people to frighten the voters away and have the elections declared invalid.

One afternoon Professor Austin invited everyone who worked in the Electoral Component to an office party. The trainers thought it was a big deal—they were finally going to meet the chief—but I knew him from way back.

It was pleasant—beer and snacks in an air-conditioned lobby. I knew most of the people: the trainers, the Radio UNTAC reporters, the admin. staff, the communications people, the warehouse and logistics people, the Computer Center management and the secretaries. After everyone was happy, Professor Austin, standing halfway up the stairs, gave a speech. He said that we could think of everything that had happened until now as a kind of rehearsal. "What we have been doing up to now is to put things in place, to set up, as it were, the machinery for an election." That was good, he said, but now the rehearsal was almost over, and we were about to go on center stage, where we would need courage. "The courage not to be intimidated, to continue to work together, to serve the Cambodian people who are depending on us to face the difficulties ahead with a courage equal to what they have shown in their enthusiasm to register and in their overwhelming desire that we go ahead with this election." He finished by thanking us for coming. He had a depth of sincerity and purpose that most of us had forgotten about.

Everyone left the room with the feeling that Professor Austin believed that more people would soon be killed. Fair enough. It was a price that we had to be willing to pay. After people start to die, we heard behind his words, don't evacuate, don't quit, don't go to the media. The core of the Electoral staff had to stick together, no matter what, if the election was going to, no matter how poorly, work.

Some foreign commentators saw the Cambodian people as having an election choice of cancer or polio—internal corruption or paralysis. Cancer was the Cambodia People's Party, the party of the State of Cambodia, the government installed by the Vietnamese. The Cambodia People's Party, CPP, was also known as Cambodia People's Properties because government officials had sold off government properties and pocketed the profits. The voice of the CPP, but not necessarily the man with the real power, was the dashing Hun Sen. (The Cambodians believed that the man with the real power was the shadowy party chief, Heng Samrin.) With one working eye thanks to a battle wound, Hun Sen campaigned on the CPP's record of restoring the country from complete barbarism and keeping the Khmer Rouge at bay. When asked about corruption in the CPP, he had a snappy rejoinder: "Is there corruption in UNTAC?" After the election, he promised to go after the Khmer Rouge—more war.

Polio was FUNCINPEC, the party of one of Sihanouk's sons, Prince Ranariddh (*Ran-a-ruet*), who looked and sounded like a younger Prince Sihanouk. Paris-educated Ranariddh claimed that a vote for him was a vote for his father. If he came back to power, mercurial Sihanouk would make himself king and include the Khmer Rouge in his government. If that happened, most people believed that when the charismatic king—the one man who could unite Cambodia—died, things would fall apart.

Cambodians had a certain nostalgia for the old, peaceful and relatively prosperous pre-1975 Sihanouk days. Everyone had forgotten that

in those days Sihanouk ruled with an iron fist—brutally crushing his
opposition with a few people, like Mr. Pol Pot, slipping through.

There were eighteen other parties on the ballot, and even though
they didn't count for rice husks, I knew about them. Nine parties had
popped into the picture in the last few months as their founders had
come back to Cambodia from overseas. They claimed that they were
thus untainted by corrupt Cambodian politics. Five parties were
breakaways from the son-of-Sihanouk party, or FUNCINPEC, who also
claimed they were not corrupt. And four parties represented former
guerilla groups or border strongmen. Every party promised peace, freedom, honesty and prosperity, with a few parties adding a strong dose of
racial hatred for even more popular support.

The leaders of six of the parties had recently returned from the United
States. They claimed to have taken the best of the American system and
incorporated it into their campaign strategy. Take the leader of REDEK,
Kim Kethavy from Long Beach, California, for example. He said in an
interview with *Free Choice*: "The first thing I will do when I become
leader is drop to my knees, bow my head to the ground and beg the U.S.
government to give us economic assistance....If we don't have America's
help, Cambodia will die forever." His political experience included managing a chain of gas stations in California, which may be why he promised to open "hundreds of car factories" after his election.

This was Cambodia's democratic future.

I never met anyone who would tell me who they were going to vote for.
Sovan did not know her mother's choice, and she would not tell me
hers. Cambodians felt that the people who announced their choice today could become the victims of political violence or intimidation tomorrow. The headquarters of the political parties all looked like for-
tresses because the people in them felt that their lives were in danger.
Politics seemed to mean, "Agree with me, or I'll kill you."

Some commentators predicted that the combination of promised election violence and the choice of cancer or polio would produce, at best, a
60 percent voter turnout. But for better or worse, UNTAC said that it
was ready with eight million ballots and fifty thousand Cambodians
hired to run the 1,561 polling sites.

The election was scheduled to begin on what Prince Sihanouk's astrologer had deemed to be a particularly auspicious day: Sunday, May
23.

5

Let's Vote on It
End of May – July 1993

The election was six days away. When I had filled out the application form to be an IPSO, I told them that yes, I would go anywhere. I was ready to put on a helmet and flak jacket and sit in a sandbagged bunker with chain-smoking Pakistani soldiers.

Just then, everything looked bad. Early Monday morning, we received two memos:

> "There has been a noticeable increase in the incidents involving shooting/threatening of UNTAC personnel by some unidentified personnel in and around Phnom Penh particularly in the late hours of the evening i.e. around midnight or thereabouts.... UNTAC personnel should restrict their movements after 22:00 hours....

and this one handwritten:

> "A reliable source has indicated that NADK will ambush and attack along Route 3 (the road that connects the southern port of Kampot with Phnom Penh)...all UNTAC elements should exercise extreme caution...."

How could things get much worse?

The phone rang. I picked it up. It wasn't for me, but, yes, Porn was in. He took the phone, listened, nodded, and started to speak in Thai. While still holding the phone, he performed a traditional Thai dance, and spelled my name in English. Something was up and a minute later Porn told me what was happening. A Thai woman in the Electoral Headquarters had been placing the polling officers in their polling stations when she saw a Thai name. In the name of Thai national security, she phoned the Thai name, Porn, and asked him where he wanted to work as an IPSO. He said that he, well, we, wanted to work near our homes, which were in the same neighborhood. It was all up to her. "Yes, just a moment please...no problem." She told Porn that he could work in the athletic complex called Olympic Stadium, and I could spend the election in Chak To Mouk, a middle school.

I started dancing too.

Our mysterious caller said that I would have a "large" polling station. A large polling station, Porn explained, would have eight seven-person teams. He had a "small" polling station with three teams. The mobile polling stations had one team apiece.

Chak To Mouk was less than ten minutes by motorcycle from my house. I checked it out that night. The school bordered the compound where the prime minister lived on posh Norodom Boulevard. Directly across the street was the headquarters of the United Nations Strategic Investigations Unit, whoever they were. Behind the metal fence in front of the school, a large central courtyard was flanked by two single-story school buildings. As this was the school the government ministers sent their children to, it did not look like it was about to collapse. Somehow, money had been found to paint it bright yellow.

THEIR MOST LIKELY TARGET

That Friday, the 110 International Polling Station Officers in Phnom Penh, one for each polling station, had a meeting with the military contingent assigned to Phnom Penh, the Ghanaian Battalion. On the edge of town on the way to the airport, "Ghanbatt" headquarters was a four-story building that once must have been a school. From the roof we could see the sprawl of the city, with just a few buildings popping over the trees. In other directions were rice fields, ponds and thatched houses. The rainy season was just beginning, and the countryside looked green and lush in the long deep shadows of late afternoon.

As the meeting began, it became immediately clear that most IPSOs had not stopped worrying about their necks. They wanted permission to order around the soldiers who would be providing the armed security at their polling stations. The Ghanaians, especially their commanding officer, thought that was crazy. He explained the situation to us in non-military terms. Up to this point, the military, in particular his men, the gallant men from Ghana, had worked very hard, considered every detail, every angle, and done everything humanly and militarily possible to insure our security. "Therefore," he continued in a bone-chilling voice, "you do not have to waste a second of your time thinking that you are going to command my men, because you are not."

He did not have to repeat himself. He had a certain military presence in that, as he spoke, I could imagine him shooting, in mid-sentence, one of his men in the head for hesitating to obey orders.

Next, the UNMO (United Nations Military Observer) spoke. He was a member of the British Special Forces. He wore camouflaged fatigues, and looked like he had just stepped out of six weeks of jungle patrol where he had lived on raw leaves and insects. His stage presence began where the Ghanaian's ended. In an accent that came right off the playing fields of Eton, he said that he could not be certain that he understood every nuance of guerrilla psychology. However, if he were a terrorist, the biggest moving target would be the truck that carried the ballot boxes and polling materials to the polling stations. "Therefore," he concluded, "I would see to it that those lorries are unloaded with minimal delay."

The provincial electoral officials, our leaders, summed things up by wishing us well and adding that, if we had any problems, we could call them on the radio.

No one found that very reassuring.

As the meeting ended, many of the IPSOs were still worried about their safety. We had been promised flak jackets and helmets, but no one knew where they were.

Porn and I tried to calm each other down. "Porn, man, have you seen your polling station?" I asked.

"This morning."

"How does it look?"

"It looks okay, but there are too many tall buildings around it. It would be easy for a sniper to shoot inside."

"You scared?"

"I think I'm gonna wear a flak vest and helmet. How about you?"

"I don't know yet."

Rumors were buzzing like mosquitoes at dusk. I could ignore the one about a government satellite with x-ray cameras able to record who people had voted for, but not the one about the Khmer Rouge who were supposedly encamped just across the river, with my polling station as their most likely target. This was related to me by an Australian who had been in the city in 1975 for Pol Pot's evacuation of Phnom Penh; he later walked into Thailand. He told me to stay low if I heard incoming mortar fire. He also reminded me that in November, during registration, someone had fired a rocket-propelled grenade from across the river that had just missed a voter registration site.

Thanks.

My friends in New Market told me that they were staying home during the election.

Setee, still a traveling translator for UNTAC administration, told me what he had heard from the provincial taxi drivers: no one wanted to come into Phnom Penh anymore. People in the provinces believed that if there was going to be trouble, it would be here.

ON YOUR MARK, GET SET...

Things were tense, but there was also a certain party atmosphere in Phnom Penh. UNTAC had splattered the city with brightly colored posters of the ballot and banners across the main streets that proclaimed in Khmer and English: "Election '93" and "Your Vote is Secret."

Radio UNTAC was now the CNN and MTV of Cambodia. The Cambodian people loved Radio UNTAC. Maybe they liked it because they thought they could trust it, or maybe they liked it because it played an odd selection of classical Khmer music and rock'n'roll in between political messages from all twenty political parties. Driving around town, you could hear it from the shops and homes. On television around Phnom Penh and in the video theaters it had set up in the provinces, UNTAC was everywhere as well. There were special programs and even a drama series that featured a regular cast of actors. One week they would explain how democracy works; another week they would demonstrate how to vote or investigate voter intimidation. The shows were done with melodrama, music and humor. I knew one of the actors, a handsome Russian man who could speak fluent Khmer. He said that he was tired of women hounding him on the street.

With Uncle UNTAC in town, freedom of the press had suddenly become a reality in Cambodia. Little kiosks that were set up to sell foreign cigarettes were now filled with local newspapers. Each paper purported to tell *the truth*, including the one that featured interviews with Martians and the story of a woman whose dead husband had told her from the grave how to make a million dollars. These were true, the editor said, because they had been copied directly from American supermarket tabloids. Anyway, despite what people read in the tabloids, there was only one thing on people's minds: the election.

The next day, Saturday, May 22, the IPSOs and their polling station teams had a pre-election rehearsal. Everything was confused. Phnom Penh was divided into nine sections with each section having an office. My section leader said that everyone was to report to her office at exactly 6:00 A.M. Everyone did. She staggered in at 6:30 and told us to go outside to pick a translator. The translators were lined up like the ladies in a Phnom Penh brothel: you're too fat, you're too thin, you smoke...I picked the first person in line. What a relief that he, Vuthy (*Vuu-tee*), could actually speak English, didn't smoke, and had a motorcycle. He drove us to our polling station, just a couple of minutes away.

The polling teams were waiting there, but their boss, the Presiding Officer, who was the second in command, was not. The manual, I remembered, said that the teams were headed by Assistant Presiding Officers. I called the eight APOs together to introduce myself. I said that, according to the *Electoral Law*, I was their leader. We talked for a minute—a few of them could speak English. They said they had been training for the election for a month. Good, I thought, you'll need it. Just then, their other leader, the Presiding Officer, arrived. She asked me if I could speak French. Sorry, no. I started to explain the duties of the IPSO to her. Never mind, she said, she understood everything and I did not have to worry. Good. In her fifties, she was the principal of a primary school. With her weathered features, big build, square jaw and ready smile, she had the look of someone who had been through the war without becoming unduly ruffled by it. Vuthy called her *Ming*, Aunt. After that she was Aunt *Ming* to me too.

A large flatbed truck drove in and we unloaded the ballot boxes, voting booths, and other equipment, including two toys—a colorless ink you could put your finger in and a little pocket ultraviolet or "black" light which made the ink visible up to seven days later.

We unpacked the equipment and the teams lined up exactly the way the polling manual said they should. I practiced a sample vote with one of my eight teams:

- The queue controller told me where to stand in line.
- One of the two identification officers looked at my finger (for signs of previous inking) and at my ID card (for the day-glow UN logo) under the pocket black light. The other identification officer checked my card number against the list of one hundred Phnom Penh cancelled voter registration cards that the Computer Center had produced.
- The ink applicator dipped the tip of my index finger into the clear watery ink.
- The ballot issuer punched a hole in my ID card and stamped a ballot before handing it to me. I marked my ballot in the flimsy cardboard voting booth.
- Finally, the ballot box controller had me put the ballot in the metal ballot box.

If they had taken their jobs any more seriously, we would have had our first election casualties right then. Ming was right—I did not have to worry.

We put everything back in the boxes, and the truck, the most likely target for terrorists, took them away. It was not yet eleven o'clock, and already I had the feeling that the provincial electoral officials had succeeded. Everyone could see that the teams were well trained and that most of the logistical problems had been solved—although no one had yet found the helmets, flak jackets and metal detectors. But those were just details.

SHE HAD FINALLY DIED

Saturday afternoon I watched a video and drank beer. At dusk, feeling sentimental, I drove my motorcycle to Sovan's house to tell her family the name of my polling station. On the way there, at the last big intersection, sat a government armored personnel carrier. The APC was waiting there to tell any invading Khmer Rouge: "Okay, chums, if you come to town you have to get past this." But it was too hot inside the tank for anyone actually to be in it, so the soldiers played cards on the ground outside. No need to overdo things.

Sovan's relatives wished me luck. Her aunt gave me a hug. What could they say?

That night I read my will and tried to arrange my things. I heard on the radio that Prince Sihanouk had made one of his rare visits home to Cambodia to wish us well. I read the polling manual again. I had another beer, forgot about the election, and thought about how much I disliked Cambodian food.

Why, I wondered, did the Cambodian people even bother to eat? Even my love, Sovan, bursting with brains and talent, *just could not cook*. I was sure that I never would have made it this far had it not been for a Vietnamese food stall in New Market. There they served the greatest iced coffee this side of heaven, and had trained a Cambodian woman to cook vegetarian *ban chow*, a Vietnamese noodle dish. She was a great cook, and had the unusual distinction of being *the world's oldest living Cambodian*. It sounds unbelievable, but it was true. After my first meal there, I was absolutely sure that there could not be an older, chain-smoking, shriveled crone this side of the grave and behind a wok in all of Cambodia. I had always wanted to take her picture, but I never took my camera to the market since I believed that she would be a goner by my next appearance. Once I was sure that she had finally died, but a month later she came back, and, thank God, started cooking again.

A LITTLE ARMY

Rain fell most of the night. It was still raining big lazy drops into the shallow puddles on the street when I stepped out of my air-conditioned room at six in the morning. It was dark, too.

I had planned on walking to the polling station—a man on a motorcycle would be an easy target for a sniper, but it was raining so I took the bike. Riding in the back alleys all the way, I parked in the Strategic Investigations Unit where they had said I could use the toilet. The toilet in the school was a horrific mess. With the bike in Strategic Investigations, I stood a fair chance of escaping if trouble came.

Inside the school there were only a few people and no one from security. The front gate was open. I asked one of the Khmer staff to try to find whoever had the key to the gate so we could lock it. He found the groundskeeper. We had to lock the gate because we could not have people streaming into the school. Crowd control would take place at the little pedestrian gate to the right.

Soon team members started arriving and going to their respective rooms. Everyone, including me, was wearing "Election '93" T-shirts. We were a team. My interpreter, Vuthy, rode in on his motorcycle and someone dropped off the Presiding Officer, Ming. The two Civilian Policemen, from India and Kenya, drove their UN truck inside the compound after we opened the gate, and parked it. Finally three Ghanaian soldiers, one of whom was the Sergeant in charge, were dropped off. The Civilian Policemen carried metal detectors. The Ghanaians wore flak jackets and carried ancient rifles whose barrels were wrapped with masking tape. I looked at my armed contingent and wondered if those rifles actually worked, and if they did, did the Ghanaians know how to use them? No one knew what had happened to my flak jacket and helmet.

The rain stopped at 6:30—just in time, since the voting equipment, with military escort, had arrived. The lead vehicle was a pickup truck with a large machine gun mounted on top of the cab. It was manned by three Ghanaian soldiers. Behind the pickup truck was the most likely target for terrorists: a large flatbed truck that carried the ballot boxes and supplies. Three more armed Ghanaians were standing by the equipment looking out for any trouble.

Everyone clamored around the truck and unloaded the supplies, com pletely forgetting the most-likely-target business. Then the trucks circled the inside of the compound and drove off.

Ming barked orders that were immediately obeyed, "You take the ballot box over there," "APO, how many ballots do you have?" "APO, where is your completed form 2019?" Those guys were a little army.

After everything was set up, it was time for Ming, the party agents, and me, the IPSO, to countersign a form to certify that each ballot box had been sealed shut with a numbered metal seal. That way, at least in theory, everyone knew that we were beginning the election with empty ballot boxes, whose seal numbers everyone knew.

Numbered seals were the keystone of the operation. The party agents, representatives of the political parties, were there to check for any cheating. They were not allowed to talk to the voters or even to tell us what party they represented, although the locals knew. The party agents were, however, allowed to watch the ballot boxes during the day, and at the end of the day's polling, they could witness us closing the ballot box slits with a numbered *plastic* seal. In the morning of the second and third

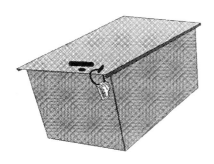

days, they could then verify that the boxes had not been tampered with during the night by witnessing us cutting the same numbered plastic seal that had held the slit closed all night. The metal seal would remain on the box until it was time to count the ballots. The system supposedly made it impossible to secretly stuff or switch a ballot box.

In theory a party could have one representative present for each ballot box. Fortunately however, only four or five parties were organized and large enough to send people to the polling stations; consequently there were only four or five party agents, out of a possible twenty, in each room. One of the party agents, in her late twenties, was gorgeous. She had a round soft face, thick sensuous lips, and almost annoyingly inviting bedroom eyes. But I never talked to her.

The ballot box security system sounded flawless, but from the first it was too good to be true: the party officials didn't understand it at all. Maybe no one had told them, or they hadn't paid attention, or they didn't care. Anyway, Ming explained the system to them by saying, "You're gonna sign this form." They quickly figured out that this must be something official. They made a scramble for pens and wrote the metal seal numbers on scraps of paper or on their palms as the APOs in each room read the numbers off.

Time was flying by. We zoomed through the eight boxes in four rooms. The APO would read each seal number aloud; I would officially click the metal seal to secure the ballot box shut; and finally Ming, the party representatives and I would sign the form.

We finished at 7:50, ten minutes before the polls were supposed to open. Already a large crowd had gathered outside.

MEETINGS WITH REMARKABLE PEOPLE

Just after eight o'clock we opened the pedestrian gate and let in the first few voters. Suddenly, from out of nowhere, a large crowd materialized in front of the classrooms.

How?

Ha! Our highly trained and dedicated Ghanaian soldiers and our highly paid Civilian Police had never considered the possibility of actually walking around the school. Had they done so, they would have noticed, behind the little houses where the teachers lived, an open gate giving access to a back alley. The local voters knew their way through this gate directly into the school.

"Couldn't we put one man at the back gate to keep people out?" I suggested to the Ghanaian sergeant.

"I cannot spare anyone." He had two men. The truth was that no one wanted to sacrifice himself in the name of democracy or risk being out in the rain.

It remained overcast.

"Can we lock it?" I asked.

"We don't have a lock."

"I have a lock."

"You have a lock?"

"My motorcycle lock."

It was then a simple matter for me to run across the street to the Strategic Investigations Unit, grab my helmet lock, which had previously been a bicycle lock, and run to the back of the school, through the swamp that was also the school's toilet, to lock the gate.

By now hundreds of people were crowding around the pedestrian gate trying to get through into the school yard. The potential voters pushed, shoved and squeezed up around the door as if we were giving away one hundred dollar bills. The gate was only big enough for two people to get through at a time, so it was fairly easy for the queue controller to open the gate, let a few people in, and close the gate. Once inside, the lowest ranking Civilian Policeman, the one from India, scanned them with the metal detector. They were then directed to one of two polling sites. The higher ranking Civilian Policeman sat in a classroom and did nothing.

In the compound there were two voting sites because there were two kinds of ballots—tendered ballots and ordinary ballots. Ordinary ballots were for people who had their voter registration card with them and were voting in the province they had registered in, Phnom Penh. They were not ordinary if their voter registration card had been lost or stolen, or if they were from another province. Most people were ordinary. The non-ordinary voters had to fill out a form stating where they were from, their name, and their voter registration number, if they had their card with them or otherwise remembered their number. That form was on the outside of an envelope that they would put their ballot into before slipping it into the tendered ballot box. The Computer Center would later check to see if indeed the "tendered ballot" was from a registered voter.

All this would be important during the counting.

The pedestrian gate worked well except that, after the people voted, no one could leave. How could they? People were packed twenty deep outside the gate. Soon we had a hundred people complaining that they wanted to leave.

Finally the Ghanaian Sergeant decided that one of his men would be able to sacrifice himself, risk everything including, if it started to rain, getting wet, and stand alone at the far gate that I had sealed with my old bicycle lock. That soldier would allow the voters to go out, but not come in. "But first," the Ghanaian Sergeant asked me, "could you show me exactly where the gate is?"

After I showed him, he asked me to show one of his men exactly where the back gate was and to unlock it for him. So I made my third trip through the swamp/toilet to the back gate, a hundred meters away.

This time, as I came back, I saw my worst nightmare: huge crowds of people were besieging the classrooms, the big front gate was wide open, and hundreds of people were streaming in from the street. I hurried to one of the classrooms where Ghanaian soldiers whom I had not seen before were blocking the doorway. "I am the IPSO in charge!" I shouted as I pushed through them. Suddenly I was under the glare of TV camera lights. As the cameras rolled, a disheveled man in muddy pants and a "Polling Official" T-shirt—me—introduced himself to the distinguished gentleman in the safari suit—the Special Representative of the United

Nations Secretary-General, Mr. Yasushi Akashi. He seemed glad to see me and shook my hand.

"How is everything?" he asked.

"Out of control. Could you ask the soldiers to help us regain control of this polling station?"

"It is very crowded now," he commented.

Judy Thompson was with him. "Didn't you know we were coming?" she asked.

"No idea at all."

She winced.

Mr. Akashi was in a hurry, I guessed. He quickly slid into his car, for which the gate had been opened in the first place, and drove out of the compound. The camera crews and reporters followed him out.

There were now crowds of people ten deep outside every classroom and near total chaos inside as the teams tried to process people. People were jumping out of the classroom windows to leave. The queue controllers did not have whatever it took to force people to wait outside, to stand in line, or otherwise act in an orderly and unnatural way. I tried to show the queue controllers how to make people enter the classrooms one by one. As long as I was there, things were under control, but as soon as I left one room for another, order collapsed. Something had to be done if we were not going to slip into a riot. We had to close the front gate.

At the front gate the Indian Civilian Policeman was in a daze. "We have to close the front gate," I said to him.

"There are too many people, sir," he said.

"But if we don't close it, the classrooms will be out of control."

"I'm sorry sir, we cannot close it. There are too many people, too many people."

That was what I had heard we could expect from CivPol. During voter registration, the UNVs had complained that CivPol would not get out of their air-conditioned vehicles to help.

As the policeman watched, three of the Cambodian staff, Vuthy, and I locked arms and slowly brought the two halves of the front gate together as people scrambled between us to get inside. We bolted the gate, and I put one man there to make certain that no one unbolted it. This still left the pedestrian entrance open, and it was now the Niagara Falls of entrance ways. Fortunately the gate was only a meter wide, so Vuthy and I were able, again by locking our arms together, to close the gate. Now the people who were just about to enter were being squashed. "Let me in! Let me in!" one woman screamed out in English.

"No one can come in until there is room in the classrooms," I shouted back.

"No, we can come in!" she pleaded. There were still crowds of ten people deep outside each classroom.

She was being squashed, but I was in charge.

"Just wait a few minutes."

We tried to tell the crowd to form a line, but that was completely hopeless.

We waited a few minutes until the crowd outside the classrooms thinned out a bit, then I had two men open the gate enough to let one person through, me.

"Okay, people," I said in Khmer, standing on my toes and facing the crowd. "Are we happy? Is this a good election?"

People laughed.

"I'm going to let you in, but only five people at a time."

I put my arms around five people, put them between me and the gate, signaled the men inside to open the gate, and let the five people shoot through. The two men shut the gate, at which time the crowd flattened me against it.

"Wait, wait!" I shouted as the crowd pressed forward.

"Wait, wait!" someone echoed back, mocking my Khmer.

"That's right," I said, "Wait, wait!"

The system worked. Five or six people would rocket through every minute or so, the Indian CivPol would scan them with the metal detector, and they would go inside. Vuthy sat on the fence the whole time, talking to the crowd, reassuring them that they were going to vote soon enough.

It would have been easy for someone to pickpocket, trip, punch me in the face, or stab me, but no one did. A few times someone in the crowd pointed out a pregnant woman or a woman carrying a baby, and the crowd would part just enough to let her through. Once, a man raised his hand to indicate that there was something I should see. I motioned a few people aside. Had someone fainted? Was there a lost child? No, there, on the ground and looking up, as always, was my friend from New Market, Mr. Four. He had come to vote. I motioned for the crowd to let him through. They did, and he crawled under my arms, through the gate, and eventually into a classroom to vote.

I did not notice, but I would guess that Mr. Four, like everyone else, wore his best clothes. To the Cambodians this was something very special: the first multi-party election in longer than most people could remember—twenty-seven years—and they were going to make the most of it. Crowding me at the gate was a sign of their enthusiasm.

By eleven o'clock the crowd had thinned out enough that I was able to leave the gate and let the two men inside take over. I slipped inside. Wow! I felt as if I had just won the heavyweight boxing championship of the world. I was elated, tired, hungry, and thirsty.

"You work very hard, my friend," the Indian policeman said to me.

"Thank you."

The other Civilian Policeman was still hiding.

With the crowd thinned out, people could now leave through the front gate. The Ghanaian soldier at the back gate had grown lonely and maybe hungry, too. He quietly left his post to join his friends sitting in chairs outside one of the classrooms.

I checked in with Ming. To her it was just another day; no problem. I had a look at what the polling teams were doing. There were still enough voters to keep every team busy.

Almost everyone on the teams was under thirty, half of them women. Everyone looked professional but relaxed, as if they had just won their own heavyweight boxing titles. As I walked from room to room to let everyone know that I was around, I questioned the card punchers. They punched the voter registration cards with a hand-held paper punch and kept the punches, the size of the letter "O," in a plastic cup as a record of how many people had voted. (If you pay people enough money, they will do just about anything.) I found that I could ask any puncher, "How many cards have you punched?" and get an instant response.

"497."

"393."

"421."

Like that.

By noon over three thousand people had voted at Chak To Mouk polling station.

THE QUEEN OF PERSIA

Sari, my old Pakistani friend, brought me lunch at noon. By chance I had met her on the street the day before and found that she had not lost her charm. Jubilant as always, she asked me what I was doing. I told her. Always the motherly type, she asked if she could bring me lunch at the polling station. "Yes," I said, "that would be wonderful."

She still looked like the cover of a fashion magazine with her model's figure, eye shadow, lipstick, and enough glamour to start a riot. She also still dressed, when she was not at a party, like the Queen of Persia. She wore jeans that fit her like ballet tights, but she also wore the long flowing shirts and the long scarves that Pakistani women like to wear. She was a delightful woman. I was sorry that I had lost touch with her, but equally glad that her husband was far away, that I was not married to her, and that we both had almost forgotten our wonderful night in bed together.

She brought me tuna fish sandwiches, orange juice, and cookies. I was lucky to know her. As we ate lunch in the shade of one of the unused school buildings, she told me, in a slight departure from her usual air of jubilation, that her marriage had fallen apart.

"Made in heaven, gone to hell," I said to ease the shock.

"Life can be a bitch," she added.

"A bastard."

She said that once she had arranged for her husband to come visit her in Cambodia and had even paid for his ticket, but then he didn't come. He didn't even call her on her birthday. Later, one of the German doctors had moved in with her. She started to cry as she told me the story...I patted her hand and tried to think of something comforting to say to one of the kindest hearts in Mrs. Penh's Phnom, whose only weakness was an inability to deal with one of the unwanted fringe benefits of working for UNTAC—unbearable loneliness.

One should never assume, I realized then, that the life of someone you lose touch with continues in a never-ending Lambada.

How About That?

In the afternoon, as the big crowd of voters thinned, another crowd thickened—the journalists. According to the *Electoral Law*, no photography was allowed inside the polling stations, so one way of meeting journalists was to tell them not to take pictures. They were all looking for a story. What was the story? No bombings, no shootings, no crazies—just wild enthusiasm. They said that everywhere it was the same story: big crowds, no problems, no story.

How about that?

It was against the rules for IPSOs to give interviews, but for what they paid us, how could I refuse when a TV crew from ABC asked to interview me? What could I say? Things were fine.

Along with the journalists came waves of observers and various dignitaries. The observers were from different human rights groups and

Meaning business, an UNTAC soldier protects a group of Vietnamese fisher families fleeing Cambodia following a series of anti-Vietnamese terrorist attacks by the Khmer Rouge.

governmental and non-governmental organizations. They would look around for a few minutes, take notes, and find nothing wrong. The dignitaries included the Chief of the American Mission, Charles Twining.

The voting continued. One voter came to me and said that his wife was sick, very sick—could he take a ballot home to her? I told him no, but if he brought her to the polling station in a car, I would open the front gate for him. A few minutes later he drove her in. She looked to be more dead than alive, but somehow, even though she could not hold her head straight, she managed to vote.

Other people came to vote who did not know how to hold a pencil. The APOs showed them how. A few rickshaw drivers stopped by, left their rickshaws outside, and came in. I was in a classroom when one strode inside. A strikingly handsome young man, built like an Olympic distance runner, he wore a Cambodian cowboy hat and clothes that looked like they either were specially made for him or had simply become part of him. His problem was that he could not read or write. One of the young women showed him how to hold a pencil and pointed to, I hoped, the party he wanted to vote for. He marked his ballot behind the cardboard voting booth and walked out a few centimeters taller. The woman who had helped him smiled at me as he left. She had understood his moment of elation.

To some of the old people, voting was a great adventure. Like so many elders in Asia, they were, now that the time was right, all smiles and affection.

Soon it was 3:30. Originally, the plan had been to sleep in the polling station, but luckily that plan had been scrapped. Then the soldiers were going to sleep in the polling station, but that plan had been dumped as well. In the end, no one in Phnom Penh was going to sleep in the polling station, and everything was going back to the district office. That plan stuck. We closed the gate precisely at 4:00 P.M. and began the scramble to pack up.

The APOs had forms that were designed to track every ballot: how many were used, lost, discarded, and how many were left. After they filled these in, they passed them on to Ming, who worked furiously to calculate the grand totals for the entire station. Meanwhile all the supplies were put back into empty ballot boxes and the rooms cleaned. Finally every ballot box slit had to be shut with a numbered plastic seal, which Ming and I did as we signed the forms and the party agents followed along.

Everything was finished by 4:30, when the flatbed truck with the military escort arrived and took the supplies back to district headquarters.

I was exhausted, but as I walked to my motorcycle my feet were not quite touching the ground. Maybe my life, Mr. Four's life, Sari's life, and everyone else's life were not worth a spit, and yet life, at times, could be just plain wonderful.

I listened to the BBC that night. The night before, two UNTAC Chinese peacekeepers had died when someone shelled their compound, but on this day no one had been killed and half of the eligible voters in Cambodia had voted. The BBC said that even some Khmer Rouge soldiers had voted. Good for them.

We had two more days to go.

It Was Our Profit

Monday morning (day two), a couple of the ballot box seals were found to be broken. When the boxes had been placed in the truck, they had been banged around, and a few of the plastic slit seals had snapped. What could we do? Everyone knew that the boxes had been under the Ghanaian guns all night and that they had not been tampered with. What could the party agents say? Later someone from district headquarters dropped by and showed us how to seal the boxes so that the slit seals would not break. Until then, everyone had simply done what was written in the Michael Maley manual.

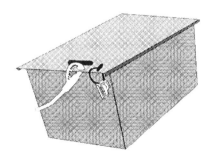

With the experience we had gained from the first day, everyone at Chak To Mouk knew exactly what to do. The Indian Civilian Policeman was happy to stay at the front gate, play with his metal detector and flirt harmlessly with the girls, while his commanding officer was equally happy to stay in one of the classrooms and read the newspaper. The Ghanaians were happy to sleep on duty on the veranda of a school building until their commanding officer from headquarters drove in and told them not to. The ever-vigilant Ming was happy to keep her staff at their stations even though business fell way down. And our friends, the party agents, were happy to doze off once in a while if the spirit moved them, which was fine.

Journalists and tourists kept coming. I told them not to take pictures and chatted with them for a minute. Only one man made any trouble—he would not stop filming with his video camera. I called for CivPol. They were finally going to get a chance to prove themselves. I called again and again. Finally, the senior CivPol officer came to the rescue, "Oh him," he said, indicating the photographer, "he's my friend. I asked him to come and take some pictures."

Oh.

Vuthy and I stayed vigilant as well, and passed the time walking from building to building or sitting under the shade of the tree at the front gate. We became the best of friends. I told him many of the things I've related here and he told me his story as well. He was born in 1970 in a village in the nearby province of Kampong Speu. He said that he was just a kid during Pol Pot's experiment in communal living, which he remembered as "not too bad" for him and his family. When the experiment was over, his family decided to give city life a try. They found a nice apartment in Phnom Penh and took up residence.

I interrupted him, "You mean you squatted in some dead family's apartment?"

"It was our profit," he said.

In Phnom Penh, the family went into business selling firewood. They did well and later sent Vuthy to a private school to study English. In 1988 Vuthy, believing that he was about to be drafted into the Vietnamese-backed army, left his family and fled to Malaysia by boat, where he spent four years in a refugee camp. With repatriation—forced resettlement—he had come back to Cambodia where his family was waiting for him in their profited apartment. Now he was working in UNTAC Headquarters as a translator and waiting for his mother to find him a wife.

"Are you married, sir?" he asked.

I thought for a minute. "No, but I could get married later this year."

On the last afternoon, Judy Thompson stopped by with an article from a Bangkok newspaper. Sovan had charmed all of Australia and had been, because of the time zones, the first person to vote in the election. I knew it.

In the end 10,029 people voted at Chak To Mouk polling station. Over six thousand people had voted the first day, about three thousand the second, and a thousand trickled in on the third day.

All ended well. As we parted, everyone shook hands and agreed that we had done a great job. At their request I gave my home address to Ming and Vuthy. I told them to write me if there was anything I could do for them.

The "fixed" polling stations closed on Tuesday afternoon, but the mobile stations had three more days to go—UNTAC thought this was enough time to helicopter or truck a mobile polling station to Cambodians living in isolated areas. And UNTAC did it! In one of the unsung logistical miracles of our time, they put a "mobile" polling station within easy reach of almost everyone on Mars. By the end of the week, 90 percent of the registered voters of Cambodia had cast ballots. The mobile teams had even hit the prisons and the hospitals.

This was UNTAC's finest hour.

KEEPING SCORE

All of the Phnom Penh IPSOs were told, just as our stations were closing on Tuesday, to report to the Phnom Penh Electoral Warehouse for ballot counting at ten o'clock Thursday morning. I arrived a little early.

By chance the same men who had protected me at Chak To Mouk were now guarding the Electoral Warehouse. The sergeant in charge asked me a stupid question: "Do you remember me?"

I told him that I did.

"Good," he said. "Can you get me an Election '93 T-shirt?"

I told him I would try.

This time I was not taking any chances. I walked around the periphery. What had formerly been two huge rice barns were now the Electoral Warehouse and the Phnom Penh Counting Center, and between them someone had recently dug a bomb shelter; UNTAC was not taking any chances either. Someone had also put up a high barbed wire fence and a few lookout posts.

This was the first time for the IPSOs to see each other again. The same people who had complained about being forced to be IPSOs now felt that they were heroes, and that it had been one of the greatest experiences of their lives. Everyone was in high spirits and full of great adventure stories, all of which were about the same. Except, that is, those stories from the people who were sent out of town, but still within the province of Phnom Penh. They told about *sleeping in their polling stations*. The UN had decided that no potential voter should be more than fifteen kilometers from a polling station. So on election day, all across the country many IPSOs were shocked when they found themselves out of hotel range and sleeping under a mosquito net in a temple, a school or a tent. Perhaps those who were surprised the most were the one thousand IPSOs who had come to Cambodia just for the election.

Niwit had been one of those who had slept outside of Phnom Penh. Not one to complain, he said it was "like a camping trip with the boy scouts." Things had gone well.

Porn was ecstatic. His polling station, Olympic Stadium, had been the busiest in Cambodia. He had called his wife Sunday night to tell her he was still alive. She said she knew that. She had just seen him on television along with me. Later he showed me his $800 flak jacket and helmet, which in the end he hadn't worn.

The electoral management called us together with a bull horn to announce that we were there to get ID cards and that we should come back the next day.

The next day, Friday, they told us that we could not begin counting as the mobile polling was just finishing. Instead, we would make certain that no one had "stuffed" the ballot boxes. This was serious. We would carefully check the forms that the APOs, POs and IPSOs had filled out to verify that their tallies were the same as the number of ballots in the boxes. That sounded like a good idea. There were, however, a few problems:

- almost no one could figure out how to do it,
- if they could, they could not read the handwriting of the locals
- or, if they knew how to do it and they could read the handwriting of the locals, they tended to find that the number of ballots that the APOs, POs, and IPSOs said were there, and the number of ballots in the boxes were slightly different.

So, very early on it became clear that we would do one of two things: (1) spend the next two weeks reconciling the numbers on the forms with the actual number of ballots, or (2) spend the next seven hours puttering around the Electoral Warehouse telling IPSO stories and complaining about the heat while quietly forgetting about the rectification.

Fortunately, management decided on number two, which gave them the day off and time to plan how we were going to do the counting. The political party officials just followed along.

Until then no one had thought much about how to do the counting. Maybe they thought it would never happen, or they had too much to worry about already. Anyway, now management announced that Mr. Akashi and the Phnom Penh government had decided yesterday that once the counting started it should continue twenty-four hours a day. This would, they believed, keep ballot boxes from disappearing or changing contents.

The Phnom Penh electoral management now came up with an ingenious and elaborate scheme for counting votes. Beginning tomorrow we would divide into two groups. Group one would work eight hours, have eight hours off, and then come back for eight more hours. Group two would do the same; everyone would continue until finished. They announced the plan. Everyone complained. Management said that we had to be ready to make a sacrifice for the UN, Cambodia, and democracy, and if we could not do that we should all leave Cambodia immediately. One man, when told this, was almost in tears. But management held fast. It was settled. A few minutes later, though, a woman whispered to her management boyfriend something about returning from outer space to planet earth. Soon, and with no visible loss of face, management decided that we would count the ballots in twelve hour shifts beginning Saturday at 8 A.M. This left us the choice of roasting all day in the airless rice barn or staying up all night. I voted for the life of a movie star.

The next day, Saturday, Mr. Akashi announced to the world that the elections had been free and fair. Someone asked him why the Khmer Rouge had stayed in the shadows throughout the election. He had the guts to say he did not know: "Their minds are unfathomable." But all the Americans knew why. Ho Chi Minh had given us a crash course in guerilla warfare in the 1970s, when his ragtag but diligent army defeated the most powerful nation on earth. Ho had said that a guerilla movement always needed a large base of popular support. Khieu Samphan and Pol Pot, who had also studied under Ho, knew that they would lose that base if they blew up the election. Better to stay in the jungle, play it cool, and wait.

Saturday night, I learned how to count:

- First, take three ballot boxes from three different districts (Phnom Penh had nine districts). Count these ballots, box-by-box, into piles of fifty. Have one of the three people on the team double-check one other person. Write down the number of ballots and then the grand total of ballots in all three boxes.
- Second, combine the ballots from all three districts into one box.
- Third, count the ballots again, sorting them by party into piles of fifty and double-check again.
- Lastly, add up and record the party totals. The grand total from the party totals should equal the total number of ballots from step one. If not, begin again.

Fortunately Niwit, a longtime poker player who had a mind for numbers, was on my team. We did not make any mistakes and the hours passed quickly.

After the first few hours it was becoming clear that with the third step, "Count by party," we were putting less than half of the ballots into the government party pile and the greater part into the son-of-Sihanouk party pile, with the other eighteen parties getting only the odd ballot. The data entry clerks had told me that the Phnom Penh people could never forgive the Phnom Penh government, "the Heng Samrin Regime" as they called it, for its corruption and brutality. I could see their point.

As we worked under the horrid fluorescent lights, in the incredible heat of the night and in the noise and wind of the fans, the political party officials walked around to see if we were putting the right ballots in the right piles. It was boring work for them and a few dozed off. But they couldn't sleep for long—we needed them.

We found that about one percent of the ballots were invalid because the voters had not marked them at all, marked more than one party, or put a mark in the margin of the ballot. On a few ballots I could tell that the voters had pressed the wrong end of the pencil into the paper. Whenever we found an improperly marked ballot, an official from a political party had to initial it to verify that it was indeed invalid.

One party, the one in the lower right-hand corner of the ballot, received more votes than they should have if they, like most of the other eighteen parties, were just getting the odd miscast vote. What happened, someone figured out later, was that many of the illiterate voters had held the ballot topside down: they had thought they were voting for the party in the upper left-hand corner, the government party.

Everything was free and fair.

There were about 498,000 voters in Phnom Penh. Someone calculated that a team of three people could count about 700 ballots an hour. If each shift had about fifty people, one shift would count about 150,000 votes, and everyone would therefore have to work two twelve-hour shifts if everyone came for both shifts. That was what happened. The counting of the ordinary ballots for Phnom Penh ended at four Monday morning. We left the tendered ballots for the Computer Center to handle.

THE TRUTH AND NOTHING BUT THE TRUTH

I was up by 9:30 Monday morning to race to the airport to meet Sovan at 10:30. But her plane had landed an hour early and I missed her. She was not at home either. She was running around town with the 130 ballots she had brought back from Australia, trying to figure out who to give them to.

By the time I caught up with her a few days later, she had heard about my cultural evening at the BK International Disco and Massage Parlor from one of the wide-eyed Khmer men in attendance. Now, in her eyes, I was fallen. Now her "gentleman" was a lowlife, a disgrace and possibly, depending on what the Khmer men had told her, guilty of sexual sin. Up to then, I'd been doing pretty well. Now I was a snake.

It's always hard to get along with women—they ask too much of men. The Thai medical community claimed that, in the 1980s, they had perfected for the world the art of re-attaching the penises that jealous Thai wives had severed from their errant husbands. I did not have to worry about becoming detached, but if looks could kill...

Well?

I decided that I would give her time to cool down and then tell her the truth.

At the end of the week, I tracked her down in the Computer Center and sat with her while she ate her lunch and stared at the wall. I told her the truth: the Thais had made me go with them to that wretched bar, and I would never go again. I had not committed anything resembling adultery, had only talked to the dancer for a minute and even that was just to be polite. In fact, I said, I had missed her, Sovan, so much and was so disgusted by the place that I had risked my life to walk home alone.

She was still staring at the wall.

"You are much more beautiful than those girls, anyway," I added.

"How many women have you said that to?" Her face was solid rock.

"None."

"Was I born yesterday?"

I was in trouble.

For a woman who had never gone on a date until she was almost thirty, she could play rough. I had thought that she would fall for the part about me risking my life.

"Have I gone out with any other Cambodian women?" I asked.

"What does that have to do with anything?"

"There is only one woman I will ever go out with in Cambodia," I declared as if taking an oath, "and she is the most beautiful woman in Phnom Penh."

"Are you feeling okay?" she asked.

She was tough.

I waited a moment. "I'm feeling fine. I've never felt better. You know, Sovan, even the best man in the world is going to do something, sometime, that you don't like. You have to learn to trust people to do the right thing."

David Portnoy/Black Star

Heavily armed Cambodian People's Armed Forces (CPAF) soldiers prepare to go out on patrol in Siem Reap against an enemy who claims, as they do, to represent the *real* Cambodia.

Bangkok Post photo library

The United Nations Transitional Authority in Cambodia, UNTAC, impressed the Cambodian people with glitz, if not real fighting power. Some parents named their children Untac.

I waited. She would not look at me.

Sometimes a man has to forget all about his own personal dignity.

"Okay," I said, "I'm sorry."

She turned away from the wall.

"Do you want to see my pictures from Australia?" she asked.

"Yes, of course, very much."

Yes, usually it is better to tell the truth.

UNTAC posted the results of the election province by province. When results started to show that the Phnom Penh government might lose, the government started complaining that there were some "irregularities," mainly broken ballot box seals. They made a stink about it but, although theoretically it looked as if someone could have cut the seals and stuffed the boxes, in fact everyone knew that no one had gotten past the UN soldiers to do it. The poor government missed the big irregularity, though: what had happened to the tendered ballots with no voter registration numbers?

What had happened was that about 90 percent of those ballots, thanks to the Computer Center, were effectively cast in the trash. When the tendered ballots that lacked voter registration numbers went to the Computer Center, the data entry clerks searched the database for the names on the tendered ballot envelopes and found just 10.2 percent of the names. Were the other 89.8 percent faking it? Was there secretly, such that none of the IPSOs noticed, widespread voter fraud? Probably not.

Probably most of those people were legitimate but, like 60 percent of the population, illiterate voters. When they registered to vote, they had given their names to the registrar, who wrote them on their voter registration cards and in the receipt books that went to the Computer Center. Seven months later, at election time, if those people had lost their card or had it stolen, they would give their name to the polling official, who would write it down for them on the tendered ballot envelope. Someone could always write a name down slightly differently the second time. The registration official's Tom Sim might have become the polling official's Thom Simm.

Ah-ha.

Ravi, the software engineer, blamed the failure directly on Hugo. I would guess that Hugo blamed Ravi. One of the Khmer supervisors told me that he had tried to explain to Hugo and Ravi how the Khmer script works, but that no one had understood him. Khmer writing has an elaborate system of subscripts and superscripts that are essential if the words are going to be spelled correctly. The search program had assumed that the data entry clerks had typed the scripts in a certain order when they could have just as easily have typed them in another. No one had cared about that.

Later I mentioned to one of the people from Complaints, Compliance and Enforcement (the UNTAC office responsible for enforcing the *Electoral Law*), that as far as I could tell the tendered ballot confirmation system did not work. The Complaints man told me that he used to go to the Computer Center with the names of registered voters whom, for one reason or another, his office had decided to de-register. He said that the Computer Center could *never* find the names on his lists. Eventually, unless he also had the voter registration numbers with him, he would not even bother to ask them to look.

In the end, it seemed that the funny little Cambodian computer consultant in New York had been right all along: the system was too complicated for Cambodia. To put it in anthropological terms: the dominant culture had tried to impose its cultural model on the subordinate culture without understanding the societal nuances of the subordinate culture that would make the dominant culture's model inappropriate. The Cambodians, who may have had experiences like this before, have a proverb that more succinctly says the same thing: "Wrong place, wrong way."

The world, however, judged the Computer Center to be the shining success of UNTAC.

So it goes.

WHERE'S THE PARTY?

After the election there was not much of a party in Phnom Penh. While the government was questioning "irregularities," one of Sihanouk's sons, Chakrapong, who worked for the Phnom Penh government, said he was founding a breakaway republic in the eastern third of the country. For a few days the country moved to the edge of another civil war. But people were too tired of war to actually fight one. Besides, the rest of the Phnom Penh government, notably the prime minister, Hun Sen, did not think that dividing the country even further was such a good idea. Thus, a few days later, Chakrapong drove his car into Vietnam. The civil war was called off, and the results of the election were honored—well, sort of.

The results were that the son-of-Sihanouk party, FUNCINPEC, received about 45 percent of the votes; the government finished second with 38 percent. A third party, the Buddhist Liberal Democratic, which once ran Site Two and was headed by one of Sihanouk's former prime ministers, Son Sann, won three percent and thus a few seats in the National Assembly. My favorite party, the American-inspired REDEK, finished last with just eleven thousand votes—so much for car factories in Cambodia.

In the end, even though no one was completely happy with the way things turned out, everyone decided to try something new, different, and untested—a nonviolent change of government, or at least a partial change. They put Sihanouk back as King, while the leader of FUNCINPEC, Ranariddh, and dashing Hun Sen became co-prime ministers. Khieu Samphan found the idea of co-prime ministers to be pretty funny, but he and his buddies were, for a while at least, left to laugh out in the jungle.

Now that the election was definitely "successful," everyone expected life in Phnom Penh to get better, but instead something went wrong, and it got worse. The markets became crowded again, but many of the people who crowded them were beggars. Many of these people were "internally displaced persons": land mines, fighting, hunger, forced relocation and the belief that they might now find something better in the city had caused them to flee the countryside. Now when you parked your car downtown, a child, widow or amputee was there to help you park it, to open the door for you, and to beg. As you walked into a store where foreigners shopped, a group of people surrounded you. Mothers pushed babies into your face and said "Baba, ngam, baba, ngam"—"*Mister, food, mister, food.*" They waited for you as you purchased your luxury goods—canned lightly salted mixed nuts, German lager beer, 100 percent pure virgin olive oil, antibacterial deodorant soap, decaffeinated dry-roasted freeze-dried coffee, and 50 percent real orange juice concentrate. They watched as you took out your American dollars or thick wad of Cambodian riels to pay. As you left the store, they greeted you again, hoping that you now had some more change to give them. If they could, they helped you into your car, shut the door for you, helped you back out and tapped on the window just before you pulled away. Could you give a bit more? Some of them could look at you very piercingly. One of the overseas Khmers wrote a letter to the newspaper saying that the beggars were stealing the beauty of Cambodia and that they lacked dignity. I think they also lacked a choice.

With an ever-increasing number of unemployed people in town, many men who had nothing else to do became motorcycle taxi drivers. If you hesitated to cross the street, a motorcycle taxi driver would stop; if you were in an office, they would be waiting outside; if you walked down the street, they would constantly drive by saying hello or raising one finger in the air to offer you a ride. Supply far outstripped demand.

Other people decided to try their luck at another possibly more lucrative profession, and became car thieves. It became the craze. At Training, Education and Communications, just as we were packing up, one of our drivers took a van across town to deliver some papers to Headquarters, and that was the last anyone saw of him or the van. A few days later a secretary drove Judy's car to the post office to mail a letter. She was only inside the post office for a minute, just long enough for someone to steal the locked car. Soon everyone had a car-stealing story and an explanation to go with it: the government was hiding them, the guys in transport had stolen the keys, the vehicles were being whisked over the border to Vietnam, people in the jungle were paying five thousand dollars per vehicle, or the Khmer Rouge were stealing them. Over a hundred vehicles were stolen! UN security tried to set up anti-theft measures, but the thieves, as they say in poker, always upped the ante.

Street crime picked up as well. We received another memorandum from UNTAC security about safety in the streets. I could not stay away from New Market, but I stopped jogging in the dark and riding my motorcycle even in daylight.

With the Phnom Penh government no longer running for election, the people who ran the city services felt they no longer had to pretend that they were not completely out of money. They admitted they were completely out of money. For the Cambodians, this meant that their electricity and water, instead of being cut off for hours at a time, were now off for days or weeks.

One night I took Sovan to one of the many UNTAC going-away parties that had started within days after the election. When I went to her house to pick her up, I found her sitting with her mother in the loft, in the dark, with the door closed. The fumes from the furniture factory's diesel engines remained heavy in the air, and it was hot enough to bake bread. "Why don't you open the door and let some air in?" I asked.

"We are afraid of the thief."

"Yes, of course, the thief." One of her relatives had recently shot at a thief and missed. The thief turned out to be their security guard robbing them.

That night it was Michael Maley's going away party for his boss,

Professor Austin. It was a real Australian party. Somehow they had managed to buy beef steaks, broil them, stack them high on a plate, put a case of beer and a bottle of whiskey beside the plate, and call that dinner. To the people from "Oz" it was "a good feed"; they "got stuck into it" and devoured it as if they were going to be hanged in the morning. Sovan and I found some peanuts and orange juice.

Since I had borrowed a truck from a friend, we left early. We both said good-bye to Professor Austin. I tried to tell him that I thought he had been the one man who had held the show together. His summary comment was, "Thank God more people weren't killed."

Michael thanked Sovan and me "for intervention at certain critical junctures," and added something about "right-oh, cheers," which was his way of saying good-bye and good luck. We wished him the same.

As we drove home most of the city was in darkness. For long stretches what little light there was came from the occasional candle, kerosene lantern, or fluorescent light connected to a car battery. The only places that were not blacked out were neighborhoods where foreigners lived. There household generators, sounding like a fleet of lawn mowers, clamored to keep jerks like me in air-conditioned splendor.

The Playmate of the Month and Death or Suicide

Later in the week the UNV office decided that, with so many people leaving town, they should hire someone for a couple of months to keep track of who was going where. I was therefore offered a job: make a database of travel information on the four hundred departing UNV district electoral supervisors.

I told Sovan about my new job.

"Oh good," she said, "now you can come to my wedding."

"Your wedding?"

"My wedding. A week from Saturday."

"That's nice. I like weddings. I had a date with another woman planned for then, but I can cancel it and come."

"Thank you so much."

This exchange, by the way, is an example of what anthropologists call "phatic speech." From the very beginning, Sovan and I had such an instant rapport that normal speech, "exchanging information," was totally out of the question. Who wants to exchange information when you can have fun?

"I'm glad you're getting married," I said. "You know, for a while I was thinking you were going to end up an old maid."

"So was I, but I found the right man at last."

"When can I meet him?"

"Saturday at 8 A.M."

"Can I come at 7:30?"

"No, eight o'clock."

It was, in fact, the wedding of her cousin Rita.

Rita had always been my candidate for Cambodian Playmate of the Month: big breasts, big hips and a big seductive smile. I liked Rita. Every time I visited her she was sitting in her hammock or lounging on the bed looking like a million dollars. She would smile at me; I would smile back. Her hair was always glowing silken black, and she always wore a new, spanking-clean, stylish outfit.

"Sovan," I asked, "is Rita lazy?"

"No! Hey guy, she is my cousin. Don't say bad things about her."

"If she isn't lazy, why doesn't she ever do any work?"

"She doesn't want to."

"But she doesn't study anything either, right?"

"I guess."

"So if she never works and doesn't go to school and doesn't do anything except lie around the house watching television all day, then she's lazy."

"She is going to America!"

"Does that mean she isn't lazy?"

"That means that we don't have to worry about her."

"Oh, I see."

Rita's mother did not know the meaning of laziness either, and even though she could not read or write, she had made a Cambodian fortune in the furniture business. That fortune and the good name of the family had attracted an American-Khmer mother to Rita. The mothers talked on the telephone. The American-Khmer mother flew to Cambodia: she felt there was potential in Rita.

Upon her return to the U.S.A., the American-Khmer mother showed Rita's picture to her son. What could he say? What could any man say? He called her. He wrote to her. He sent her a heart-shaped poster of himself with her image superimposed beside him. She liked it. He wrote that he loved her. He became engaged to her. He flew to Cambodia. A few days later, on his wedding day, I met him and immediately felt that I was shaking hands with the legendary Prince Charming. He had lived in the U.S.A. for eleven years and seemed very pleasant. I tried not to show that I thought he was going to a prison from which there was no escape save death or suicide. "So she's the girl for you," I said.

"It was just supposed to be, I guess," he said as the professional wedding director dressed him in rented, traditional Cambodian wedding clothes to make him look like a prince. He had about six more changes to go. At various times during his wedding he would look like a saint, an ancient soldier, a priest, a lover, a businessman and, when he put on his rented tuxedo, like someone going to the high school prom.

"But aren't there Cambodian women in America?" I asked. There are almost a quarter of a million Cambodians in the U.S.A.

"There are, but most of them aren't the kind of girls that you'd want to marry. For fun yes, but marriage no."

"Yes, of course."

Sovan was listening.

"Ask him how old he is," she said to me.

"How old are you?"

"Twenty-four."

"Then it's time," I said prophetically, "And time for Rita too." Rita was eighteen.

Their marriage ceremony, like most Cambodian marriage ceremonies, lasted all day and half the night. Eventually, I fell asleep, but I know that the ceremonies went something like this: wake-up ceremony, get-dressed ceremony, enter-monks-for-the-chanting ceremony, wait-while-the-band-plays-traditional-music, breakfast for a hundred people, more music, cigarette-smoking ceremony during which the bride lights the husband's cigarette, haircutting ceremony with hired priests and comedians, reception, dinner for two hundred, rock and roll party and dancing until midnight, phallic-tree-planting ceremony (whatever that is), and at 2 A.M., closing ceremony. The Cambodians may be the only people on earth who are relaxed enough for an eighteen-hour marriage ceremony, which they say is the rushed version of the traditional three-day ceremony.

The groom had planned to spend two months in Cambodia, but he went back to the U.S.A. three weeks and six picnics later. After all, as he said, "There's nothing to do in Cambodia." He left his bride, who could not speak ten words of English, behind to work out her visa problems.

Making himself perfectly clear is Yasushi Akashi, the head of
UNTAC. To the left stands UNTAC's military chief, Lt.-Gen. John
Sanderson.

Prince Norodom Sihanouk, the head of the Supreme National
Council during the year of UNTAC, returns to Cambodia for his
coronation as the UN mission winds down.

6 Most Likely Fat and Happy

With the election over and UNTAC safely on the way out of Cambodia, we could end our story here. Now that I think about it, however, there are a few things of a personal nature that I may have glossed over earlier. I can elaborate on them now, and mention a few other things as they come to me.

TRIBUTE TO GAUGUIN

Everyone always said that Sovan was beautiful. She was, although it took me some time to fully appreciate it. I had to know her for a while to notice that when she entered a room the focus shifted a bit, as if Princess Grace of Monaco or the youthful Jacqueline Kennedy had just stepped in. She had class. There is a myth in the west that all Asian women are graceful; they aren't, but she was. In everything she did, from washing her clothes to combing her hair, there was a certain element of attention, of thoroughness, of that special something that belongs to ballerinas and the emperor's daughters. Gauguin could paint that kind of grace into his portraits of the women of Tahiti, but his models were rather chubby. Sovan was long and thin.

MYSTICAL TRANSVESTITE

Early one afternoon I drove Sovan to the UNTAC medical clinic, and afterwards, as it was still the UNTAC lunch hour, we dropped by Maxi's house.

Maxi was from India. Some of the people who knew her felt that she had an unusually large store of intuition, insight and mental acuity, while others found her nosy, meddlesome and inane. I liked her and gave her the benefit of the doubt. Sovan liked her, too. Maxi was, everyone agreed, a talker and would lecture us on everything from spiritualism to urine therapy. Mystics tend to look different. Sovan said that because Maxi jogged and lifted weights, she looked like a man. I didn't think so. Yes, she was solid muscle, but with her deep-set dark eyes, high cheekbones, broad shoulders, breasts that shot straight out of her chest, and hair braided straight down her back, she looked more like some sort of mystical transvestite than like a man.

As soon as we entered her spacious apartment, Maxi had to, as always, give me a hug and a kiss on the cheek which Sovan, as always, pretended not to see. Cambodian adults do not express affection in public.

Maxi demanded that we sit in the living room while she whipped up some instant noodles for us in the kitchen. The electricity was off, so the generator, which sounded like an unmuffled motorcycle, was running outside.

"The doctor dropped everything when he saw Sovan," I shouted out over the noise of the generator from the deep, soft sofa.

"No, he didn't!" Sovan yelled to Maxi.

"Yes, he did," I said. "He postponed his lunch so that he could be alone with her. Maxi, listen, the doctor wouldn't let me into his office. He wanted to be alone with Sovan!"

"Stop it!" we heard Maxi shouting back from the kitchen. "You're embarrassing Sovan."

"I'm telling you what happened. She's beautiful and the doctor was attracted."

"Maxi, don't believe him!" Sovan shouted.

"You are attractive," Maxi had stuck her head into the living room for a second, "but he shouldn't carry on like this."

"He always exaggerates!" Sovan thought that shouting like this was funny.

I wasn't exaggerating. Sovan liked to be told she was beautiful and I never minded telling her. We were a perfect match.

After she fixed the noodles, Maxi had Sovan and me sit on either side of her on the couch so that our conversation could be more relaxed. Lately she had been reading about anagrams. She wanted to show us how different "meaningful" words could be formed if the letters of our names were rearranged. This meant, at least in my case, that she could rearrange letters all day.

Late one afternoon Maxi and I went jogging together around Independence Monument.

"Could you," she paused, "be serious about Sovan?"

"Yes."

"Good, because I think that she is serious about you, and I wouldn't like to see her hurt."

"I think that she is serious too, but she says she isn't."

"She's shy. And, you know, in Asia a girl has to be careful, very careful, about expressing her feelings."

"I think so."

"But if you are sincere she is bound to see it, bound to see it."

"If I were any more sincere, I'd be dead." Maybe Maxi really did have an excess of women's intuition.

"Serious, yes, good. But you have to give her time, too."

I took Maxi's advice to heart. A few times I tried to mention my seriousness to Sovan. She would always end the discussion with, "You are my best friend."

"Good."

Other times, if things were getting too serious, she would end the discussion with, "Are you crazy?" She taught me how to say it in Khmer: *"Luuk chakuut tay?"*

Now, though, time was running out.

But things looked good. Setee's future in-laws had invited him and his mother to live with them after the marriage. Sovan told me the wedding was now planned for December. After that she would have no place to live. No place to live? Plus, she said, with UNTAC closing down, she did not know what she was going to do next. What would she like to do? She had recently taken the test that foreigners have to take to be admitted to an American university, the TOEFL (Test of English as a Foreign Language), and had scored unusually high. There are no American universities in Cambodia. Yes! As a final Asian hint, she told me that she did not want me to leave and that she would not be happy in Cambodia without me.

Foreigners should always look for these subtle hints in Asia. Things were falling into place.

BEER, SALTED PEANUTS AND "A GIRL"

Two weeks after the election all the terminals in the Computer Center were in boxes ready to be shipped back to New York. Other computers were put up for sale along with most of the huge supply of office equipment and vehicles that UNTAC had brought to Cambodia. The international staff of the Computer Center left the country, as did Judy, Porn and the trainers. Niwit and Sari decided to stay a bit longer. They were not quite ready to deal with divorce or the four-thousand-dollar-a-month drop in salary that leaving Cambodia would entail, so they both took jobs in the Procurement and Inventory Control Unit, the UNTAC cleanup department. They came to know each other there. Small world. Most of the data entry clerks were sent to different UNTAC departments. Some of them made a database of every UNTAC vehicle; others were sent to make a database of every soldier in Cambodia. Sovan took a dummy's job as a secretary's assistant at UNTAC Headquarters. She thought that her job would last a few more months. I knew that mine would last until July 25.

My job was easy. Every UNV who was leaving Cambodia had to talk to me before leaving. I would interview them about their travel itinerary and enter it onto a database. After that, they could get their ticket home. I talked to them as I typed in their data. Most were from the Indian subcontinent, but others were Irish, English, French, Italian and Japanese, with a few Fijians and other exotics. Some of them had had it rough, living in the middle of nowhere with no electricity or running water and the sound of artillery terrifying them to sleep at night. A few people had had close calls. Two people had their houses shot up. One woman crawled out the back door and into a swamp as her house was being machine-gunned. A man hid under the bed as his room was sprayed with automatic rifle fire. One group of UNVs, evacuated from the would-be breakaway republic of Sihanouk's errant son, had had it especially rough. They had been forced to pack and get out in a flash; as they parted, popular sentiment had temporarily turned against UNTAC. The Cambodians who had worked with UNTAC suddenly had to choose between their new friends and popular sentiment. They chose popular sentiment. For those UNVs, then, it was a bitter departure. Other people had been robbed by their landlords. I heard all the stories that one always hears from Westerners living in the third world. No one was sad about leaving. Of the 350 UNVs whom I processed, only one person stayed even one day longer than she had to: Tanya Lieberman. Tanya had been quoted in *Time* magazine just before the election, in the lead paragraph of their cover story on Cambodia. She had told *Time* her belief that, after she had organized her district, the military would take over for her and run the election without her. The military didn't, but somehow everything had worked out, and now she was going back to the same place to study the Khmer language. As she would no longer be working for UNTAC, she believed that this time she would not be a target. Everyone else could not leave fast enough.

Some of the people who came through had seen me around the Computer Center or had even known me in the old AEPU days, and we were now old friends. One day two departing Pakistani men wanted to take me to lunch. Why not? They told me stories of their lives as district electoral supervisors. They had more responsibility and more money than they had ever had before. One of them had been in charge of a large district and had 250 people working for him. As lunch progressed, they said that they had both remained faithful to their wives. Yes, they said, it had taken them a while to accustom themselves to working with Cambodian women, because in Pakistan women are not allowed to work outside the home, which saves their honor and insures harmony in the work place. But after the initial shock of seeing women in the office, things had gone well, and indeed both of them were now certain that it was possible, at least in theory, to work with women. Sari had told me that she hated almost all Pakistani men.

"True," one of them concluded very seriously. "True, yes, yes, I remained very true to my wife. It was just that when I am drinking, I must have a girl. I have got to have a girl, so okay, when I was drunk I took a girl."

I nodded as if to indicate that yes, of course, that was natural: beer, salted peanuts and "a girl." It was natural.

"But just a few times," he added. "Not more than ten times, I'm sure."

"Not more than ten times," his friend agreed, indicating he had acted naturally as well.

Many of the people I helped issue tickets to had paired up and were now going to a different country than the one they had come from, but I heard of only one marriage—an American UNV had married a Cambodian woman. He was fat and happy.

FAT AND HAPPY

Time was passing quickly. I thought that being the second UNV man to marry a Cambodian woman would make me fat and happy too. This would be the first time I'd ever asked someone to marry me, and I knew it wouldn't be easy. For one thing, I knew that Sovan could be stubborn and that she would not budge at all until she was certain beyond any doubt that I would go through with it. But I had confidence: she loved me, her family liked me, there was no divorce in my immediate family, I was not divorced, I was a former university lecturer, and I had tested negatively for AIDS, twice. Wasn't that enough?

After rehearsing my lines about five hundred times, one afternoon I decided to confront Sovan man-to-woman.

"You know," I said, "we could talk about continuing our relationship."

We were outside her aunt's house. Sovan was in a hammock. I was sitting on a chair. Children, babies, relatives and furniture factory cus tomers were, as always, everywhere.

"Oh yes," she said, "I want to. I'll write you letters, very sweet letters." As she said this she gracefully wrote me a letter in the air with her long fingers.

"No, I mean staying together."

"Yes, if you work in Cambodia you can stay for lunch at my house sometimes."

Couldn't she ever be serious? I was as serious as I'd ever been in my life. "I mean, our relationship continuing with you coming with me to another country."

"But that is impossible. I don't have a visa."

"They give visas for spouses."

"But I don't have a husband overseas."

"But you could, you know?"

"No one is going to marry me."

"I know someone who might."

"Might! Easy to say. What good is might?"

"You might want to, you know, wear a white dress, have a big dinner, invite lots of people."

"I don't have the confidence to do it."

"Don't worry, we can find a dress that fits, and if the food is good and we hire a good band, people will come to the ceremony."

"Let's not talk about things that are impossible."

"What's impossible? I read in a magazine that lots of people get married."

"It is a big problem."

"Then why do so many people do it?"

"It's a big problem for people like me to marry people like you."

Round one for Sovan, but the fight was not over.

After that, I had more courage, but every time it was the same conversation with different endings: "I want to stay here to help my country." "I don't want to get into a situation where there are expectations I cannot fulfill." (Whatever that meant.) "I tried to go to America for eight years and in the end failed. I do not want to fail again."

I had to repeat to myself Maxi's advice again and again: "Patience."

An American at the International Outreach Project had married a Cambodian woman. Sovan once had me ask him about the technicalities of international marriage. He said that, after a fifty dollar bribe to a government official, it was not a problem. When she heard this, Sovan found other excuses.

I went back to Maxi and told her everything. She listened and tried to think of something wise to say. She told me that in this part of the world foreign men, especially American men, had earned a reputation for sleaziness (her word was "butterfly"). A girl, especially a good girl, she said, had to walk like a tiger through the jungle. "Major Thom should not be discouraged," she concluded.

Sometimes I ran into former data entry clerks around town. They always asked when I was leaving Cambodia and if Sovan was coming with me. One of the women interrogated me downtown on the street one day.

"No, she doesn't want to go," I said.

"She wants to."

"She says she doesn't want to."

"Everyone wants to."

"But she says she doesn't want to."

"Don't believe her."

"Okay, I won't believe her."

She then explained that if Sovan were serious about not going with me, perhaps *she* could be a stand-in. That was a nice offer. By coincidence, that particular young lady was exactly half my age and bore a striking resemblance to my mother. Somehow the chemistry was not right.

New Sheets on the Bed

Why would anyone, I wondered, stay in Cambodia if she could possibly avoid it? If I'd been born a Cambodian man, I'm not sure I would have tried dancing across a minefield to get out, but I wouldn't have hesitated to marry an obese woman, a smoker or even a French or Australian woman if it would have helped get me a visa into another country. We could always divorce later. How could she let this be the final irony— not to walk through the door when at last it was open?

Time was running out. Soon I would be leaving Cambodia. One afternoon I met Sovan at her house. She had just come back from shopping.

"What did you buy?"

She showed me a sheet-and-pillow case set. The motif was brightly colored flowers, the kind of thing you might find in an upscale hotel.

"Oh, how nice," I said, "Who did you buy them for?"

"For me."

"Yes, of course, for you." The diesel engines would sometimes leave a thick layer of soot over everything in the loft, which had left the old sheets permanently gray. But why buy new sheets, I thought, if you're going to leave Cambodia with me? But she wasn't planning to leave. This was her home and she was going to give it some class.

I could not believe it. No Asian woman ever goes out with a foreign man almost every weekend for a year and then does not marry him. I was still convinced that our movie would have a happy ending. It would make such a good movie, too: cynical and lost intellectual meets and falls for the savant queen of Cambodia. They design the ballot for a successful election. And at the end of the movie they fly off together to Honolulu, honeymoon capital of the world. Who needs *The Killing Fields* when you can have *Love Story?*

Three hundred UNVs left Cambodia in June, along with over one thousand UNTAC staff: every plane out of Cambodia was fully booked. The next month, another hundred UNVs left the country. On July 25, it would be my turn.

I ran around town and said good-bye to everyone except Sergei, who was out. Sari gave me a final hug and Maxi a final kiss. Maxi said she had fallen in love with an UNTAC man from Chile and was going to visit him there. I wished her luck.

I had two going away parties. The first one was a luncheon that I hosted in a restaurant near Wat Phnom. Along with Sovan came four people I had worked with in the Computer Center and before that in the old AEPU days. Now considered some of UNTAC's most skilled data entry people, they were making a database of the 130,000 soldiers in Cambodia who were not Khmer Rouge. (As a goodwill gesture intended to help insure the new government's stability, UNTAC had decided to pay the soldiers three months' wages.) After Hugo, they said, their new boss, a woman from California, was a saint. Their big problem was what they were going to do after UNTAC left Cambodia. Working for thirty dollars a month again was going to be rough. I don't know how they had come to feel about me, but for me they had gone from being those smiling Cambodians whom "old Cambodia hands" liked to talk about, to being just ordinary people with all of the anxieties, worries, depressions, hopes and fears of anyone else. I would miss them, and I think they knew it.

The second party took place the night before I left. Sovan and I went to the best hotel in Cambodia, the Cambodiana, for dinner. It was air-conditioned, the lights were soft, and candles flickered on the soft white tablecloths.

For the last week I had been helping her copy computer software, and she had been helping me buy souvenirs. Tonight was the first chance in what seemed a long time, as on a lazy Cambodian picnic, just to sit and talk. For the first time she asked about my home in the United States. "It's a farm," I said, "and from the farmhouse where my parents live you can't see any other houses."

"It sounds lonely," she said.

"Americans usually say I'm lucky to live there."

"Is it cold?"

I told her how cold it can be in the winter in the northeastern United States.

"Too cold," she said.

"Children, even Cambodian children, think snow is wonderful. You wake up in the morning, look outside, and everything is pure white."

"I like Cambodia."

"Then come visit in the summer."

We talked about our plans. Her dream was to build a house somewhere around Phnom Penh and to live there with her mother. Maybe later she would try to study computers in the United States. "Will you come to visit me if I do?" she asked.

"If I'm there."

"Where do you think you'll be?"

"I don't know. I travel around. This time I think I'll stay in Thailand for a while and then visit Australia and New Zealand."

"Just travel around with no home and no permanent job?"

"You know, I tried to find a Cambodian woman who would marry me so I could settle down with her, but in the end I think it didn't quite work out. So yes, why should I do anything else?"

"You should get a job and a nice house."

"And be even more lonely?"

What could she say?

The restaurant had a buffet that featured spaghetti, garlic bread, salad, French onion soup, and mixed vegetables. There were cakes for dessert. She tried everything, but said she preferred Thai food.

"So next week," I said, "go to a Thai restaurant with a different foreigner."

"I won't go out again."

"But you like going out."

"Not anymore."

After dinner, I took her straight home. We had said everything, and I had not yet finished packing.

It was a 7:30 A.M. flight. Since it was a commercial and not an UNTAC flight, the travel agent had told me to be at the airport at 6 A.M.

I drove the UN truck to Sovan's house at 5:30. It was just getting light, but as this was a special day, everyone was up. I climbed the ladder to the loft. Sovan's mother, Om, who had always made sure that Sovan did not forget to feed me, asked me to hold the kerosene lantern close to my face so that she could take a final look. I held the lantern and, as Sovan was watching, I parodied a few "high-fashion poses" for their amusement. Om, who had never really known what to think of me, laughed along with Sovan. I pressed my palms into the prayer position and bowed my head to Om who, since she was older, did not "sompiah" back. "If you come to Cambodia again," she said, "come right back here."

"Thank you, I will." I wished her well and climbed down the ladder.

The rest of the family came to the airport in their own car, while I drove Sovan and Setee, who had come back to Phnom Penh for the occasion.

Setee shared his sister's anxiety about the future. In spite of everything, he, along with every other Cambodian who worked for UNTAC, or even for an upscale restaurant, hotel, bar, supermarket, or brothel, had never wanted the year of UNTAC to end. And here it was ending with the departure of yet another foreigner. I had given Setee a camera and a Walkman, but no matter what I gave him or Sovan, how could it be enough?

Cambodia was one place that I hoped not to see again for a very long time. I'd had enough. Yes, it was a beautiful country; yes, it had tremendous potential; yes, I never had any real quarrels with the Cambodian people who had always returned any kindness tenfold. But yes, it was also one never-ending and personally dangerous nightmare for anyone who felt even a little of the suffering of those around him. UNTAC and the UNVs, who would be completely gone by early 1994, were "short-timers." We were just here for the quick and highly publicized fix and gone tomorrow to the next highly paid and glamorous, quick-fix, air-conditioned mission. The NGOs had been right all along—there was no such thing as a magic mandate or a miraculous 2.8 billion-dollar overnight conversion from anarchy and barbarism to order and democracy. For better or worse, Cambodia would stay the same, or, now that it had seen and tasted a shining example of greed and materialism, become worse.

In April of 1975, the Cambodians who worked for the American Embassy went to the airport with their American bosses and shook hands with the people whose peace plan had gone, to say the least, horribly awry. After that, the Yankees walked into their helicopters and flew away to the next air-conditioned office; and here we were doing it again ...

> Bye, bye Miss American pie,
> drove my Chevy to the levee,
> but the levee was dry, ...
> singing, this will be the day that I die,
> this will be the day that I die

The Cambodians who had worked at the embassy and who for sentimental reasons had decided to stay in Cambodia, were shortly thereafter murdered. These people, whom I called my friends, would shortly suffer a lowering of living standards and a lot of disappointment when their lives did not improve, but just went on.

Who was I, anyway? Just a tourist who never stopped complaining about the food? Someone who had grown tired of the weather in Honolulu, Hawaii, the Japanese honeymoon capital of America? I was just visiting, thank you, and now that my vacation was over, it was time to go home. Thanks for the good time. I've enjoyed meeting you; it's been fun, and seeing your suffering has been interesting. Who knows, maybe I'll even write a book about it sometime.

So, yes, Sovan, you can have your pride, your smile, your beauty, your grace, your intelligence, your laughter, and your country. And I can have my American passport and my life. I can use the money I've saved eating in New Market to travel economy class with my laptop computer wherever I like. After a couple of months of mucking around in Thailand, New Zealand will be warm enough for me to hike in the mountains. I'll buy a good backpack and lots of supplies. I won't worry about security, and I'll try to gain some weight, to relax for a while...hey, I deserve it, don't I?

Sovan, please don't haunt my dreams.

The ticket counter was closed when we arrived at six, so we had time for breakfast in the airport restaurant—rice noodles with mung bean sprouts and basil covered in a spicy peanut sauce. Sovan's aunt, Ming, told me how much she would miss me. After all, I had always been there, with Sovan, on the family picnics. Indeed, she said, she had known both of us almost the same length of time, about one year. I told her I felt the same way. One of Sovan's little nephews, whom I had met while riding an elephant, had come to say good-bye. I told him to practice his swimming. If I ever came back to Cambodia, I expected him to be able to swim, as I had done, across the river at Kien Svay. He laughed.

On the way to the airport, Sovan had given me a beautiful Khmer cotton scarf. Now I slipped her a little amputee-made cotton purse. Later, her mother would find hidden in the purse, along with a note from me, the fifty dollars I had always wanted her to spend to get a driver's license.

We finished breakfast. I tried to pay for everyone, but Ming, claiming that I might need my Cambodian riels again, insisted on paying with her American dollars.

We walked out of the restaurant and stood under the DEPARTURE sign. Everyone shook hands with me, except Ming who, as she was over fifty, could give me a hug. I dried my eyes and posed for a last picture with Sovan.

"Like a dream, Sovan," I whispered into her ear as I turned to go inside the terminal. "From the first moment to the last, like a dream."

She nodded, claimed we would meet again, and forced a painful smile.

The airline agent examined my ticket and handed me a boarding pass. Customs absentmindedly stamped my passport. I was a little late. The other passengers were already leaving the terminal. As I turned to go, almost in slow motion, I looked back. Sovan was still looking through the window, one hand cupped against the glass to help her see, the other waving as if wiping the glass clean. I waved again, turned away, and hurried out onto the tarmac.

Constructed in the twelfth century, Angkor Wat was almost totally reclaimed by the surrounding forest until 1908, when the French began to restore it. The temple complex is called the "soul of Cambodia," and is the symbol of Cambodian national identity.

Appendix A
A few names and definitions as the year of UNTAC begins
(Persons are arranged alphabetically by second name)

AEPU stands for Advanced Electoral Planning Unit. A part of UNTAC, its mission is to take a survey of the possible voters of Cambodia so that UNTAC can plan where to send voter registration teams and later locate polling stations.

AK-47 is the weapon of choice in Cambodia. Designed by the Russian engineer Mikhail Timofeyevich Kalashnikov in 1947, it is officially called the Avtomat Kalashnikova. At the turn of a switch, it can be changed from semiautomatic to fully automatic, firing at a rate of six hundred rounds per minute. At least thirty million have been produced worldwide.

Yasushi Akashi, 61, from Japan, joined the United Nations in 1957 and was chosen, after working as Under-secretary General for Disarmament Affairs, to be the Special Representative of the Secretary-General and Head of Mission in Cambodia.

Reginald Austin, from Zimbabwe, is the Chief Electoral Officer of UNTAC. He was Dean of the Faculty of Law at the University of Zimbabwe and lecturer in international law at the University of London for eighteen years. He worked as an election consultant to different political parties and governments in Africa and published numerous books on law and elections in Africa before coming to Cambodia.

B-40 Rocket is the shoulder-held bazooka popular with all sides in the Cambodian civil war. Originally developed by the Soviets, it was refined by the Chinese. Its rocket-propelled grenade is accurate up to 500 meters.

Norodom Chakrapong, 47, is Deputy Prime Minister of the State of Cambodia. He is the half-brother and arch-rival of Norodom Ranariddh.

CPP is the party behind the State of Cambodia, also known as the Phnom Penh government. In 1979, the party, then the only party in the Vietnamese-installed government, called itself the People's Revolutionary Party of Kampuchea. As hard-line communists, the party collectivized agriculture and regulated commerce. Before the arrival of UNTAC, however, the collectives were disbanded, free enterprise was embraced, and the party changed its name to Cambodian People's Party. It is headed by Hun Sen and Heng Samrin.

DK, PDK, and **NADK** stand for the government of Democratic Kampuchea, the Party of Democratic Kampuchea, and the National Army of Democratic Kampuchea, all referring to what the Khmer Rouge like to call themselves.

FUNCINPEC is the Front Uni National Pour Un Cambodge Indépendent, Neutre, Pacifique Et Cooperatif founded by Prince Sihanouk in 1981, but, as of 1990, headed by his loyal son Prince Ranariddh. It is the only real non-Khmer Rouge opposition to the 1992 Phnom Penh government.

Khmer is synonymous with Cambodian.

Khmer Republic is the name Lon Nol gave to his 1970-75 government, which replaced Sihanouk's Kingdom of Cambodia.

Lon Nol served in the French colonial forces, then became Minister of Defense under Sihanouk for most of the 1954-70 period. With what many considered American help, he led the overthrow of Sihanouk in March 1970 and withdrew to the U.S. in April 1975, on the eve of the defeat of the Khmer Republic, of which he was head of state. He died in 1986 in Hawaii.

Pol Pot, 64, was born Saloth Sar. His sister was a consort of King Monivong (ruled 1927-1941) for a time. When Sar was six years old, in 1934 or 1935, his parents sent him from his provincial home in Kampong Thom to live with his sister and brother in Phnom Penh. In 1949, he received a Cambodian government scholarship to study in Paris, where he became a member of the French Communist party. He returned to Phnom Penh in 1953 and worked as a teacher in Phnom Penh into the 1960s. In 1962, he became secretary of the Cambodian Communist Party's Central Committee. Fearing the police after Sihanouk asked Lon Nol to investigate anti-government demonstrations, he fled Phnom Penh for the countryside in 1963. He visited Communist China in 1965 – 1966 just as that country was beginning what, for him, was the impressive "Cultural Revolution"; he later visited Vietnam. Sar visited those countries again in 1970; the year that Sihanouk was ousted and fighting broke out between the Cambodian communists, their Vietnamese allies, and the Lon Nol government. Sihanouk visited Sar in the countryside in 1973 to show his support for the anti-Lon Nol movement. By the end of 1973, the North Vietnamese had withdrawn their armed forces from Cambodia, but by then the Khmer Rouge had an army of perhaps sixty thousand men. Sar finally returned to Phnom Penh on April 23, 1975. The rest, as they say, is history.

One of Pol Pot's sisters lives quietly in the State of Cambodia province of Kampong Thom.

See David Chandler's excellent Brother Number One, for a political biography of Pol Pot.

Norodom Ranaridd, 48, is the son of Sihanouk and half-brother of the one-year-younger Chakrapong. As the president of FUNCINPEC, he represents the only real threat to the dominance of the CPP or Cambodian People's Party. To Westerners, at least, Ranariddh looks and sounds like his father did thirty years ago.

Khieu Sampha, 60, studied in Paris in the early 1950s and earned a Ph.D. in Economics for his thesis Cambodia's Economy and Industrial Development. Returning to Phnom Penh, he helped establish a French-language newspaper. He was a member of Sihanouk's cabinet in 1962 and a member of the National Assembly from 1962 until 1967 when he fled to the countryside in fear of government repression.

In 1976 he became Head of State of Democratic Kampuchea, replacing Sihanouk. In 1979 he replaced Pol Pot as Prime Minister of Democratic Kampuchea. Currently one of the two representatives of the Party of Democratic

Kampuchea in the Supreme National Council, he doesn't like people to refer to his party by the term Sihanouk coined for them, Khmer Rouge.

His brother, a former newspaper editor himself, lives quietly in Phnom Penh.

Lieutenant-General John Sanderson, from Australia, is the Force Commander of the Military Component of UNTAC.

Hun Sen, 42, is the Prime Minister of the State of Cambodia. Originally an officer in the Khmer Rouge, he and other future leaders of the Cambodia People's Party, including Chea Sim, the chairman of the National Assembly, and Heng Samrin, the Secretary General of the CPP, fled Cambodia for Vietnam in 1977 and 1978 to escape the paranoid clutches of the Khmer Rouge. Like Khieu Samphan, he has some charm and represents the "nice face" of his party.

Norodom Sihanouk, 70, became the king of Cambodia in 1941 at the age of 18 and functioned as part of the French and, for six months, Japanese colonial apparatus. In 1952, he began to maneuver politically for independence from the French. He gave the throne to his father in 1955 and ruled the country from then until 1970 as its political leader. He ruled with his own brand of authoritarianism, repression, paternalism and royal benevolence, which included resurrecting the royal ballet.

After he was overthrown in 1970, he became "Head of State" for what would become the Khmer Rouge government. In 1976, however, Pol Pot put him under house arrest and replaced him with Khieu Samphan.

Pol Pot asked Sihanouk to represent Democratic Kampuchea at the United Nations in early 1979, just before the Vietnamese invasion.

In 1981 he founded FUNCINPEC, a liberation front aimed at ending the Vietnamese occupation. FUNCINPEC became a political party in 1992 with Sihanouk's son, Prince Ranariddh, as president.

In 1992, he became the head of the Supreme National Council.

Worshipped by some, with tremendous popular support in the countryside, and despised by others, he once described Pol Pot as the only other Cambodian with charisma.

SOC stands for the State of Cambodia, the government originally installed by the Vietnamese. From 1979 until 1991, it was known as the People's Republic of Kampuchea.

SNC, or Supreme National Council, was created by the Paris Peace Agreement to be "the unique legitimate body and source of authority in which, throughout the transitional period, the sovereignty, independence and unity of Cambodia are enshrined." SNC is under the presidency of Prince Sihanouk with representatives from the four factions who signed the Paris Agreement. The Paris Agreement, however, gave the power necessary to implement the agreement to the United Nations.

UNTAC, the United Nations Transitional Authority in Cambodia, was outlined in a report by the United Nations Secretary-General which contained the plan for the implementation of the Paris Agreement.

Appendix B
The 1900 year countdown to UNTAC

First century A.D.: What Cambodians like to call the first Khmer kingdom comes into existence. There is extensive trade with China and India, with Indian religion, arts and the bureaucratic elite making strong impressions.

Ninth century: Classical Khmer architecture is firmly established under the reign of Jayavarman II (reigns 802-850).

Tenth century: Yasovarman (reigns 889 to 910) moves his capital to Siem Reap where he founds the first city of Angkor. Except for brief intervals, the capital remains there for four centuries.

Twelfth century: At the height of the Khmer Empire, Suryavarman II (reigns 1112 to 1152) builds Angkor Wat, the masterpiece of Khmer architecture. His armies range into much of present day Thailand and Vietnam.

Late twelfth century: Jayavarman VII (reigns 1181 to 1201) builds the last of the great Khmer buildings, Bayon, the center of Angkor Thom, near Angkor Wat.

1369, 1388, and 1431: The Thais repeatedly capture Angkor.

1434: The capital shifts to Phnom Penh.

Sixteenth century: Thais and Vietnamese begin to shrink the Khmer Empire.

End of 18th century: Cambodia is reduced to a buffer state between Vietnam and Thailand.

1863: King Norodom I (reigns 1859 to 1904) consents to let Cambodia become a French protectorate.

1908: French begin reconstruction of Angkor Wat, which has been virtually lost in the jungle. French also piece together Cambodian history by translating ancient inscriptions.

1941: Norodom Sihanouk becomes King of Cambodia.

1945: French resume control at the end of World War II.

1951: Khmer People's Party, the first Cambodian communist party, forms. Members of this party will later be claimed as founding fathers by both the Khmer Rouge and the CPP, the party that evolved out of the Vietnamese-installed Phnom Penh government.

November 9, 1953: Cambodia declares independence.

May 1954: At the Geneva conference, the French agree to withdraw from Cambodia.

March 1955: Norodom Sihanouk abdicates the throne and his father, Norodom Suramarit, becomes king. Sihanouk becomes premier after a general election in September.

1960: King Norodom Suramarit dies and Prince Norodom Sihanouk becomes head of state, but not king.

1963: Sihanouk accuses the U.S. Central Intelligence Agency of fostering rebellion in Cambodia and renounces all U.S. economic, military and cultural aid.

1965: The U.S. has 300,000 troops stationed in Vietnam. Cambodia breaks diplomatic relations with Washington.

1966: For the first time in eleven years members of the Cambodian National Assembly are elected from among candidates not personally selected by Sihanouk.

1969: The U.S. begins massive bombing of the Ho Chi Minh trail that runs through Cambodia.

March 18, 1970: With what Sihanouk suspects is U.S. government help, he is pushed out of office, and what many Cambodians consider the golden age of modern Cambodia comes to an end.

April 30, 1970: American President Richard Nixon announces that American forces have staged an "incursion" into Cambodia to attack North Vietnamese sanctuaries. Huge anti-war demonstrations erupt across the United States with four students shot by National Guard troops at Kent State University. The incursions last until July.

Late 1970: American troop strength in Vietnam is down to 280,000 from a high of 540,000 in 1968.

1972: Two million Cambodians are made homeless by the war in Cambodia.

March 29, 1973: Last American troops leave Vietnam.

August 6, 1973: An American B-52 bomber mistakenly drops its load of bombs on its ground-based radar beacon, instead of the target coordinates, and wipes out most of the Mekong ferry port of Neak Luong.

August 14, 1973: Americans stop bombing Cambodia.

April 12, 1975: The American Embassy staff evacuates Phnom Penh by helicopter. Most Cambodian cabinet members and embassy staff, who are offered a way out, decide to stay in Cambodia.

April 17, 1975: The Khmer Rouge enter Phnom Penh and the Lon Nol regime collapses. Year Zero begins with the "Angka," as Pol Pot calls his movement, turning back the clock in Cambodia as the cities are emptied in a move to "pure" communism.

April 29, 1975: The U.S. ambassador to Vietnam leaves Saigon as the last Americans are evacuated. Thousands of Vietnamese flee Vietnam in a chaotic exodus. Over fifty thousand Americans have died in the Vietnam war.

April 30, 1975: The North Vietnamese enter Saigon and the government of South Vietnam surrenders.

December 25, 1978: Vietnam invades Cambodia.

January 7, 1979: The Vietnamese "liberate" Phnom Penh, and the Khmer Rouge regroup in the dense jungles near the Thai border. The "People's Republic of Kampuchea" is installed by the Vietnamese with former Khmer Rouge military men, who earlier fled the Khmer Rouge to Vietnam, in charge. Cambodia's seat at the UN continues to be occupied by the Khmer Rouge, as the world body refuses to recognize the Vietnamese-installed government in Phnom Penh. After 1982, the seat is taken by the Coalition Government of Democratic Kampuchea, which includes Sihanouk. The United States leads an economic embargo of Cambodia and Vietnam.

October 5, 1979: The first aid donations arrive at the Thai-Cambodian border in response to the massive rush of Khmer refugees.
    Over the next thirteen years, over half a million Cambodians will enter Thailand. Many will succeed in re-settling overseas while 370,000 others will eventually be returned to Cambodia.

October 14, 1979: First international airlifts of relief supplies to Phnom Penh begin.

October 22, 1979: Thais announce the creation of the Khao I Dang Holding center in Thailand for Cambodians being considered for resettlement in third countries.

April 6, 1980: The Phnom Penh government reintroduces the riel as the standard currency of Cambodia.

1982: The United Nations declares the emergency in Cambodia to be over and Western aid to Cambodia is reduced. This results in what Eva Mysliwiec describes in her aptly entitled Punishing the Poor: the International Isolation of Kampuchea.

Early 1985: Vietnamese troops push Khmer Rouge and opposition forces across the Thai border and into "border camps" in Thailand. The Khmer Rouge regroup deeper in the Pailin area of Cambodia.

Late 1985: Site Two refugee camp becomes the largest concentration of displaced Cambodians on the Thai-Cambodian border.

September 1989: Vietnam claims it has withdrawn all of its troops from Cambodia, thus offering the first hope of an international settlement. Pol Pot resigns as military commander of the Khmer Rouge, but is still believed to be "Brother Number One," the guiding force behind all KR activities.

1990: Aid to Cambodia from Vietnam, the Soviet Union and the Eastern block ends, and more international organizations and embassies open in Phnom Penh.

October 23, 1991: The five permanent members of the United Nations Security Council, as well as Australia, Indonesia, Japan and other countries, joined by Prince Norodom Sihanouk and the four factions representing jointly the people of Cambodia, agree on a framework and process for peace in Cambodia and sign "The Agreement on a Comprehensive Political Settlement of the Cambodia Conflict."

The agreement provides for a cease-fire, the withdrawal of all foreign forces from Cambodia, the return of the estimated 370,000 refugees, the release of the prisoners of war, and the reconstruction and rehabilitation of the country.

"Phase II" of the agreement requires the forces of the four factions—the State of Cambodia (SOC), the Khmer People's National Liberation Front (KPLNF), the United Front for an Independent, Neutral, Peaceful and Cooperative Cambodia (FUNCINPEC) and the Party of Democratic Kampuchea (PDK)—to regroup, canton their forces under UNTAC supervision, and surrender their arms.

October 23, 1991: Sihanouk returns to Phnom Penh.

January 1992: The U.S. economic embargo of Cambodia ends.

March 15, 1992: Mr. Akashi arrives in Cambodia and UNTAC officially begins.

March 22, 1992: The author arrives in Cambodia.

Sources

Chandler, David P. *Brother Number One*, St. Leonards, Australia: Allen and Unwin, 1993

Isaacs, Arnold R. *Without Honor*, London: The John Hopkins University Press, 1983

Karnow, Stanley *Vietnam, A History*, Harmondsworth, England: Penguin Books Ltd., 1986

Mason, Linda and Roger Brown *Rice, Rivalry, and Politics: Managing Cambodian Relief*, Notre Dame, Indiana: University of Notre Dame Press, 1983

Mysliwiec, Eva *Punishing the Poor: the International Isolation of Kampuchea*, Oxford: Oxfam, 1988

Shawcross, William *Sideshow: Kissinger, Nixon and the Destruction of Cambodia*, New York: Simon and Schuster, 1979